FINE LINES: Spring 2019
Volume 28 Issue 1

ISBN: 978-1-79506-989-2

Cover photo "Don't Mess with Mother Nature: Texas Panhandle" photo by Derek Burdeny, derekburdenyphotography.com

Fine Lines logo designed by Kristy Stark Knapp, Knapp Studios
Book and cover design by Michael Campbell, MC Writing Services

~ Spring 2019 ~

VOLUME 28 ISSUE 1

Edited by

David Martin

CONTENTS

ABOUT *FINE LINES*

Fine Lines is published by Fine Lines, Inc., a 501 (c) 3 non-profit corporation. David Martin is the managing editor. In this quarterly publication, we share poetry and prose by writers of all ages in an attempt to add clarity and passion to our lives. Support is provided through donations, all of which are tax deductible. Join us in creating the lives we desire through the written word.

Composition is hard work. We celebrate its rewards in each issue. Share this publication with others who love creativity. We encourage authors and artists of all ages. Our national mailing list reaches every state. Increased literacy and effective, creative communication is critical for all.

Fine Lines editors believe writing of life's experiences brings order to chaos, beauty to existence, and celebration to the mysterious.

DONATIONS

Contributions are tax deductible. When you support *Fine Lines,* we send e-letters with *Fine Lines* news, upcoming events, the inside scoop on special issues, and provide copies to students who have no means to buy this publication. You will add to their literacy, too.

We offer two methods of payment for your *Fine Lines* donations:

- U.S. residents should make checks payable to *Fine Lines.* Please include your name, address, and email with your donation, and send to:

Fine Lines
PO Box 241713
Omaha, NE 68124

- We also accept credit card payments via PayPal.

SUBMISSIONS

- We accept submissions via email, file attachments, CDs formatted in MS Word for PCs, and laser-printed hard copies.
- Editors reply when writing is accepted for publication, and if a stamped, self-addressed envelope or email address is provided.
- Submissions must not include overt abuse, sexuality, profanity, drugs, alcohol, or violence.
- Do not send "class projects." Teachers may copy *Fine Lines* issues for their classes and submit student work for publication when they act as members and sponsors.
- Address changes and correspondence should be sent to the *Fine Lines* email address: fine-lines@cox.net

We encourage readers to respond to the ideas expressed by our authors. Letters to the editor may be printed in future issues after editing for length and clarity. Reader feedback is important to us. We support writers and artists with hope and direction. Write on.

Never say you know the last word
about any human heart.

HENRY JAMES

DEDICATION

This volume of *Fine Lines* shall henceforth and forever be dedicated to Dr. Seuss. For writers, it is all about the words, which enchant, confound, elude, and inspire. Ted Geisel took 236 little sight words and created a miracle: *The Cat in the Hat,* which is the first book millions of children the world round have read independently for sixty-one years. I proudly count myself among them. Oh, the places we've seen, the creatures we've met, and the adventures we've shared. While he was at it, the good doctor revolutionized the children's literature industry, based on the simple notion that playing with words is fun! His books have sold over 650 million copies. Not bad for a big cat in a bow tie and a striped hat with 236 words. Wowza!

Marcia Calhoun Forecki

Where Writers Grow
Image by Kristi Bolling

WRITERS WRITE ANY WAY THEY CAN

"I am free to grow, and I hope to grow into a kind and successful person. Normally, these two ideas do not seem to go together in today's world, but I want to make them work. I want to grow into someone my mom would be proud to see in one of her boys. *Fine Lines* is where writers grow. I like that. Write on."

Jacob Clarys
University of Nebraska at Omaha

Fine Lines
Writer's Critique Group
meets the 3rd Thursday of each month at
Concierge Marketing
4822 S 133rd St., Ste. 200
6:30–8:30pm
Bring 6–8 copies of your writing for peer editing.
We start and end on time.

heavenly hairdo

TRACY AHRENS

wind blows, brushing tattered tips and sturdy shafts —
tresses trimmed by bolts, gusts and icy glaze.

earthen cords extend.

elemental conditioners strengthen —
rain rinses,
sun soaks,
scalp secures organic stimulation.

in time, strands shed as roots rot.
saplings stretch to succeed.

avian accents highlight leafy locks
seasonally dyed to celebrate.

we wander in this woody mane,
friends and foes of the filaments.

Listening to the Squirrel

DUANE ANDERSON

The squirrel is talking,
but I do not know who it is talking to
or what it is saying since I am
not familiar with its language

and I am not sure how I could learn it
if it truly is a language
and not just the sounds it makes
letting everyone know where it is.

I guess I am content that I am
knowledgeable in one language,
knowing that I could never learn
all the languages spoken on earth,

let alone all in the animal world.
Was it telling everyone within earshot
that it was in the tree
and wanted no other visitors or

just liked to hear itself chatter?
Now the squirrel has stopped making its
sounds, and I still have no clue
why it made the sounds it did.

Though I could not see the squirrel
with all the leaves covering its
place in the tree, and I knew
my place was not in the tree with it

due to a lack of climbing skills like the
squirrel and my fear of heights. I will let the
squirrel rule the tree world and continue
my listening as it makes the sounds it does.

Love

SARAH ASAD

I desire to stop loving you.
I demand — stop this madness.
Vulnerable it's making my being,
As my heart floods with tears.

Akin to the Moon that beckons the Sea,
No matter how hard I try,
The water never reaches its Beloved.
Pathetic how torn to pieces,
Just as shattered glass, I become.

I've been weakened by my affection
For you whom I pray for with my being.
It tears me to shreds as a tattered doll
Staring with resigned listlessness.

Therefore, I command, take it back,
All of it, every last drop, this Love,
The one that makes me weak.
Yes, that one, the one that tires me.

Without Love, I will be at peace,
For the fragility will follow it away,
A far distance away… far far away.
Despite peace, despite pain,
Is life worth living without Love?

How I Eat M&Ms

CATHY BECK

I eat only solid color M&Ms.
Unless I don't.
I eat only three M&Ms at a time.
Or five M&Ms at a time.
But never two. Or four. Or six.

I will eat multiple colors
As long as they are all different colors.
But it can't be two yellow and one brown.
Or one red and two blue.
Or even one red, one blue, one orange, and two brown.

They need to be all different colors
Or all the same color.
Like Red, Red, Red
Or Yellow, Yellow, Yellow
It doesn't matter if they are mixed M&Ms

Like plain and peanut and mint
As long as they are all the same
Or all different colors
Some people will eat three different colors in one gulp.
Yuck!

Some people will only consume red M&Ms.
Some will only eat brown.
Some will (horrors!) eat four at one time
(My brain would go *"Tilt, Tilt, Tilt"*)
My daughter separates them all by color

And then eats them any way she wants
How do you eat M&Ms?
Do you let them melt in your hand?
Do you pay attention to the colors?
Does it matter if you grab a handful of four M&Ms?

Does it drive you absolutely bonkers
The way crazy people like me eat M&Ms?
Because I think it's really quite normal.

Boys at Play
photo by Barb Motes

Write On – Right On!

JOSEPH S. BENSON

Ally invited me to attend *Fine Lines* writers' camp.
After some thought, I said, "There's no reason I can't."
Camp sounded interesting, and we'd have time together.
My daughter drove us to Omaha in beautiful weather.

Ally said I'd like David Martin, have no fear,
and she hoped Bob would be back again this year.
He is an octogenarian, a retired librarian too,
and writes so well you feel what he's written is meant for you.

I didn't expect camp to make me so excited.
Creativity, artistry, and comradery were ignited.
I became enthralled by everyone's passion.
It piques my interest when people act in this fashion.

Back in the sixties, we had our own jargon.
We'd say "far out," when we agreed with a person.
"Right on" was a cheer for things we enjoyed.
Surfer dudes and hippies this language employed.

Our Fearless Leader taught us to cheer, "Write on!"
Fine Lines Camp taught me that "Write On" is "Right On!"

Momma and Heinrick

J ELEANOR BONET

Ameli sat silent and unmoving in the high-backed rocking chair, reliving her anticipation of their first child. She could say no more prayers, besides this seemingly endless night was finally almost over. Instead of dwelling on sorrow, she let her mind wander until it settled on a happy memory of that first pregnancy. Eric, when she told him he was to be a father, pulled the dusty, broken remains of the old rocker from the barn attic where he and Ameli's grandpa had left it. In secret, Eric worked with the skill of loving concentration and repaired the broken seat and polished the old wood until it shone like Ameli's happy eyes.

None of her sisters wanted the rocker because it was broken and old, yet no one would toss it to the burn pile, not because it was too good to be burned in the winter fest but because Ameli would cry such pitiful tears each year that it was brought out to be tossed away. She told Eric she inherited it by default when they married and moved to Eric's parent's home-place. She made him fetch it despite his grumbling about how silly it was to move it from one barn to the other. She did not realize it, but Eric paid attention to her sentimental chatter at the breakfast table. She spoke longingly of when she would sit in it holding her babies and told her childhood stories of being rocked to sleep in it held tight in her grandma's arms. Ameli's favorite memory was of the time when all three sisters sat giggling and squealing as Grandpa tilted them way back on the rockers, and tickled them until they wiggled like fish in a puddle. When the wooden seat snapped, it sounded like a rifle shot, and the giggling girls went suddenly silent.

"Oh, oh," Grampa said to the girls, now tumbling onto the floor as he tipped the chair upright, "we be in the trouble now, girlies." That was when Ameli knew for sure that Grandpa was afraid of Grandma's tears.

"And we were in big trouble," she chuckled, as she told the story again, while Eric joined here in bed on their first night in their new bedroom. "Oh! How my momma scolded us all and sent us girls to bed and my papa to the barn," Ameli giggled. "I know that if we had not snapped the seat, I would not have that chair because my oldest sister gets all my Momma's inheritance. But the broken chair was not good enough for her, so Momma let me claim it." She laughed as she snuggled into Eric's arms, and they fell asleep. She dreamt of babies that night and rocking them in that rocker.

That winter, when she was in her ninth month, Eric surprised Ameli. "Soon enough, you will be a grandma, rocking away the hours by the stove," he teased, when he presented the rocker to her in the tiny nursery. She was overcome with joy and cried, but Eric knew they were tears of happiness and because pregnant women seemed to cry at any instigation. Through her tears, she complimented him on the perfect repair work and the glowing shine of the freshly waxed wood.

"Let me be a momma, first, before you make me a grandma by the fire," she chided and leaned against him. "Thank you, dear. It makes me so happy." They stood, silent in their shared happiness looking at his masterpiece. He imagined her singing, as she rocked and hummed in the chair, knitting another bunch of little booties and bonnets, even though the baby-chest was filled to overflowing.

Then, Ameli turned and mischievously pinched Eric's cheek, "And you! You sounded like a grandpa already the way you huffed and puffed your way up those stairs." It was her turn to tease, and they hugged each other as content as they could be anticipating the arrival of their first born. Ameli shifted her feet, arching and rubbing her back in discomfort.

Eric knew she was tired and said, "Come, sit in it, you need to rest your back." He held it steady, as she eased herself awkwardly into the chair, finally settling in with a sigh of great relief. Eric chuckled at her pose, like a bowlegged queen on her throne, smiling up at him and glowing with joy.

"We better get to supper. I smell the bread is done." Ameli grunted in her effort to tip herself forward out of the chair and started to rise but fell back into the rocker. She groaned in frustration with the realization she was stuck, it made her frown like an angry child. Eric laughed until he cried from the effort, the sight of Ameli struggling to stand up was too comical not to laugh. She was only days away from giving birth, and her belly was simply too heavy for her leverage herself out of the rocker. He knew she hated being helpless. So, he laughed.

"Eric! Help me, Eric! Don't just stand there laughing at me, you dummy," she scolded. As only an embarrassed and angry wife can do, she gave him a look that knocked the wind out of him without even touching him. He was getting to know that look well, it appeared more and more often the closer her delivery time came.

His laughter may have been knocked out of him, but there was still a twinkle in his eyes, as he obediently came to her aid. He knew lifting her was going to be a cumbersome challenge. "I would hug you, dear, but you are too fat." He rubbed her big belly and asked, "Knock-knock, who's in there?" He burst out laughing again, as he heard her swear at him and nearly land a smack on his head. She never swore, and that made it all the funnier. He sputtered as he tried not to laugh, saying, "But, dear, what if I can't get you out or I drop you?"

"Then, you get to be the midwife. Don't be such a worry-wart. Just help me up!" They both grunted, as he again tried, awkwardly, reaching around her belly to his arms under hers, and finally, he gave a mighty pull as she pushed with all her might. They were both breathless from the effort and laughing like children at play by the time she was finally standing. Ameli punched his arm, nonetheless, to make a point. "Never laugh at a pregnant woman, and don't you ever tell your wife she is fat. Remember, she cooks your food!" She shook her finger at his nose saying, "And don't you dare tell your mother I cussed, either."

Ameli's good humor had come easily, then, in those days before her first born came into the world. She knew it would do so again, after enough time had passed, but at this moment, hours after Heinrick had breathed his last shallow breath, an almost imperceptible smile was all that could find her lips. Sitting in her beautiful rocking chair, sorrow dominated her being, and she almost forgot to breathe.

In the far corner of the nursery, a flame flickered weakly in a soot-dimmed lantern, casting a hazy light over the roughhewn cradle Grandpa pulled from the attic, as he had each time Ameli announced she was expecting. His chest would swell with pride, as he set it respectfully in the center of the nursery next to her rocking chair and declare in always the same way, "Dis here is for sure the best cradle ever made since God put Jesus Christ in da manger. Dis here cradle is a piece o' do old country. Yah, is oak wood from Sweden. It's been bed for a hundred babies in our family, dat's for sure. Yah, ever since dar was Vikings in dragon ships, dar been our babies in it! Yah, dat's so!" The thought of some giant Norseman with battle scars and big, thick hands like Grandpa's carefully carving the little bed for his child, perhaps a son, perhaps a daughter, caused her trembling lips to smile slightly. It was a tiny cradle for a tiny child but filled with such big love, over and over, through the centuries, since it was made. Such acts of love mean so much.

A larger lamp sat perched high on another of the honored heirlooms passed down from mother to daughter, Ameli's grandma's immigrant chest, another castoff from her sisters. It traveled across the sea from Sweden to Minnesota carrying all her great-grandma's linens, pots and yarns from the old country. From the height of the trunk on its long legs, meant to keep it safe from curious mice, the lamplight illuminated the bowed head of Ameli's daughter, making her white nightgown shine brightly against the shadows. Ameli sighed, it was as though an angel kneeled beside Heinrick's cradle, and her lips could no longer hold even a small smile. She struggled to focus her gaze, but all, save the cradle and girl, were blurred through the glistening tears she felt spilling onto her limp hands loosely folded in her lap. Silent and still, she watched Lisle's little hand move in slow sweeps, petting the soft curls on her brother's tiny head. Lisle's shiny, straight, Viking-blonde hair, made golden by the lamplight, hung down into the cradle. In comparison, the baby's wispy, chestnut-brown ringlets were darkly dull. So lifeless.

As soon as he was born, Ameli had seen Heinrick's dark hair and heard his gasping cries when the midwife set him on her chest. Her tears of heartbreak swept away in an instant all the pains of childbirth, leaving in its wake only those of a now familiar sorrow. Familiar, because she had felt such pains twice before and knew they could come again each time she gave birth. Once the midwife placed him in her arms, Ameli held Heinrick against her bosom almost all day and through the night for the whole of his short life. Only Eric, the gentle man she joyously married and loved with all her soul, could convince her to let the baby rest in the cradle, and she could sleep in the daybed near him.

"Ameli, please, sweetheart, let him sleep in the cradle of his ancestors, where he can be warm in his bed shawl Grandma made him. I will sit here and watch him while you sleep." As he had done before with his other two sons, Eric lifted Heinrick gently from Ameli's tired arms and laid him in the only bed this son would ever know. Then, he carried his exhausted, grieving wife to the daybed he built for this purpose, to let her rest easy near her babies. Lisle took her place on the little stool beside the cradle and looked at her brother.

Through her childish eyes, Lisle watched these loving acts become almost a ritual. When she was two, Johann died, and she jealously longed simply to be the only one held by Momma and cherished by Papa. When she was four, Niels died, and she cried when Momma cried, because Momma cried. But not understanding this new emotion, this sympathy, she wanted Papa to hold her tight and stop Momma's tears so they would all feel good again. Sometimes, when her brothers were in their bed, she crawled onto the daybed and slept with Momma, wanting to help her but wanting more to be told what it all meant. This time, with Heinrick, she was older and understood more because of those rituals.

One thing was the same each time a brother was born; Lisle always felt enthralled by the obvious and constant love between her parents. They never hid it. It never wavered. She wanted to be a part of it and share in it with them, but by some awareness beyond her child's mind, she knew it was not hers to share. Now, in her sixth year, her third brother, Heinrick, had come into her world and left it like the others. Lisle was understanding more of what that heart-rending clash of feelings meant, and she had a growing desire to comfort rather than be comforted.

She was aware in this moment, kneeling beside her baby brother, his body so still and silent in his cradle, that Heinrick was no longer inside the pale, peaceful face. He had come and then gone like his older brothers. Grandma had explained in her calm and wise way, "Lisle, Heinrick is with God in Heaven playing with his big brothers. He is not in that body anymore." But still, Lisle wondered where he had truly gone. Heaven must be a very big place with choirs of angels and countless ancestors of all the people in the whole wide world. Can Heaven be crowded like church on Christmas Eve, when all the families of all the farm folk in the county filled the sanctuary? Would he get lost like the lambs that walk too far away from the ewes in a big herd of sheep? Would he be calling for his momma, too, like one of those lambs?

As she wondered in silent concern for her baby brother, Lisle tucked his bed shawl around him, feeling the wavy texture of its rippling patterns, so finely knitted across a thousand rows. She straightened all the wayward strands of fringe and asked whoever it was that could hear her thoughts, would Heinrick be forever asleep in Heaven, always wrapped in his blanket's warmth? "I think you will, little brother," she said to him, knowing he would hear her.

Grandma had spent many weeks happily knitting the bed shawl, as she chatted a sing-song of gossip, her words unconsciously synchronized to the needles' rhythmic tac-tac-tac. Lisle remembered every hero and villain brought to life in Grandma's tales of warrior queens

and adventuresome men gone to fight monsters beyond the edge of
the world. She shared in her ancestors' glory and their misery in the
old country's frozen winters. Sweden, where only the dead stayed
behind while the strong sailed west in search of a new, safer, richer
homeland in America. Where famine and war could not follow.

In her aged wisdom, stoked with sarcastic humor, Grandma also
solved all the mysteries of misbehaving neighbors and children. It
was so hard to keep a secret from Grandma. With a meandering path
of observations, guesses, and suspicions, she was led almost always
to the truth of the situation. She knew amazingly curious things, too,
including why cows need bag balm, and bulls sometimes need a good
bop on the nose. She recited rhymes that taught the women how to
cure their men and babies of common ills. She knew exactly which
teas and salves would gently treat the elders suffering incurable diseases. She was wonderful and so confidently silly.

"You always hope for the best, expect the worst, give thanks for
the good that comes, and live with what you must," Grandma would
say with a shrug. "But, my Lisle, always be a good, kind person. Think
before you speak and be generous to others."

Lisle held that wisdom close to her heart. Tac-tac-tac, the past
and present merged as myths. Family history and daily happenings
became lessons for living a good life. Somehow Lisle could hold
the convoluted strings of stories, gossip, medicine, and adages more
clearly in her mind because she listened as she watched Grandma's
fast-moving fingers transform that ball of powder blue yarn into Heinrick's bed shawl. Tac-tac-tac. It seemed the tales of heroes and healing
were being knitted into that shawl.

There were some Grandma stories the elders would laugh and
slap each other's backs over. No knitting was happening during those
raucous encounters, but the steins were full and the food plentiful for
such times. All that boisterousness, over things that made no sense,
caused Lisle's head to spin. What was all that funny about how Becker's baby-making was so powerful he could do it from Sweden? Mrs.

Becker had a lot of babies. So what? How could Mr. Becker's two years in Sweden matter? For heaven's sake, Lisle wondered, why did that tidbit of gossip make all the grownups giggle and behave like naughty children throwing spitballs in school? Finally, she would stamp her foot and ask, "What's so funny?" But her frowning inquisition would only make them laugh even more.

Between bouts of laughter, Grandma would nod at Lisle and say, "I will tell that one again when you are older, child." Then everyone would sputter and laugh again, soon complaining of sore cheeks and bellies.

Lisle smiled and shook her head at that particular memory. She murmured to Heinrick, as if he could hear and understand, "Sore cheeks and bellies indeed, little brother. Does that make you laugh, too? Do babies laugh in Heaven? Surely, they would never cry."

Grandma's voice and laughter would never leave Lisle's memory. To her little-girl ears, it was magic and music to watch the pastel blue, wiggle and jump its way off the round yarn-ball, to flow quickly and smoothly through wrinkly fingers and be tautly twisted onto the noisy needle-tips then off again to reappear as patterned waves on Heinrick's beautiful baby-blue blanket. Lisle's own pink baby blanket, now safely stored in Momma's cedar chest along with all her baby clothes, had been created in that same happy way. She could almost feel it still, keeping her safe and warm in her baby bed. The pink cloud-like blanket had made her feel special, just as Heinrick's must make him feel, and she was a little sad when Momma packed it in the chest. Lisle had no doubt in her mind or heart that he could feel it just as she did. Of course, he would sleep in Heaven, wouldn't he? Forever safe and warm with it tucked around him.

Being six years old, she no longer needed her blanket or tiny clothes, but everyone said she would want them for her own babies someday. "So that you can wrap them in your Grandma's love," Aunt Hanna said. And of course, some day, Lisle would do just that, but only for the girl babies and only until Momma knitted them their own bed shawls. It was a marvel how Grandmas always knew if a baby would be born a boy or a girl, so they could knit the proper color blanket in time for the birth; blue for a boy and pink for a girl. Lisle wondered what the trick was to knowing that. Or was it the Grandma's yarn choice that made the baby come out a boy?

Well, Mrs. Hansen must have bad luck at guessing, because she knitted blue bed shawls every time her daughter Hilda was expecting. Despite that, it was a girl every time. So, every time, Mrs. Hansen gave the blue blanket to the needy folks in town. Grandma said no one should ever keep a gift made and not given to its intended person; doing so only brought bad luck. The orphans and poor folks needed blankets, and being generous brought good luck. Mrs. Hansen continued tempting fate by always buying blue yarn and then trying to cancel out bad luck by giving away the blankets. "Surely, good luck will come my way soon," she said, when her sixth granddaughter was born.

Grandma felt bad for Mrs. Hansen and told her, "So, then, my friend, after so many granddaughters, you maybe just need to buy pink yarn. The baby is sure to be a boy then, by thunder." Sure enough, that's what happened. Lisle had no idea what thunder had to do with it, but it worked. All the Hansen family shouted and cried for joy that day Hilda had a boy. It was a big party for his naming day and baptism but Hilda announced she was done having babies now that she finally had given her mother a son. Not to be left out, her husband, Sven, laughed and asked, "And what about me?"

"You, my love, will be too busy working to feed all these children. You won't have any energy for that hanky-panky stuff." And everyone, even Hilda and Sven, slapped backs and knees and laughed until they bent over with hurting bellies and cheeks.

Lisle put her chin on the edge of the cradle and spoke softly to her baby brother, "Life is confusing sometimes, Heinrick," she sighed, "but our grandma, she is so wise. And babies do make people happy."

Ameli rose from the daybed to go back to the rocker and invited Lisle to come along. "Come sit with Momma, Lisle. I need a hug. Do you?" Momma's voice was so low and so very sad, hearing it, Lisle felt like a heavy sack of wet wool had been set across her little shoulders.

"Coming, Momma," Lisle responded in a tone that matched her mother's. She leaned into the cradle, kissing Heinrick on his cold forehead and Ameli pick him up to hold him a while longer. "Sleep tight little brother, I love you." Such simple and familiar words, so innocently profound when spoken by a child.

"Oh! God in Heaven!" Momma cried out softly and fell into the rocker holding Heinrick to her. She rolled her head against the back of the rocker and a moan came from deep within as her sorrow forced itself from her breast. The floodgates of anguish opened at the sound of those words, the very ones Eric and she said each night, as they put Lisle to bed. The unstoppable eruption of emotions too-long-held suppressed escaped her tightly controlled demeanor. Loss, love, and longing washed over her, and she began to cry in great gulping sobs. Her body ached to hold and suckle her son. She desperately wanted his soft, warm cheek to rest against hers. Her lips burned to kiss his forehead and feel him still alive.

Heinrick was her third son, lost, as were his two brothers before him, to a sickness no one could cure. Knowing her prayers for a healthy son would not be answered, she prayed anyway at dawn every day and as she lay awake at night. She hoped, foolishly believed herself prepared for the inevitable. This time, she told herself, if it were another son, she would withstand the pain. She knew but would not admit that the pain for a third son, even though it might be familiar and controlled, would never be any less than that felt at the first loss of a child, or the second. How could it be? How could a mother love one son less than another? How could she not cry now, as she had in the past for Johann and Niels? She cried for each of them again, as she sat holding Heinrick's cold cheek to tear-washed face. She cried, too, for the guilt that gripped her at the thought of having prayed so hard, asking God if he might give her another daughter and no more sons. From the knowledge of many generations of mothers, passed down to her in that long line, she knew daughters would always be born healthy and live long, strong lives but sons, unless they were a first-born child, would die at birth. If she could never have a healthy son, why was she tortured like this? But she was not the first woman in her linage to go through this, and she could at least take some comfort in knowing she had no real fault in this sorrow. But she suffered.

"Why?" The whispered exclamation was past her lips before she could stop it, and another wave of anguished sobs convulsed her exhausted body, as she placed Heinrick in his cradle.

Lisle ran across the room to hug Momma and let her hold on very tightly, even though it hurt to be pressed so against her mother's chest. Lisle didn't mind it, because it was still more painful hearing her mother gasp for air between sobs. Lisle was crying, too, and could think of nothing to do but speak the words of comfort used so often to soothe her own tears.

She tried to make her voice calm and soothing as she said, "Momma, I love you. Don't cry. It'll be okay. Hush now. Hush now. I am here. Shush, now."

Those few phrases seemed to work their healing magic on Momma, just as they always had on Lisle. Momma relaxed her tight hug and felt Lisle's small hand patting her back, as if the mother were the child and the child had become the mother. Ameli, whispered, "You are so good, my dolly. You will be such a wonderful momma when you grow up."

In that loving embrace, they both were able to release their grief less tempestuously, letting hot, salty tears flow unabated down their cheeks, washing away some of the sorrow. Lisle cried more for her mother than for Heinrick. He was safe in Heaven; Momma was here and so sad. Momma's agonizing grief could be quieted only by love, which could take them beyond the painful moment and back into the good memories, so they could survive. This was something Lisle knew, not from a lesson learned, but from a place where such knowledge exists as truth, a place where ancestral Vikings and their cradles live within her.

At last, Momma took a deep, deep breath and let it out slowly. Giving Lisle one last great hug, blessing her with a kiss on her forehead, Ameli lifted her daughter onto her lap and felt herself much relieved. Lisle, too, gave a great sigh and relaxed against her mother's shoulder. The burden of that wet wooly weight was lifted and she knew Momma was now back to being Momma. "I love you," Lisle whispered.

"I love you, too, my dolly. You are such a good, kind girl. We will miss little Heinrick. He would have grown up and been a good, kind boy, too, with a big sister like you to teach him." They smiled and wiped away each other's tears, and sat wrapped in a special love known only between daughters and mothers. No one had to tell Lisle that this was a love she could always come to and find, even if she had angered Momma. It did not matter if Momma was not with her, she could and would feel it constantly. She sighed again and relaxed completely in that embrace of unconditional love.

The pain was off their chests, allowed to lift like fog in sunlight. They could sit in peaceful silence now, looking at Heinrick, as dawn came toward the house, as dawn always comes in the fall, rolling across the pastures turning dew to diamonds and the willows to shimmering gold. The soft morning light washed across the room to make the dust motes sparkle like fairies floating over Heinrick's bed. Lisle smiled up at Momma and asked, "Do you suppose Heinrick, Johann, and Niels are playing with the dust-fairies by the cradle?"

Momma smiled, too, "I am sure they are, silly dolly."

Then, as if they had been waiting for that exact moment when sunshine would fill the nursery, the rest of the household began to enter, stepping carefully to not make noise. Each of them, Grandma and Grandpa, Sven the stable boy, Netty the house maid, and Mrs. Jespersen the neighbor, all came to first touch the baby and bless him then hug Momma and kiss Lisle's cheek. Their voices were low, hushed in respect and weighted down with sorrow. Their gazes were steady, meant to give strength to those who would be grieving the most. The only one missing was Papa. No one asked after him, it would be rude. Besides, they knew where he would be.

Sven stood respectfully to one side of Grandpa and whispered to the old man, "The Mister, sir, he's in the pasture. He's with his cows, sir. He would not speak, when I asked could I go to the house. But I did, sir. I came here, sir." Sven seemed insecure and nervous at having to say so much at once, wanting very badly to be told he had done the right thing.

"Yah, Sven, we know. He will be there for a bit. He'll be wanting to make peace with God, before he comes to the house. It will be good that he is with the critters now and working. You just pay your respects here and then go do your chores." The old man patted the young man's shoulder to show Sven both his presence and his words were appreciated.

The shy young man moved closer to the misses but kept the proper distance. "I am that sorry, Mrs. Ericson. Heinrick was a handsome son. That he was. He was sure to be a good, kind boy. And Missy Lisle, you do good being here with your Momma." Mother and daughter looked up at him, the elder smiled gently, and the younger reached out to touch his calloused but well-scrubbed hand. He looked at her hand on his and was especially glad he had taken extra time to carefully clean up before coming to the house. His forehead furrowed in concentration, as he struggled to understand the swirl of strange emotions.

He was overcome by their kindness, given even in their great sorrow, but it was the warmth of Lisle's little hand on his that made him cry. He felt hot tears come out of his burning eyes and slip down his face. He was again insecure, nervous and embarrassed, too. Sven knew men should not cry, at least not in front of others, but little Lisle could do that to him, make him cry or make him smile as no one else could. Spellbound, Sven looked down into Lisle's blue-as-the-sky eyes, still red-rimmed and over-bright from crying, and suddenly, he felt at peace.

"I better go do chores now, Mrs. Ericson." He saw great sorrow in her eyes, a sorrow he knew well. He felt his heart take a huge, slow, thumping beat, the same as it had done when he had seen his mother

and father suddenly dead of the fever that had come to the town.
He knew that morning, seeing them in their bed, they were not just
asleep, but it had taken him until the next morning to believe they
were dead. It was at daybreak he realized he was not in a nightmare,
and he would not be waking up from it to find his mother singing as
she made him breakfast. In the early sun of spring, as a six-year-old
boy, he had walked five miles to the church to tell the minister what
happened and then, still alone, turned and walked back. He sat at the
kitchen table listening to the sounds of the farm until Mr. Ericson
came to pack his things and bring him to this house to live. Sven knew
that out of his sorrow had come great good for him, and he prayed
that the same might happen for this good, kind family. The town knew
that the Ericsons could have no sons and would need young men to
help them.

His own painful memories swirled around in his mind making
his loss seem less distant in the presence of this fresh sadness. With
great effort, Sven closed his mind to the bad memories and chose to
be grateful for what he had today. He turned hesitantly, not wanting
to move away from Lisle's gaze and warm touch, anguishing over
needing to leave but yearning to stay with her, yet wishing he could
run away. He moved quickly, yet made sure to take the proper time to
shake hands with each mourner in order of their rank in the household ending the ritual with a slight nod to Netty the housemaid. It was
good manners to look each person in the eye, despite the brimming
tears. Sven's frown deepened, as he struggled to keep his emotions
controlled. It was important to take his leave of them, as a man should.
Once he had nodded to Netty and she nodded her silent good-bye,
he ducked his tall frame through the nursery door, hoping no one had
seen his unmanly tears.

Of course, they all had seen Sven's tears, though no one would ever
mention it to him. Such things were understood and remembered
as they should be. Everyone respected him more as a man for having
cried yet been strong enough to do the right thing the proper way.

By shaking each person's hand while looking them in the eye, he had
shown himself to be the best kind of man — a good man. Tears could
not diminish his actions or their respect for him.

"He is a good boy, that Sven Jorgenson. It is good that we took him
in when his momma and papa died," Grandpa spoke to Grandma,
but in a voice meant to be heard by all. Grandma nodded her head
and wiped her eyes. She found she could not speak; it was hard on
her heart to see Ameli and Lisle in that rocker for a third time in four
years. It pained her to watch her Eric suffer through the loss of three
sons, yet she was proud he could still be such a good man and be like
a father to Sven, someone else's child. She tried not to think about
how much she wanted her boy to have his own son and not have to
take in another's under his wing, that was an unkind thought and she
blushed. She shrugged off these mean thoughts and held her husband's hand tightly. Unkind thoughts only bring more bad luck.

Everyone else responded to Grandpa's comment by saying, "Yah,
is good." Heads nodded in affirmation of both Sven's good character
and the worthiness of the family that had taken him in. Mrs. Jespersen
was Sven's aunt, a widow living with her spinster daughter and so was
unable to take in Sven, all those years ago. When she asked Lisle's
family if they could use a strong helper on their farm, it was just after
they lost their first son, Johann. She knew then that Sven could be the
son the Ericsons would never have of their own blood. Sven was the
first child of a first son, so probably his children would not suffer the
fate of Eric's three sons. He could be a good father of many sons. His
mother was not from the same village back in Sweden as the Ericsons.
That, too, was a good thing.

"Sven's momma and papa are in Heaven now, little Lisle, so they'll
for sure be watching over your little brothers," Mrs. Jespersen's matter-
of-fact way of comforting mother and child was meant to confirm the
cycle of life and death and the strange but loving ways of God and
Heaven. She would never speak out loud her thoughts about Eric
and Ameli's loss of sons. It was not her place. Neither would she tell

anyone but God of her prayers for Lisle and Sven coming together to have sons of their own. Well, maybe, she would have a talk with Eric's mother-in-law about this.

It was also not spoken of that baby Heinrick's passing after only three days of life was not unexpected, though no one wished for it either. He had been weak since birth, and Dr. Daniel Magnusson, who came when Heinrick was born, warned Papa that his son's heart would not let him live past the first few days. "You know, Eric, it will be as it has been with your other two sons." His voice was very low, in empathy for his friend, but both men knew he spoke of death as a simple fact of life, to sugarcoat things is disrespectful, so he spoke man-to-man, friend-to-friend, in a way meant to lend reason and strength to a man he loved as a brother. Daniel often saw the soul-rending pain of such loss in his service as a doctor and was aware that, as with any wound, sorrow must be cauterized and treated swiftly, so it can be cured. Hiding or ignoring it only made it fester, prolong the pain, and led to more death.

Eric nodded and said in near anger, "Yah, Daniel, I know. I know! I will not have sons to help me on the farm or carry my name to give to their sons. I know. I know. Johann, Niels, and Heinrick are named after the brothers Ameli and I lost to the famine in Sweden. It is to remind us that life is often hard and short, and we are not the only ones to have lost a child."

That night, after Heinrick was born, Lisle stood at the kitchen door, quietly keeping herself in a shadow. She felt frozen by new emotions rising to the surface when overhearing her father speak through clinched teeth. She had not heard him speak like this before and she wanted to go hug him, but then he sighed and pounded his legs with his big fists. Lisle was surprised he did not cry out in pain from the force of the blows, and she kept still, watching his face intently. He rose suddenly and launched himself across the room to pound the wall. He seemed to want to hurt himself. To destroy something. Was it the pain inside of him that made him so angry, so violent?

Daniel said in a low undemanding tone, "Eric, let it pass." Both doctor and daughter knew by instinct that such strong emotions must be released before they did the grieving father harm. Eric must purge all his pent-up frustration and gut-wrenching grief before he could go to his wife. "You need time alone to get it off your chest, my friend. Go breathe and think awhile. Go to your fields and pray."

"Yah, I hear you, Daniel. I am no good to anyone, now. I'll go tend the cows they need me. It's milking time. Ameli will need to rest and be alone a bit, too." The men shook hands in the way life-long friends do, knowing that their silence speaks their sentiments in ways words cannot. As he turned to accept Daniel's embrace of empathy, Eric saw Lisle in the doorway. His voice shook, but he smiled at her and said, "Papa will be back, dolly. I need to tend the cows. OK? Go to your Momma, Lisle. Yah?"

"Yah, Papa. I will do that. You go milk the poor cows and come back better. Yah?" Daniel grinned and exchanged a knowing look with Eric. Lisle's voice was like her mother's, tender but a little bossy. Ameli could tell you what to do, give you an unrefusable order, and it sounded like a simple request, because she said it so you heard it coated in honey. And, you did it, even if you did not want to do it.

"Yah, dolly. I will do that." She watched Papa walk in his normal, steady, long strides, as he headed toward the barn. His cows, in their own kind of discomfort caused by late milking, spotted him and started lowing. He called to them by name, and they meandered toward him forming in single file, ready to go to their stalls. Somehow the everydayness of the sight loosened his control. He was down by the pasture gate before he let go his emotions. He had waited so his daughter could not see him cry or hear him shout to the sky, "Why was a boy not born first?"

Eric was unaware that she did not have to hear him because it would not occur to him that she was in the kitchen when the women talked about making and having and raising babies. It was for that same reason that Lisle knew he would cry and cuss and then he would pray. He would, in his own good time, come back to the house ready to comfort and not be comforted. Lisle knew she was a first child in a family where that might mean she would only have sisters. The full significance of that fact was never hidden from her, but in her child's way she understood, too, that God took the burden of blame, and she was never made to feel it on her young heart. "Life is what it is, and we live it," was said so often in her home that Lisle simply knew it to be a fundamental truth.

Momma and Papa's family trees were well known, even the branches from the old country. Everyone was aware, a dark-haired boy born a second child would have a short life. Still, every mealtime was filled with hoping and praying for a miracle of life, but part of life is death. Even so, each new sorrow at such a birth was as great as with any child's death. Knowing it would happen did not ease the pain of it. Even Lisle, though still a child, understood that praying for a miracle did not mean it would happen.

Her very practical and open family included even the littlest children in conversations about procreation, birth, death, and all such things, whether it was about how a farm cat ended up with a litter of kittens or how the deer being dressed to feed them for the winter was alive once. Life was to be respected and appreciated. These things, family trees, and sickly babies, deaths of children born healthy and taken by a dreaded childhood disease, old folks dying from unseen strokes, and even strong men from an insect bite, were part of life and never spoken of in whispers in the dark. Instead, there were quiet, matter-of-fact conversations spoken while the women washed dishes and men played cards. All those who died were remembered in evening prayers. "You cannot let death kill life," Grandma said as she slammed the frying pan full of chicken onto the stove. "By thunder this is going to be one heck of a good supper!" Her favorite hen having come to a sudden end, she was not about to waste it. "Gone but not forgotten. All transgressions forgiven, if sometimes not forgotten so easy. Death, Lisle, when understood as a part of life, is something you can live with and not worry over all the time. You mourn a death, but you do not fear dying."

The day Heinrick died, when early morning light-filled room, Lisle, waiting for Papa by Heinrick's crib and in Momma's arms, remembered her Grandma's lessons and felt included in what was happening in her home. She watched the mourners offer condolences with simple declarations of acceptance and affirmation of their common beliefs. Everyone sharing in the love and comfort offered by each visitor was proper and good.

"You do the best you can; the rest is up to God in Heaven," Mrs. Jespersen said to Grandma.

"Life goes on. You live it as best you can," Netty spoke shyly to Lisle from the corner.

"You are a good woman. My son is a lucky man," Grandma said to Momma, patting her cheek and kissing her forehead.

With each comment, everyone responded with nodding heads and murmured, "Yah, that's right." It reminded Lisle of the way everyone in church would say, "Amen," at the end of a prayer or hymn. Soothing waves of comfort swirled around the room on small sighs of sympathy and touched all the firmly nodded heads, washing everyone in a communal sense of relief. What need is there to speak it, if you all share the thought? They each believed and therefore understood without words; fate is fate, and we all die, so, between birth and death, come what may, we live our lives the best we can. They all lived knowing that no one can ask more of anyone, nor expect more of themselves. Those raised in a household of God's love, expect honesty, respect, and kindness for and from all others. So, those often-repeated sayings and responses, taught and learned, unchanged generation after generation, carry a profound significance. A person simply lives by them because they are right and good guides, learned from watching others live by them.

"Och, just pay attention. You will learn," Grandpa would say, if Lisle showed childish frustration at her unsuccessful attempts to form letters in her notebook. Over and over, as he taught her to write, he would gently guide her hand and say, "Watch and learn, little girl." Whether writing or living, Lisle realized that a person can learn a great deal by watching and listening to the elders. She did it often and loved their voices. Sitting near them, she could hear the women chatting over their knitting, while they canned fruit, and nursed their babies. Lisle learned from men's conversations by sitting near the porch window, while they relaxed outside in rocking chairs of sun-faded wood, discussing the cows' sore udders, while sipping an evening beer over a game of checkers. Lisle learned how to be a part of life in her world by listening to those beloved voices share jokes, stories of daily chores, celebrations, sorrows, and hopes. She became attuned to the binding ties woven into the subtle variations of tones of voice, intensity of gaze, and quality of touch. She was too young to think of her life in complicated terms of habits, ritual expressions and body language, but she was unconsciously absorbing the morality of her family, as she watched and listened, participated and questioned, imitated and acted out.

In her child's mind, as she sat on Momma's lap in the sunshine watching the interactions played out around Heinrick's cradle, Lisle felt as she had when she watched her grandma knitting her brothers' blankets. Life, she thought, is like the tangled ball of yarn that can be transformed and become orderly and comforting in the hands of a loving person. It is through the tac-tac-tac of knowing, sharing, teaching, and learning that we come to see the patterns of how to live a good and kind life. This is how we may come to live together well.

In the quiet, after all the visitors left, Lisle could not keep her eyes open any longer. "I am sleepy, Momma."

"Yes, dolly, you can sleep now," Momma said softly and kissed her sweet daughter's forehead. Lisle's eyes closed, and she was about to drift off to sleep in one of the safest places in the whole wide world. Then, Momma lifted her arm and said, "Eric. You have come."

"Papa?" Lisle came wide awake and stretched out her arms to him. "Papa!" She felt so happy to see him, her voice was filled with joy even though sadness had been all around her. He stood so tall and straight, filling the room with his presence more than his bulk. He lifted Lisle into his strong arms and bent to kiss his wife's forehead.

"I am done with milking. I am here now." He looked over Lisle's shoulder, as she hugged his neck like a bear cub hanging on for dear life. Ameli smiled, and her sorrowful burden seemed lifted by the long and loving gaze from Eric.

From their place in the hallway, Grandma and Grandpa listened.

"Lisle, you go to bed now, yah? Go with Grandma. That's my dolly." Papa handed her over to his mother. "Momma and I want to be alone awhile with Heinrick."

"Yah, Papa. I know." She kissed his whiskery-rough cheek and hugged him extra hard, then took his face between her little hands and looked him in the eye. "Papa, it will be all right. We love each other."

Papa touched his forehead to hers and said, "You are a good and kind person, Lisle. I love you, too."

Grandma waved at Lisle. "We go now," she said holding her finger to her lips. She tugged on Grandpa's sleeve in a quick jerk to silence him as he was about to speak. The visitors who had greeted Papa as he came up the stairway into the nursery began to file out of the room.

"Yah, is good," they said in unison, like a chorus at church saying its final "Amen."

Puffed Up Winter Chickadee
drawing by Geoff FitzGerald

Get to Know One of Our *Fine Lines* Editors

STU BURNS

Wendy Lundeen

Stu Burns: Who is Wendy Lundeen the person apart from Wendy Lundeen the writer and editor? How do you define yourself in terms of personal history, career, family, education, and all those strange and wonderful things that composite the human experience?

WL: My dad was a WWII Prisoner of War, and because of him, I define myself as patriotic and devoted to serving the United States of America by exercising my freedoms and privileges. I even volunteered on a presidential campaign. He had a strong work ethic and was kind to all. He was a lover of God, America, his family, life, nature, poetry, and was a wonderful role model. I like to think I am moving his passions forward into the future — to my grandchildren.

Mom was a seamstress, quilter, gardener, singer, lover of music, movies, reading and family. Because of her, I love music and singing. I adore movies and never miss the Academy Awards. I enjoy seeing the fashions. Maybe, because Mom was a model, I followed her into that realm.

I was born at Offutt Air Force Base, Omaha, NE, when my parents came here from Iowa with Mom's parents to deliver Dad to catch a train to Kansas City where he would travel to the Korean War. Mom went into labor, and I am the only family member born in this state.

I began my career late in life. I was 43, almost 44, when I began teaching Spanish at Omaha Central High School in 1994. Besides being a mom and "yaya," this is probably the most rewarding and fulfilling role of my life. I love teaching and adore everything Spanish. I moved to Buffett Middle School where I taught 8th grade Spanish. That was quite enjoyable. The students allowed me to be an entertainer. They accepted my singing and putting concepts to music and raps.

SB: What work of yours, writing or otherwise, are you most proud of?

WL: I am proud of the travel stories I have written and some of my poetry. I am most proud of sharing about and bringing awareness to my grandsons' terminal illness. They have Duchenne Muscular Dystrophy. I have been ripped apart by this devastating impact on their lives, and writing helps me cope. All is not lost until they take their last breath, and I continue fighting for them. I am proud that I can help other people feel their pain, sorrows, JOY, and love.

I also love my other work: acting in the *Nutcracker* at Bellevue Little Theater every December as "OMA" — and other onstage per-formances, such as, *Tea House of the August Moon* — Atlantic, Iowa when I was 15; *Bye Birdie* at Burke High School at 17 — *Sleeping Beauty* (Kabuki Style) at Emmy Gifford Children's Theater in the early 1980s, *Children of Eden* 2011, *Brigadoon* 2013, *A Grand Night For Singing* 2014, all at Bellevue Little Theater. I also love to sing. I have been singing in church choirs since I was 14. I sang with NE Choral Arts and Voices of Omaha and have sung at weddings and funerals. I am proud of the solos I sing at my church.

SB: How did you get started with Fine Lines?

WL: I met David Martin at Central High School when I began teaching Spanish in 1994. He asked me to be a travel editor, and it was great to share the beauty and excitement about other parts of the world. When my grandsons were diagnosed with their terminal illness, my interest shifted, and I began writing from my heart about them.

SB: How do you approach the editing process? How do you feel your own identity as a writer affects the work you do as an editor?

WL: I admit I begin reading works of poetry as if they will rhyme — my technique — and when they do, it's easier for me. When they don't, sometimes, I feel I must work harder to interpret and/ or understand what the writer is trying to convey. I work hard to find meaning in the words and even apply meaning from my own frame of reference. That's all I have, really. I rarely edit prose but enjoy a good story. Of course, I watch for misspellings, errors in punctuation, and alignment.

SB: Is there anything you've read in your time at Fine Lines that has stuck with you? If so, can you describe it and how it had such an impact?

WL: There is a piece in the 2008 winter edition by Maddison Grigsby. I take it out from time to time to remind myself what really matters in life. She was a senior in high school when she wrote it. Her heart is in the right place, and when I think back to when I was her age, I know I was self-absorbed and in "MY" world. Her thoughtfulness, compassion, and kindness are evident. This was at the time my grandson was diagnosed with his illness, and this piece puts everything into perspective for me. Maddison is eloquent, articulate, and full of heart. I felt sad for the orphans and happy at her realizations as a young child about what matters in life. I was elated about the senior citizen who could "dance" in a wheelchair. When my grandson "danced" in his wheelchair last year, Maddison's story came to mind. "You were created by God, and no matter where you go, who you meet, or what you become, you are here for a purpose. Never forget how special you are." We all want to be loved, and we are all special. She is grateful and she asks us to thank someone.

SB: Is there anything you would like to share that the questions above did not address?

WL: I have learned so much from being a part of *Fine Lines*, and I am so grateful for all the wonderful friendships and relationships that have been created as a result of my participation. I know there are many unwritten, unfinished, prophetic, profound, magical works waiting to splash all over our blank pages. I am grateful for the opportunity to be in the position of teaching and encouraging young writers to express themselves at the *Fine Lines* Writing Camp every summer. I am honored to be in the presence of great minds year after year. Write on!

Stop saying I wish
Start saying I will

Lurking Shadows

JAYME BUSSING

The unseen glint of a blade within the shadows. The assassin stalks her prey amongst the dark crevasses of the streets, soft-soled boots poise as they shift ever so slightly. Studying. Watching. Waiting. A soft whisper of cloth falls on only the deft ears of vermin, slinking amongst the muck of the underworld, afraid of the light, of those who dwell there.

For the briefest moment, there's a dazzling gleam from the assassin's side, a blade coated in a thin veil promising demise. The pin prick of light is enough to catch the prey's peripheral vision. They turn to inspect the surprise treasure — perhaps a stray gold piece fallen from the purse of a clumsy merchant — only to find a swath of darkness looming before them, the air oddly still. Stifling despite the cool dampness of the night. There is nothing.

There's a pause, their face an open mask to the imaginative horrors that lurk within the human mind, within the dark corners of nightmares. With a slow turn, the prey begins their slow retreat once more, unaware of the terror to unfold. The assassin's muscles are tense, coiled to strike like a black asp. Her gloved hand tightens its grip, spurred by the knowledge of her target's destination and the time constraints that tighten like ropes the longer she waits.

She moves to strike, dagger poised in hand and itching for the kill, when another presence sets her muscles rigid, frozen in place. A curtly dressed man strolls into vision, his hands buried within his pockets, picturesque in his nonchalance. His eyes, however, scan the showy streets around him, looking for things that go bump in the night. A greasy smile slips over his lips once the prey enters his searching gaze.

The assassin's eyes narrow as she watches the encounter, her prey smiling as though they weren't afraid, they weren't sweetly intoxicated with expensive wine.

Her target hands over a thick parcel of parchment from beneath their fine robes, the slimy newcomer replacing it easily inside his own, the two talking idly as if the transaction hasn't happened. The assassin silently adds a new target to her list. She needs those documents.

The two offer friendly farewells and depart their separate ways, allowing the assassin to resume her silent stalking. Her constraints grow tighter with each step, purpose-driven and limited.

A turn away from the desired destination, the light of the moon is cloaked by the delicate fabric of clouds, snuffing out the remaining glow and offering the predator liberating freedom. She darts forward across the narrow streets, a wraith against the inky scenery, reaping a single soul as she passes.

The victim whispers their final breath, falling onto the cobblestone with a muffled thud. Moonlight kisses the protruding dagger, the blade glittering like a fine jewel as the clouds disperse.

The assassin is gone, her next target on the move.

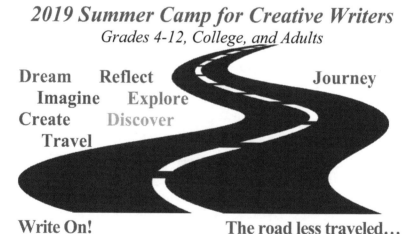

A Sunny Square of Sidewalk

MARY CAMPBELL

For the past few months, since I was diagnosed with stage-4 lung cancer, I've felt my life contracting. Time is a gift that arrives in little packets, not the vast, mysterious plain it was when I thought I'd live forever. This has happened before, when my children were newborns, for example, and I got to be a stay-at-home mom for a while. Nothing that happened before they were born and nothing that was going to happen when I went back to work mattered much. The only things in sharp focus were the baby and the new routine: warm bathwater, fresh clothes, mealtime, and overpowering love.

These days, metaphorically, I'm playing Barbies with little kids in a sunny square of sidewalk. I've developed the spontaneous mindfulness of children. My new superpower is the ability to shut off guilt and regret, anxiety and fear, living inside the spatial perimeter of that square and the temporal boundary of that hour. Physically, I'm warmed and comforted by sunlight and toddler kisses.

This works great for me, but people have questions. They want to know what I'm *doing* about the cancer and what's going to happen when the chemo stops working. They'd probably like to know how long I'm going to live, too, but, politely, they don't ask. Still, it seems as if I should care about these questions, and right now I don't. I have to trust that when I need certain answers, I'll get them. Meanwhile, I let the questions bounce off my square of sidewalk. Otherwise they interrupt my dancing.

In the weeks and months B.C. (Before Cancer), I fretted. My life seemed too small. Rather than appreciating the sunrises and sunsets I was dependably receiving, I chafed at limitations. I wanted to be out there in the world, doing things, going to concerts, riding my e-bike, waltzing in a pavilion, and meeting friends for lunch. Truth be told, I longed to buy a mini-motor home and take to the road. These days A.D. (After Diagnosis), I'm enchanted by late-summer sounds — katydids, crickets, and the change in the pitch of children's voices, as they wring every drop of joy out of the final days of summer vacation.

A cancer diagnosis has an unexpected cushion: people treat you like you're special — or maybe you just feel special, and people react accordingly. It's as if they think you're particularly brave or strong when, really, all you are is unusually conscious. Your cancer gives them something to do to demonstrate their love for you. Trust me on this — every card, letter, phone call, email — every token of friend-ship means the world. Don't for a minute think the little things don't matter. Maybe, they can't cure cancer, but the hugs warm my heart, and the prayers keep me afloat.

To be continued…

Shoreline Golf Course – Early Spring

BUD CASSIDAY

I golfed today with my friend Jerry.
We've golfed together for 35 years now give or take.
He won $1.75 from me today.
Other days I win from him. Most times Bob
joins us, but not today.
We talked about our work.
We talked about fishing, and hawks, and found
a large feather on the first fairway.
Other days we've found leftover
bones from a hawk's meal, or perhaps an owl's,
seen coyotes and foxes.
One time I found a large carp carcass snatched
from Carter Lake on a fairway,
partly eaten and partly decomposed.
That must have been a tasty meal.
We noticed the eagle's nest on hole #9
has fallen into disrepair since its
last residents, three little white headed
eaglets we could see above the branched rim of
the aerie several years ago.
But they are long gone and may have started
their own aeries by now.
We talked about various great shots we had made
once upon a time hoping that we might recreate
some of those moments today.
We talked about our kids and his girlfriend's dog,
politics, and religion, war and peace.

I made a long birdie putt on the first hole
and went on to miss about a dozen really good putts
in the round.
Golf is like that, sometimes. Well, more like most
of the time.
Contrails crisscrossed overhead,
and they became long, narrow, puffed clouds,
joining the others,
gradually moving across the sky,
carried on the wind high above.
It's nice walking out there on the green grass,
among the grey trees, under the blue and white skies.

White Tail Buck
photo by Barb Motes

Sentinel Peak:
Poems of the Desert People

DAVID CATALÁN

For my father Francisco Catalán
who labored in the Arizona copper mines
drank the sacred saguaro wine
and shared the Sonoran desert
with his O'odham brothers

CREATION

The earth is young and unfinished
Silent darkness sleeps upon its face
Earthmaker breathes a mighty cloud into the sky
Brings it down to the soil in torrents of rain
Digging flowing rivers and wandering canyons

Earthmaker walks upon the ground in heavy steps
Raising flattened mesas and sacred mountains
The new sky meets the growing earth
Where they touch living things arise
The saguaro, ocotillo, palo verde, and mesquite
Coyote, snake, rabbit, lizard, and deer
The air vibrates with buzzard, raven, and eagle
Elder Brother reaches into the ocean clay
And brings forth the people to be named O'odham
The people speak and the earth knows the power of words
The people sing and the earth knows the power of music
The people dance and the earth knows the power of motion
The people drink the saguaro wine
Clouds bring rain to replenish the thirsty earth
The desert blossoms with living entities
Corn and beans to sustain the people
Creatures that walk and slither across the earth
Feathered gliders that soar through the air
Majestic plants that keep a watch over the new land
The people show gratitude to Elder Brother
The people celebrate His creations
The people seek the blessings of life
As they travel on the spiritual journey through the Maze

THE MAZE

The Man in the Maze is Elder Brother
He is a symbol of every human of his creation
A being who starts his journey at the beginning of life
Then is destined to twist and turn toward a goal
Through the consequences of choices made
Through respect for the living desert
And a bond made with its creatures
Through reverence of the mountains
And the refuge sought in its caves
Through the sharing of earthly gifts

And the gratitude shown by those who receive them
Sorrow may be found in a path of the Maze
Pain may be felt in sickness and old age
Hunger may be revealed when the rains do not come
Joy may bloom in the birth of new life
Fulfillment may satisfy in achievement
Each step taken on the path of the Maze
Is a moment in life
From Birth to Death
Death comes when the center of the Maze is reached
When goals are met and dreams become reality
When Elder Brother sends down his blessings
Which fall upon his sons and daughters
In readiness for the Sun God to greet them
Leading them on the final path to the next world

I'ITOI

The creator god has always dwelled among his desert people
He is their maker and their protector
Today he lives in a cave upon *Baboquivari Mountain*
An old man resting from many earthly labors
Forever vigilant and watchful over his domain
Much as a loving parent is mindful of his children
I'itoi nurtures memories too many to count
Of bringing light into a darkened void
Of bringing people unto the earth from the underworld
Of teaching his children the art of survival
Of naming them with sacred identities
The *Hohokam*
The *Tohono O'odham*
The *Akimel O'odham*
Even the *Papago* to fight his wars
I'itoi was also a god of vengeance
Punishing his people for acts of unkindness
Through war, flood, and famine

Blinding enemies
Cleansing the land for new beginnings
Guiding the people through the Maze
Illuminating the path to well-being
Bestowing the gift of the *Himdag*
A balance
A harmony
A vision
Whereby desert people are sustained

Feminism Is Multifaceted
image by Amanda Caillau

Liaison Between Societies

JACOB CLARYS

A *liaison* (lee-AY-zon) is a French word meaning "bond," and there is only one bond between all civilizations, music. Looking through a band choral book, the selections include pieces written less than one hundred years ago and those that range all the way to seven hundred years ago. Although the differences are dramatic, it is the ideas survived, and modern music has grown from them. Music is a fundamental principle in human life, but what makes it so special, and why does it show up in every civilization to date? Music is one of the best forms of communication; it is beneficial to health; it is an economic booster, a cultural definer, and it brings people together.

Music is one of the best forms of communication and predates language itself. Historians can find traces of music from all time periods, but sometimes, there is only music and no formal language. Before a unified language was created, ancient people used melodies, whistles, and drums to communicate with others. This is because the song is the universal language of mankind. During the U.S. Civil War, Union and Confederate troops would use "Bugle Boys" and the drum corps to signal an attack, retreat, and as a command. Everyone understood what it meant, because it is hardwired, or we are born with it. The Civil War was most definitely not the first conflict to utilize music. Every civilization from the ancient Hebrews and the Greeks to modern times has used it. Music breaks the language barrier. David Ludden said, "Higher pitch, more fluctuations in pitch and rhythm, and faster tempo convey happiness, while the opposite conveys sadness. People from two different countries can understand and appreciate the same music." This is possible because people can detect similarities in emotion within one's own language. If music was required everywhere, the overall ability to communicate would increase and would prompt people to be more direct in interactions.

Music is beneficial to health. More specifically, it can help with embryonic development. Studies show that playing music for an unborn child provides benefits that are crucial to maturation. Listening to a relaxing song or singing lullabies sends calming chemicals throughout the body and into the placenta, facilitating bonding and relaxation. Playing lullabies communicates to children that it is time to relax and go to bed. Music also helps to stimulate the augmentation of their growing brains. Music isn't just helpful for children, it helps all ages. Music is seen as stress relief for teens, and studies prove that people who learn to play instruments are less likely to have dementia. Music therapy helps mental health patients with developmental and learning disabilities, Alzheimer's disease, other age-related conditions, substance abuse problems, brain injuries, physical disabilities, and chronic pain, including mothers in labor.

Music is an economic booster and will always be a staple in society. The music industry produces around forty-seven billion dollars annually. This is another reason why music has stayed intertwined in the fabric of humanity. In today's world, many people pay inflated prices to see their favorite artists and bands perform at concerts. Not only do people pay to see musicians, but they pay to learn how to play.

Music is a defining part of a culture. Another reason music is prevalent in history is because it represents different cultures and their time periods. In the early twentieth century, jazz was popular in the United States, predominantly in the African American communities, because it helped to express their struggles. The "Roaring Twenties" were all about defying societal standards, and jazz was the perfect outlet. It combines spontaneity and freedom in the music to create a cultural masterpiece that depicted a story of struggle.

Music brings people together. One of the most fascinating things about human history is that no matter what culture, there is always a form of music connecting fourteenth-century Europe to twenty-first century North America. It is fascinating that despite the differences in culture, race, ethnicity, time, and place, there has always been someone performing a piece relevant and emotional music that represents the people.

Like Karl Paulnack said, "Music is a basic need for human survival." It is the lifeline that all cling to and have for thousands of years. It is what people turn to in hardship; it is what commemorates the start of a relationship in marriage and is what lays the deceased to rest. Because of all this emotion presented in music, people are brought together by this emotional bond. Where there is emotion, connectivity follows. Richard Wagner's "Elsa's procession to the Cathedral" may in fact be the most beautiful piece I have ever played because the emotion can be heard throughout. The piece is like a book everyone can read, and each note is worth a thousand words. It is music like this that drives society and brings it together despite many differences.

"It is powerful at the level of the social group because it facilitates communication which goes beyond words, enables meanings to be shared, and promotes the development and maintenance of individual, group, cultural and national identities" (*The Powerful Role of Music in Society*). It is common to believe that each group in humanity is distinctly different, but that is incorrect. The connecting factor is music, making us not so different after all. Music, hardwired into our very genetic codes, has been around since the birth of humanity. It is one of the best forms of communication and predates language, it is beneficial to health, it is an economic booster, a cultural definer, and it brings people together.

Grass-Fed Blues

STUART CODD

The arsenal of meats, condiments, and vegetables combined with the cacophony of voices emanating all around the food truck was deafening. The Washington State Fair holds its busiest crowd all year round. Here in Puyallup, the atmosphere during festival season is like none other, with the Pacific Northwest sun firing with all its might onto the landscape. To Andre's left, vast aisles of cars lined up like a bunch of toy cars presented on a shelf. On his right, the taco truck sat adjacent to his burger truck ten meters away, and in the distance, the various large-scale amusement park rides crowded around each other. Andre was hoping for a large profit today, as his own food truck business almost went broke last month.

"Hey, babe, do you know where the extra grass-fed beef is?" Andre glanced behind him, and his wife Sasha stood there with a large hunk of meat in her hands. The white apron tied around her was stained brown and yellow with all the meat and grease to prepare for opening day. Despite being married for three years, Andrew was still taken aback by how perfect she was in his eyes, even when she denied it.

Standing at his height of 5'9, Sasha had a long face with defined eyebrows, which other women would've been envious of. Every morning, Andre would slouch over to the kitchen in their studio apartment in downtown Seattle to see her making eggs and bacon in a pair of faded overalls and a red shirt, her standard uniform as an up and coming artist. The recession of 2008 left them hard-pressed for money, which was why Andre took a job as a food truck driver. His uniform, aside from the apron and hat he wore on the job, was standard cheap jeans and shirts from the nearest Goodwill. Since Sasha's work wasn't well known, she hadn't been able to sell her paintings as much as she hoped. In their studio, the kitchen area sat next to their king-sized bed with a stack of paintings leaning against the wall in front of it. Sasha pointed to the drawers by the refrigerator; the mini-freezer they had next to it.

"Yeah, they're in the bottom drawer on your left," Sasha replied. Andre hoped that this grass-fed beef wouldn't be a waste of money today. Grass-fed beef was expensive, but there were always some families that asked about the quality of the meat, and then they would walk away disappointed. Every time Andre pulled out the beef, Sasha fell victim to his constant complaints about how expensive the meat was.

"Oh, good. I would pound some more meat if I were you. You never know how much you need at events like these," Andre advised Sasha. She proceeded to lift a 10-pound package of beef out of the mini-freezer.

"Try not to pout about the meat today, please? It doesn't look good, if the customers see us arguing in here," Sasha reminded him, taking out a meat mallet. Turning away, Andre started shredding the lettuce with the *thump, thump, thump* of Sasha's mallet pummeling the meat behind him.

Andre sighed, "Yeah, but if it was just you, I wouldn't have to order all this meat. I wish people wouldn't have to be so particular about what kind of meat they were eating; they don't realize how *expensive* grass-fed meat is." He took out a container full of tomatoes and chose a knife from the assortment he laid out next to the sink and began dicing the tomatoes. Andre knew from experience that getting agitated while using a knife is never a good idea, but he wasn't thinking about that. He was obsessing over the $300 he spent picking up the 10-pound package of grass-fed beef he ordered along with the cheaper meat.

"Well, you're the artist. Artists need to have eclectic taste." Andre made no attempt to hide the grumpiness in his voice.

"What's gotten into you? This is going to be our busiest day of the year! You don't get to be mean, until the end of the day when we're packing up," Sasha glared at him.

"Sasha, we've been cooped up in this food truck for five years now, and it doesn't look as though things are going to pick up anytime soon. Unless you've got a few thousand dollars buried somewhere." Andre moved toward the onions and set to work, choosing another knife.

"Well, I may have something coming that can turn things around for us." The excitement in her voice rose with each word; when she reached the word "us," it was like a mouse had been caught in a trap.

"Don't tell me your art has been accepted into one of those 'art shows' again," Andre spat. Sasha could see a dark cloud forming over Andre's head, and it seemed that it was to cause a downpour.

Sasha's art was accepted at art shows before, but she never had sold any. Time and time again, some entitled college kid from Seattle University had the audacity to critique Sasha's work in front of potential buyers. Andre felt like a bull trapped in the cage before being set loose, whenever he saw this unfold. He had trouble sleeping every night, because when he was about to fall asleep, his eyes fell upon Sasha's latest painting of a man riding a bike through the park a few blocks away from them. Lately, the stack of paintings was overflowing into the kitchen, which didn't bode well for either Sasha or Andre. It pained him to watch her fail at her shows, especially since her favorite painting of a man making pottery still sat in their apartment. She spent weeks painting that piece, while Andre was in north Seattle selling burgers.

"I managed to sell a couple of paintings last week, didn't I?" Her feeble attempt to cheer him up fell on deaf ears.

"Your parents don't count," Andre pointed out, glumly.

"Wow, first the meat, now the paintings. Am I going to have to deal with this the whole day?"

"I hope not," Andre's cloud rumbled with thunder.

"Well, I hope that your attitude improves, or else we're not going to sell anything, today. Anyways, an art collector is interested in one of my paintings. He wants the pottery one, Andre! The pottery one!"

It was fortunate that not many people had arrived at the amusement park, yet, so they couldn't hear the commotion coming from Sasha and Andre's truck.

"When does the curator want to look at the piece?" Andre appeared concerned. After the decline of the economy, Andre became skeptical of everything, especially promises. He believed no one could come through for him, whenever he was in a deep hole, as he always had to climb himself out of it. After the collapse, he lost his job working at a construction firm downtown. Andre's friends who were employed gave him some leads on new jobs and promised they would put in a good word for him. However, they didn't come through, and he was denied at each interview; his resume and interview skills were never what the employers were looking for. It wasn't until luck came to him in the form of a newspaper ad calling for a food truck worker that he found some redemption.

"The curator said sometime next week." Sasha's face glowed like candles on a birthday cake.

"Okay, okay. Listen. I'm sorry, Sasha, but these guys waltz in with their nice suits and flaunt around their money that they insist they have, but when it comes time to pay up, they don't come up with anything! Therefore, we can't trust anyone right now!" He became red in the face, and his thundercloud was shooting lightning bolts. "I've been through enough, Sasha, enough! I just want life to be more consistent than it is, and that includes eating real natural meat, instead of killing themselves on this fake, cheap stuff we're preparing!" The pace of his dicing moved faster with his face becoming more contorted along with the fumes of the onions he cut. Sasha's worry rose each time the dicing went faster, fearing that Andre would cut himself.

"Honey! Slow down before you hurt yourself or me!" Sasha backed into the corner of the truck, as Andre brought the knife down too early and sliced his hand open. Blood began running as if it were from a leaking pipe.

"Oh, damn! Sasha! Can you hand me one of those old rags?" Andre said through sharp gasps. He tried to cover up the cut with his free hand, but the blood seeped through his fingers.

Sasha handed him a rag. "Jesus, Andre. Go to the bathroom and clean that up before you get blood all over the workspace." As he started toward the bathroom, Sasha called after him, "Make it quick! More people are starting to show up for the fair!"

Sasha was right. Now, that it was later in the morning, more people started to show up at the fairgrounds. Couples surveyed the food trucks, arguing about what food they wanted for lunch. Keeping his head down, he strolled forward, covering his hands, making it look as though he was carrying something.

Why does this always happen to me? Andre thought. *Every year, Sasha would set me up with a comment, and I end up the bad guy with the bleeding hand. Hmph.*

The cut was pretty deep, so Andre moved carefully with the gauze and cloth to cover the wound. Since Andre cut his hand several times before, he became an expert in patching himself up. Sasha did have a point. Andre always treated this job with contempt. He should've been grateful that he had a job at all. Losing the construction job made him unpleasant to be around. Andre admired Sasha for tolerating his behavior for so long; he couldn't imagine how she must've been feeling all these years having dealt with his behavior and constantly failing at selling her paintings. He resolved to work on his temper, for Sasha's sake. Satisfied that he wasn't gushing blood anymore, he set out back to his truck. As he opened the door, he was taken aback by how neat the inside of the truck appeared. All the buns were neatly piled into a basket across from the register, appearing as though they were aching to be picked for the first burger. The vegetables and condiments were all lined up, as if they were set to march in a parade, and the various cheeses stacked up like a refurbished Jenga tower.

"Thanks, Sasha, it looks great in here. Are we all set for today?" The spatulas hung above the truck window, and the knives sat ready for work, their blades gleaming in the late morning light.

"Yeah. I'm glad that your hand is okay. Now, we can open up."

"If enough people buy the grass-fed beef, then, I'll be happy."

Sasha sighed. "Again, with the snide comments. You know, why can't you just — oh, what's the use? You're just going to yell at me again in front of the customers."

"Sasha, I know I haven't treated you or our situation with much optimism. I wish we could live comfortably enough so we wouldn't have to stress about how much money we'd spend on food and paint. I want you to be happy and content, and it's been hard with all the challenges we've faced over the years." Andre had trouble meeting her eyes, while confessing how he felt.

"Andre, it's okay, I understand. I know you've been our main source of income. Everything will be fine; it'll just take some time. We've made it this far, so I think we're doing pretty well despite everything we've been through."

"Thanks, babe. I'll be on my best behavior for today!" He gave Sasha the biggest smile he could muster.

She proceeded to put her disposable gloves on. "Look, Andre. Here comes our first customer!"

Both standing up straight, they welcomed the young couple who arrived at their food truck.

Eyeing Andre's menu, the boy asked, "Do you really sell grass-fed burgers here?"

"Yes, indeed, we do! Fresh from Eastern Washington. What would you like on your burger, you and your lady?" Andre proceeded to place two patties on the grill. The sizzling that came from the barbecue made him lean back and relax.

"We'll have the Southern special, with the barbecue sauce, please." The boy proceeded to take cash out of his wallet.

Well, Andre thought. *Maybe, today will turn out well after all.*

After serving the couple their burgers, Andre and Sasha watched them walk away through the parking lot. Several people caught sight of what they carried and started to file toward Andre's food truck. Glancing at each other, Andre and Sasha set to work.

The Magic Toaster

LINCOLN CRAIG
5th Grade, Buffett Middle School

Linc thought he had a regular toaster, but soon, he discovered it was quite an interesting toaster.

One day, he woke up in the morning and started to make some toast. He put in one slice of bread, and he did this every morning. When it was done, the toaster went, "DING," and two pieces of toast came flying out! Linc thought to himself, "I remember putting one piece in."

The next morning, he put in one Pop-Tart and said, "OK, one Pop-Tart is in the toaster for sure." Soon, he heard, "DING!" Two Pop-Tarts came shooting out of the toaster.

"Hmmmmmmm, this is interesting," Linc said.

Then, he remembered the videogame he was borrowing. "What if I duplicate this game, so I could keep one and give the other back to my friend?" He put the game in the toaster, and DING it worked! "I am going to duplicate my money now." He put in one dollar, and out came two dollars!

Then, he had an amazing idea. "I have always wanted a twin brother." He put his hand in and pushed the toast button. Sadly, he was electrocuted. The toaster shorted out and did not work.

The lesson of this story is: Do *not* put your hand in a toaster!

Night-Table Tableaux

WILLIAM DORESKI

The brass-bottom lamp by the bed
casts a green light on the abstraction
you've become in your old age.
The telephone on its recharger
coughs up occasional messages
that crosscut the silence preferred
by objects arranged as still-lives
to rectify angles and planes.
Although you're lacking motive
you could enter this genre scene
by extending your arm to grasp
the book bound in plain red cloth.
But would the book read you the way
the lamplight does? Would pages
flutter with flirtatious phrases
that would tinkle on the old pine floor?
All so deliberate. The green light
emanates not just from the lamp
but from the will you impose
on the objects that define you.

A Crisp Autumn Day

MARINN DRICKEY
7th grade, St. Cecilia School, Omaha, NE

Pumpkins in the cornfields
gold among the brown

Leaves of rust and scarlet
trembling slowly down

Birds travel southward
lovely time to play

Nothing is as pleasant
as a crisp autumn day.

Ranthambhore – Gave a Lift
photo by Kim McNealy Sosin

The Intruder

SOPHIA DRICKEY
10th grade, Duchesne Academy, Omaha, NE

My house is on fire
It's being burned to the ground
The intruder did this
My heart is pounding in my chest
Tears falling down my face
The intruder did this
My head is spinning quickly
Sharp ringing in my ears
The intruder did this
I am standing outside the burning house
I am clenching my fists and chanting the words
But the house is still on fire
And not everyone can get out alive

---

*Do not be satisfied with the stories that
come before you. Unfold your own myth.*

RUMI

¿Quien, Yo? No, Yo.

ROBERT KLEIN ENGLER

¡Ekhah! Están tocando la fuga de la muerte otra vez.
La oigo en el doblez seco de periódicos.
La oigo en el viento de acero del subterráneo
cuando el tren ruge con un eco de tumbas.

Veo los ojos que gritan, pero nadie cuida.
Mañana, las mejillas lisas de jóvenes sentirán
el moho de lagrimas. Es siempre esta manera,
las lanas del estado amortiguan sus gritos.

¿Usted ve la manera que él los mira?
Hay un fuego de hornos en sus ojos.
Vendrán. Espere y vea. A la cara de noche,
nunca es importante la muerte.

Mañana, el pelo brillante de jóvenes
sabrá el polvo de cenizas.
¿Usted ve la manera que él los mira?
Hay alambre de púas en su vistazo,

Pero la gente mira lejos porque nadie cuida.
Es siempre como esto, una almohada
de oro amortigua los suspiros de la duda.
Están jugando la fuga de la muerte otra vez.

La oigo en la inflamación seca de periódicos.
La oigo en el dínamo de puertas que cierran.
El tren confunde con un dirge de mentiras.
¡Ekhah! Vienen para nosotros todos.

Who, Me? Not Me.

ROBERT KLEIN ENGLER

Ekhah! They are playing the death fugue again.
I hear it in the dry fold of newspapers.
I hear it in the steel wind of the subway
When the train roars with the echo of tombs.

I see eyes screaming, but no one notices.
Tomorrow, the smooth cheeks of young men
Will feel the rust of tears. It is always this way,
The wool of the state muffles their cries.

Do you see the way he looks at them?
There is a fire from ovens in his eyes.
They will come. Wait and see.
The closing in of darkness never minds.

Tomorrow, the shining hair of young men
Will know the dust of ashes.
Do you see the way he looks at them?
There is barbed wire in his glance,

But people look away because no one cares.
It is always like this, a pillow of riches
Muffles their gasp of doubt.
They are playing the death fugue again.

I hear it in the dry kindling of newspapers.
I hear it in the dynamo of closing doors.
The train rattles with a dirge of lies.
Ekhah! They come for us all.

Home

CA'BREA FIELDS

Located in the Midwest,
A warm welcoming home to
Four fortune five-hundred companies
I am from Omaha, Nebraska
A city where everyone
Knows someone who is somebody
A state people landmark
As the corn place
A place with multiple opportunities
For jobs, education, and activities
An open downtown area
For children, adults, and visitors
A safely protected location
Where anyone can feel themselves
A zoo where smells direct
But help individuals discover
A discovery for souls
Some never want to leave
Omaha, Nebraska is a place
I gladly can call home.

My Grandfather Told Me

KRISTI FITZGERALD

My grandfather told me
I had a lovely voice
even though my parents
told me to be quiet

He asked me to sing
and recorded it on tape
that he listened to so much
the tape broke
I told him I'd sing for him
in person

My grandfather told me
It would be ok
when I fell on the ice
outside his house
He bandaged my knee
even though I knew I would get in trouble
for ripping my tights
so he took me to buy new tights
and said it would be our secret.

My grandfather told me
he would always be there-
to hold out his hand
and welcome me home

My grandfather told me
I was a beautiful artist
even though my parents threw
my pictures away

He saved every single picture
I ever drew for him
in a closet that I found
after he died

My grandfather told me
that I mattered,
that I was smart,
and that he loved me
even though my parents
told me I was stupid
and they didn't want me

My grandfather told me
to come live with him
when I was a teenager
and could no longer live
with my parents
and all his grown kids were gone;
he said he was my parents now

My grandfather told me
he would always be there-
to hold out his hand
and welcome me home

My grandfather told me,
on my wedding day,
that he could go now;
That I had someone he trusted
to take care of me.
I smiled but I didn't listen
thinking he would be with me forever

My grandfather told me
he missed my grandmother
and wanted to be with her

but that he would always be with me
even though he had to leave

My grandfather told me
he needed to cross over
so when the time came,
he would be there
to take my hand
and welcome me home

Feminism Is Equality
image by Amanda Caillau

Special Teas

MARCIA CALHOUN FORECKI

Dalia Thomas woke in empty air. No noises or smells, just silent empty air hung in her attic bedroom. If not for the roses on the wallpaper covering rough board walls or the stains on the cushion of the reading chair, Dalia might have believed she had been whisked away in the night to, where? Absent the smell of salt and grease from bacon being fried in the kitchen below her. Stilled the clanging of pans, the whisking of eggs in the blue bowl. Without the scratch of a knife on toasted bread, no whistle from the tea kettle complaining on a hot stove, no tapping of running feet, no sniffling noses, no calls of "me first," or "that's mine," and no slamming of doors whatsoever in the house below Dalia's rented attic bedroom, she might have been justified in assuming her capture by angels or fairies.

Dalia rose from the small bed, more of a cot in the small pyramid room, slipped on yesterday's cotton anklets and her pink chenille robe. She descended the steep attic stairs and peeked into the children's bedroom. They were both asleep as if this were not a school day. A Wednesday to be precise. Dalia walked on through the empty kitchen and listened at the bedroom door of Mr. and Mrs. Barczak, whose house it was, whose children were sleeping, and whose absence was beginning to unsettle Dalia. She heard no talking or snoring through the bedroom door, so she opened it a crack and peered in. The room was empty and silent.

"There surely is an explanation," Dalia thought. "Maybe Mr. and Mrs. Barczak are downstairs." Old Mrs. Barczak, the children's grandmother, lived there. She owned an apothecary shop of sorts, where she sold homemade cold remedies and love potions, among other wonders. On a sign in the window were words written in a modified

Cyrillic alphabet for American readers: "Medicines Made, Fortunes Told." Dalia had only seen the old lady occasionally in the kitchen when she came up to share a meal with the family. Most of the time she stayed downstairs in her own rooms and received her customers or busied herself with her herbs and berries.

Approaching the door to the first floor, Dalia listened carefully to the silence. She cracked the door and peered into the sitting room where Old Mrs. Barczak greeted her customers. There sat the old lady in her rocking chair facing the front door. *She'll know where the Barczaks have gone*, Dalia thought.

"Ma'am? Is everything all right?"

Dalia entered the room and stood before the old lady. A little chain of crochet lay at her feet, where it had slid from her hands in her last moment. She was as dead as she could possibly be.

The Barczaks had a telephone. The house was modern, after all, built no later than 1915. The Barczaks lived frugally, as did everyone in the 1930's, later to be known as the Great Depression. But a telephone was considered a necessity and the Barczaks generously allowed neighbors lacking one to use theirs without charge. Dalia ran upstairs to call the sheriff. He would know what must be done.

"Now, you stay with those children and don't leave them until I get there," he said.

Dalia went into their bedroom and checked that they were still alive. As she approached the girl with a mirror to see if she was breathing, young Helga awoke and began to cry. Dalia went over to Henry's bed and placed the mirror in front of his face. He immediately woke up and upon seeing his reflection began to scream. "Quiet, children. Get dressed and I'll make your breakfast."

The children rubbed their eyes and began to slowly climb out of their beds. Dalia sliced the bread for toast. She set the blue bowl on the counter and looked in the pie holder where Mrs. Barczak kept her eggs. *At least the first part of the children's day would be to specifications*, she thought. *Maybe it will strengthen them for what is to come.* Dalia was certain that very soon, their little lives would take an unforeseeable path.

The Sheriff arrived as the children were eating scrambled eggs and rye toast. "Well, the old lady's dead as a … ."

"Sheriff, please. The children didn't know about their grandmother."

"Your granny's dead, children," he said. "No sign of your parents either. Looks like no school for you today."

Helga and Henry stared at the tall sheriff, balls of wet toast still in their mouths.

"Who is going to take care of the children?" Dalia asked.

"Can't you do it? I've got my hands full with the grandmother and finding the parents."

"I've got to go to school. I just rent a room here so I can go to high school."

"Well, no school for you today, either. It's just one day. I'm sure the folks will be back soon. Probably just went out to make arrangements."

Maybe, thought Dalia. *One or both of them awoke early, went to check on the old lady, and ran out to fetch help expecting to return before the children awoke.* Dalia told the Sheriff she would stay with Helga and Henry if he would square her absence with Mr. Cook, the principal at the high school. The Sheriff said he would, but did not.

Old Mrs. Barczak's earthly coil was taken away and put into cold storage at the mortuary, awaiting her son's return with his wife. The funeral would have to wait. The Sheriff called all the Barczaks' relatives, neighbors, church members and friends, but no one had any idea where the couple had gone so suddenly. No one remembered them talking about taking a trip or feeling sick. Dalia had searched the house for a note indicating what the Barczaks' plans might be. She found a few articles of clothing left in the bureau, a pair of socks, a nightgown, a flannel shirt with a torn breast pocket, and a string of red sequins, but nothing useful.

The Sheriff returned in the afternoon to inform Dalia of his various failures during the day. "If I let my imagination go, I'd say this was some kind of Communist plot," the Sheriff said.

"Well, the Barczaks were not communists, I'm sure of that."

"What was their specialty? You seem to know enough about them," he said.

"Acrobats or fire-eaters. Something physical, I'm sure of it."

"Hard way to make a living in Missouri," the sheriff mumbled. He opened Mrs. Barczak's top bureau drawer and caressed the silk garments inside. Dalia wondered what clues to the whereabouts of the children's parents might be hidden in the smooth folds of an old woman's undergarments, most likely saved as reminders of an ill-spent, well-spent youth.

"Maybe I should just call my father and have him come pick me up in the De Soto."

"Don't do that, yet. I'm deputizing you to stay with the children."

When the spectacle of the removal of Old Mrs. Barczak was completed, Dalia had settled the children in their bedroom and read to them from her English textbook the story of "The Jumping Frog of Calaveras County" by Mark Twain and a poem by Robert Frost. When Helga and Henry became restless, they went outside to play on the big wrap-around porch of the house.

The Barczak home was a three-story, white Matterhorn of a house. It stood elevated over Troost Avenue by a set of eight steps up from the sidewalk. The first floor where Olga Barczak dispensed her cures and gave hope to the lovelorn had once been a dentist's office. The family lived on the second, and a series of high school students from surrounding farms and villages rented the attic room to attend high school in town. Dalia's own parents lived on a homestead outside of the school bus route. Dalia's parents paid the Barczaks eight dollars a month for her room and board. Dalia was also expected to help with the children and chores around the house.

Dalia got on well with the children, and with the old gypsy woman downstairs. Olga Barczak was from Poland. She had come to the U.S. with her parents and married Mr. Barczak when she was only sixteen. Townspeople believed that Olga's parents gave old Mr. Barczak some kind of potion to make him fall in love with young Olga. He was thirty-nine at the time. He had been a captain in Missouri's 9th Confederate Battalion, Sharpshooters, and moved to Joplin after the war.

After chasing one another around the porch and competitive rope jumping, won by Helga with 314 consecutive jumps without a miss, it was lunch time. Dalia looked for something to feed the children. In the kitchen she found eggs, of course, home-canned jars of deep red cabbage, store-bought tins of green beans, cheese, and Clabber Girl baking powder. Returning to the loaf of rye bread, Dalia made cheese sandwiches. Dalia did not partake. The prospect of other meals hung over Dalia's head, and she had no money to buy food.

Dalia called the Sheriff. "Have you found any relatives yet?" she inquired.

"Not yet. It may take some time to find someone to come, if they come at all."

"If they come!"

"We have to give them a little time. You'll be all right until then."

"I hope the old lady kept some canned goods downstairs, or some money. Otherwise, how am I supposed to feed the children?"

"I'll ask a church to send over some groceries. In the meantime, try to be patient."

The Sheriff had good intentions, but he did not share her sense of urgency. Dalia was due to take a typing speed test at the end of the week, and outside of the classroom she had no machine on which to practice. Her shifting from lower to upper case remained clumsy at times. Dalia searched Old Mrs. Barczak's rooms for food. She heard the door open, and thinking it might be the Sheriff returning, opened the front door. A lady with a tight permanent wave in her hair and white gloves on her hands stood in the entrance way. She pulled at the fingers of her gloves as if to remove them and then pulled the gloves on tightly again.

"Is Madame Olga here?" the woman asked.

"No, she isn't," Dalia replied.

"Oh my. When will she be back?"

"Not for a long time. Can I help you? I'm kind of in charge of things."

"Well, I'm here to pick up a package. Madame Olga was putting together some 'tea' for me." The woman pulled a few folded dollars out of her purse. "I hope it is ready."

"I'll just check. What kind of package was it?"

"Something for my husband. Something to make him more interested," the woman whispered. "Madame said she would put something together I could brew as a tea."

"Of course," Dalia said. "I'll be right back."

In the old woman's work room, Dalia found jars of herbs and crushed berries. She looked around in the cabinets for a package but found none. What Dalia did find, in the back of a drawer, was a well-thumbed, small notebook containing what looked like recipes. She found one labeled, "*dla maz.*" She recognized the word for husband and slid her finger down the page. Old Mrs. Barczak learned her potion craft from dowagers in Poland, but as she could not write the names of the herbs she had drawn the leaves of each plant. Having no indication of the quantity of each ingredient, Dalia did her best, as she had been taught always to do. When she could not find the herb indicated, she substituted based on smell. She avoided any musky or acrid smelling leaves.

When Dalia had blended a concoction that smelled fruity and woody, she tied it up in a small waxed paper bag and returned to the front room where her customer waited. The woman placed the sachet under her nose, and believing that it smelled exactly as she expected a male aphrodisiac should, pulled five dollars from the inside the palm of her glove and handed it to Dalia.

Up the stairs Dalia bounded. "Wash your face, Henry. Put on your coat, Helga. We are going to the market to get food for dinner."

"Ice cream!" Henry cried.

The next day and the next after that, nervous women appeared at the front door, all eager for packages from Madame Olga. Dalia listened to their requirements, a husband who would rather read the paper than talk to his wife, a secretary whose boss refused to give her a raise in pay, a young man who had survived the Battle of Belleau Wood in 1918, but trembled before his mother-in-law, and a very well-dressed matron who wanted nothing more than to be a grandmother but whose son was dragging his feet in the finding of a wife.

The days passed pleasantly enough for Dalia and the Barczak children. Each day a few dollars came in from Madame Olga's clients. Each day, Dalia and the children shopped for food and toys. Her friends from school sometimes called to see when she was returning. She even received a call from Eddie, the boy who sat next to her in biology class.

"I'm afraid I'm so far behind I'll never catch up," Dalia said.

"You'll be fine. Just come back soon, okay?"

"I'm surprised you even noticed I was gone," Dalia said.

"I noticed."

Dalia immediately called the Sheriff and told him he had to find someone to take the children soon so she could go back to school.

"I'm doing my best, but these people are kind of nervous around authority figures. Some speak only a little English. I'm doing my best. Just hold on a few more days."

Dalia agreed to carry on to the end of the week.

One day, at the butcher shop, waiting to pay for a pullet to roast for the children's dinner, Dalia heard a woman whisper some very distressing news to the counterman. She reported that one of her neighbors was very angry at Madame Olga's assistant. It seems that after giving her husband some special tea, he had begun building a tree house because, as he freely admitted, he had fallen in love with a certain squirrel. Another woman complained that her boyfriend, instead of proposing marriage to her, had overnight turned a bright shade of Belinda rose pink. "My neighbor bought a potion to help him sleep so he could be more alert at his job, but was fired instead because he couldn't stop his legs from dancing under his desk."

"Well," said the butcher. "They should all go and get their money back."

Dalia left the pullet wrapped on the counter and hurried home. After a short phone call, she gathered the children.

"I have wonderful news. My friend is coming soon. He has a car and will take us for a ride in the country. Have you ever seen a real farm? We can have a picnic if you like."

"When is he coming? When, when?" Henry cried. He suffered the most being stuck in the house so many days without his schoolmates."

"Very soon. Now, each of you put a jacket and a few toys in a bag. Hurry. My friend will be in very soon."

Eddie transported Dalia and the children to her parents' farm before anyone came looking for Madame Olga's assistant. He arrived in the nick of time. As Eddie was pulling up to the house, a determined woman in a tight permanent wave was marching down the street in the direction of the house. When she saw Dalia descending the stairs, she called out, "Wait. I have to talk to you. What was that tea you sold me?"

"The store is closed," Dalia said. She pushed the children into the back seat of the car, and slid into the front seat beside Eddie.

"Wait," the woman cried. Into the dust stirred by Eddie's tires she said, "It worked. I'm going to be a grandmother. Twins!"

At the farm, Henry and Helga had no end of fun playing with the dogs and chasing the chickens. Dalia's father called the Sheriff. "See here, you can't just dump these children on my family. We're glad to help out where we can, but this is too much. If no relatives want to come forward for the children, then the county will have to provide for them." The Sheriff agreed to pick up the children the next day.

That afternoon, Dalia led the children in hiking to the end of the road to collect the mail. They passed a tree with a paper nailed to the trunk, announcing the coming of a circus to Baxter Springs. Among the acts listed were Alfredo and his wild lions, Lorenzo and his dancing Dalmatians, clowns, elephants, and the Flying Barczaks."

Dalia said. "Children, we're going to the circus tonight."

"Hurrah!" the children shouted.

Eddie drove Dalia and the children to Baxter Springs. At the circus grounds, she peered behind every tent flap and knocked on every painted wagon's door until she found a man in a suit. Dalia approached him with her chin extended in determined angle.

"I'm here to see the Barczaks."

Helga and Henry ran up behind her. While the man in the suit shrugged and held up his palms indicating he did not understand what Dalia was saying, a rhythmic creaking came from the large tent directly ahead. The children burst into laughter and ran toward the tent. Dalia and Eddie followed. Inside the tent, high above the ground, Mr. and Mrs. Barczak swung on bars toward and away from each other. Mrs. Barczak wore tight pink underwear. A necklace of red sequins was sewn around the neckline of her knit shirt. Seeing their children below squealing and laughing, the couple slid down a thick rope to the ground.

Dalia explained that Old Mrs. Barczak had departed without notice, and that she had been caring for the children since that time.

Mr. Barczak shook Eddie's hand leaving chalk on his palms. Mrs. Barczak kissed Henry and Helga, and turned to Dalia.

"You have saved our children. How can we ever repay you this great debt?" she asked.

"I just did my best," said Dalia. "They were no trouble, really."

"But, you must let us repay you and your husband," said Mr. Barczak.

Eddie blushed and walked to the thick rope and gave it a few testing yanks.

"Really, it is not necessary. I was deputized by the Sheriff, you see."

The Barczak's gave up trying to reward Dalia and nodded happily.

"There is one thing you could do for me," said Dalia.

"Of course," said Mr. Barczak. "I will arrange free tickets to all the performances for you and your family."

"That would be very nice, thank you. Truthfully, I was going to ask if I might keep this book," Dalia said. She pulled the tattered little book from her coat pocket.

"*Babcia*'s old recipe book? I haven't seen that in years," said Mrs. Barczak. "Of course you may have it."

Eddie touched Mr. Barczak's shoulder and stepped to the side. "What is it, young man?" asked Mr. Barczak.

"Don't you feel uneasy in these depressed times, taking precious nickels from people who need them for food and fuel?"

Mr. Barczak placed his hands on Eddie's shoulders and spoke in a low, paternal tone. "Son, in times like these people need the circus more than ever."

Eddie and Dalia sat with the children to watch every performance of the Flying Barczaks in Baxter Springs. The couple's costumes glittered in the spotlight as they climbed a rope ladder up to a little platform. After waving to the crowd below, they began to swing back and forth. Mr. Barczak hung upside down from his knees. Mrs. Barczak swung out to him and jumped toward him. Dalia thought she hung in the air at least a full minute. During that time, the air was empty. There was no sound from the audience who had sucked in their breath vowing not to exhale until Mrs. Barczak was safe. The musicians, who placed a trumpet and a drum, went silent. Dalia squeezed Eddie's hand. The drummer struck his symbol each time Mr. Barczak caught his wife. Henry and Helga screamed their approval. When the Barczaks descended on the thick rope, the children ran to them. They bowed to the delighted audience, and ran out of the ring with their parents.

Eddie drove Dalia to her parents' home.

"I guess you'll be coming back to school tomorrow," he said.

"I have to find a place to live in town. The bus doesn't come out this far."

"I supposed I could drive you, if your parents say it's all right."

Dalia's mother was pleased to have her daughter home. She was reluctant to have Eddie drive her to and from school each day, but as time passed, the Thomases came to admire Eddie for his manners and his fastidious devotion to their daughter.

Dalia showed her mother the book of herbs that had belonged to the old woman. Some of the drawings she recognized right away. "This is St. John's Wort and here is chamomile. This one I believe is hops. It's used in beer, but is also good for toothaches and sore throats. My grandmother used it."

Mr. Thomas dug up a patch near the cellar for Dalia's herb garden. She visited the library in town and tried to identify as many of the other herbs as she could. Dalia learned that anise is easily grown in Missouri and as a tea it comforts stomach complaints. A neighbor with family in Kentucky grew angelica, and reluctantly let Dalia have some seeds for her garden. "It's a powerful remedy for ladies' difficulties, including childbirth. I'm trusting that you are not after the plant for purposes a young girl should have no need." Dalia assured her that she maintained a life as pure as the clusters of tiny, white flowers of the angelica plant.

Dalia discovered other herbs and their cleansing, relieving or restoring properties. From library books she learned about measuring herbs for teas and poultices. She found references to "a baby's fist-full" of some ingredient. Liquids were sometimes measured by something called an "imperial thimble." The more Dalia learned, the more determined she became to create special teas to sell as remedies. Eddie suggested she take ads in newspapers and sell her teas by mail.

"I have to make sure that the teas are not harmful," said Dalia, recalling the unfortunate but blessedly temporary effects of some of her earlier concoctions.

"Try them out on me," Eddie said.

No doubt Eddie regretted his words when his toenails began to grow at a fearful rate. For a month he had to trim them twice a day to protect his boots. One particularly bitter brew caused the hair on his body to turn white and then fall out completely, never to grow back. Fortunately, he was only affected below the neck. Eddie was good natured about Dalia's experiments, and only scolded her once, when an effervescent drink made him think baby ants were cavorting on his tongue. He poured the remainder of the cup into the radiator of his truck and swore he never had another leak.

In 1940, Dalia and Eddie married. They lived in a small house on Dalia's parents' property and Eddie divided his time helping both his father and father-in-law. Dalia's Special Teas were mildly successful, and she earned enough to buy curtains and pillow cases from the Sears and Roebuck catalog. In 1942, Eddie returned to his wife from a trip into Baxter Springs. He carried two pieces of paper. One was an induction notice, ordering Edward Blair Addison to report to Fort Leonard Wood for basic training in the United States Army. The other paper Eddie had torn from a store window display. It was a flyer announcing a special circus performance in Baxter Springs that very Saturday. Featured prominently was a picture of the Flying Barczaks. Eddie decided to show Dalia the flyer first and save the induction notice for later.

"It's Henry and Helga," Dalia said as she examined the flyer.

"They must be grown by now," said Eddie.

"Will you take me, Eddie?"

"Of course, I will, honey."

That Saturday, Eddie and Dalia arrived at the circus grounds early. They quickly located Helga and Henry who recognized them at once. "My, you are so lovely, Helga. And, Henry, such muscles. Don't you dare drop your sister, now," Dalia said. She was so delighted to see her friends after so many years. "How are your parents?"

"They are well. Papa runs the circus, now. Come and say hello," Henry said.

Memories were exchanged and news of recent years related. "I knew you would marry," said Mrs. Barczak. "I only wish I saw children in your future."

"Mama, please," said Helga. "Pay her no mind. She is the circus fortune teller. When I tell you how she does it you will not pay her predictions any mind at all."

Helga and Henry hurried off to prepare for their performance. Dalia and Mrs. Barczak retired to a tent where the middle-aged woman painted herself into a warted crone for her fortune telling act. Eddie talked to Mr. Barczak about the circus.

"How is business? Are people willing to spend their money on entertainment when the war looms before us for who knows how long?" said Eddie.

"Have you been called up?" Mr. Barczak asked.

"Yes, but Dalia doesn't know yet."

Mr. Barczak took Eddie by the hand and pulled him close. "God protect you, my boy." He slapped Eddie on the back and led him toward the big top. Scores of people were milling around the attractions.

"I guess business is good," said Eddie.

"In times like these, people need the circus more than ever," said Mr. Barczak. He donned a top hat and strode away. Eddie found the seat Dalia had saved for him next to her. He held Dalia when the fire-eater frightened her, and let her squeeze his hands while Helga and Henry swung, and flipped, and flew above their heads. The cymbals rang each time Henry caught his sister. Eddie let Dalia's happiness flow over him until the moon was high.

Oh, Nebraska!

DOREEN FRICK

In order for this story to make sense, let me take you back a few years and a few thousand miles to the first time I saw Nebraska. I'm not sure I could have told you the name of its capital or state bird or made sense of a sand hill, but that's not what called me here. It wasn't the corn or the meadowlark, the rolling grasses or the migration of cranes, a job, or a friend. It was something you can't put down on paper unless you tell a story. In order to set the scene for that first-coming to the Heartland, let me take you further back to my roots, back to a warm August morn when my mother brought me into the world I would grow to love.

I was long-awaited and much longed-for. Mom put in her order for a girl with dark black hair and deep Irish-Arab roots. I guess she didn't remember praying for a fiery-tempered, brooding poet that Thanksgiving when she conceived me. That must have been the added bonus God gave her for being such a saint.

The baby she birthed had big bags under swollen brown eyes, and when that seven-pounder cried out her first hello to Philadelphia, Mom thought she'd never get any sleep. After the required two-week stay, my mom begged for just another day of peace. The doctor agreed. He knew she was going home to a lot of work. Her own mother was dying in the downstairs bedroom, and her blind father was living with them as well. This lady was going to need all the rest she could get.

My grandmother died a few days after Mom brought me home from the hospital. Mom took me to her room and laid me in my grandmother's unsteady arms. That was my one and only hello. I'm sure it was a heartbreaking one.

Life was full for this generation and full of stress. Dad traveled a lot. Mom was an only child, carrying the weight of a lot of pressure I have

only recently begun to examine, but she was Scotch-Irish and determined. After her mother's death, she emptied and sold her parents'
home, moved her father in with us and got his cataracts operated on
so he could see again. All the while, I clung to Mom. In every picture,
I'm either crying or look like I've been crying. Mom said I refused
to walk or give up my two AM feedings; she carried me everywhere
and dutifully brought the bottle to my crib, until I was twenty-seven
months old, and she was once again throwing up every morning
because she was expecting my sister.

What? Someone else will be joining the family? I wasn't anxious to
share Mom's attention and swore I'd never leave my mother. My mom
was a Philadelphia girl. I grew up with an accent and attitude and
figured I'd always be one, too.

My parents went on to have even more children and more businesses. Eventually, my dad would settle on one: writing books, and
that's how I got to Nebraska the first time. Dad was on a speaking tour
and asked my husband to drive him across the country. I went along
for the ride and sat in the back seat and took notes.

When we got to the Heartland, I saw rows and rows of corn, big
blue skies with clouds as huge as oceans, windmills, sunflowers, and
people hungry to shake dad's hand and ask him to autograph their
books. This would be my father's last tour; he was seventy-seven, and
my mom had Alzheimer's, so he would not want to leave her anymore.

Dad cried the day we took off for the book tour. My daughter was
staying with Mom, and each night, Dad would call and talk to Mom,
and my daughter said my mom would cry, as I watched my Dad on the
other end; he was crying, too, so their conversations were short. I was
in my fiftieth year, a time period which lingers in my mind because it
was a changing year for me. I was seeing long-distance love, aging love,
and it was the first time I'd ever seen a photo of my grandmother, the
one who held me just before she left this Earth.

My parents just moved into a smaller place, and as I was helping
them unpack, I spied a very old chest and began sorting through the

crumbling photo albums stored inside. There in the bottom was a lovely picture of a woman, who I very much wanted to know. This woman had her hair in a bun. Her chin resembled my own daughters' chins. She was a woman with impeccable posture, huge eyes, lovely skin, and I fell in love with my grandmother on that day.

I would say something stirred in my soul that year; something very deep was awakened, and the yearning for connection had taken hold. I took the picture home. I thought about Mary Jane, the grandmother who left this world just as I entered it.

The book tour to Nebraska (and many other states) had a feeling that began to take hold on me, as we drove through the heart of America. Maybe, it was because my own mom was beginning to fade, memories growing dim, the time shortening, and the quickening of my own soul as all I knew and loved was beginning to crumble. Maybe, it was the perfect storm of energy and depression that made me look for something to anchor me. To steady me. To give me new hopes and dreams. Who can say why a place and a time remain in your heart, except that they do?

There is no right time to explore your past. I probably began searching the day my grandmother held me as a baby. Who knows what babies and children feel? So much we cannot remember remains locked deep in our souls, felt more than expressed? All I know is there's something inside me that's made me keenly aware of other people's longings and deeply held secrets.

One day, when I was sixteen, I met the boy of my dreams, and on our very first phone call he asked me out on a date. He told me in the safety and secrecy of that phone booth that his mother never even took him home from the hospital. He said it so matter-of-factly; he had no idea where his mother was.

I felt something prick at my own heart, and in that one sentence, I saw a boy still aching for connection to his family.

Where are you Antonia?

In 1988, our fourth-grader was given an assignment: fill in a genealogy chart. That weekend project started the ball rolling, maybe not so much with the son, but with his mother. Something stirred in my thirty-something soul.

Fortunately, my sister had just gotten married, and on one of the trips, she and her new husband took, they visited family and stopped at graves in Scranton and Philadelphia, Pennsylvania, opening a piece of history that was new to me. The chart began with promise and a pencil. Our son was making phone calls, and I was picking brains. To fill in the rest of the blanks, I figured we'd glean some details from my husband's stepmother and his seventy-year-old mom whom we'd just met. That was our real find that year. At age thirty-six, my husband met his birth mom.

As soon as he met her, I knew he was hers. Same sense of humor. Same dry wit. Was she surprised we showed up at her door? Yes. And no. She loaded us up with photos of her family, far and wide, an old Bible with remembrances and birth certificates and a marriage license and newspaper clippings. She had three sons, and now one of them had sought her out. A lady who thought she was on death's door lived another twenty years crocheting Afghans for our four kids. These half-grown grandchildren she was finally able to hug and love into adulthood.

Receiving all this information about this long-lost family far and wide tends to overwhelm me. Cousins and aunts and uncles carry no history with them or memories, and they begin swirling around somewhere in the brain until they find a home in one's heart. We focused on getting to know birth mother Myrtle. The rest of the clan would have to wait.

Many busy and productive years passed. I had children of my own to raise and get off to school and life and careers, and most of what we'd marked on that poster board from long-ago sat gathering dust in the closet of the little boy who finished the assignment many moons in the past and was packing up his things and heading off to college.

He let me keep the poster, which to the best of our knowledge was as complete as it would ever get, and a year later, the house was sold, and we moved far from the graves and relatives and history we discovered back in the day. We lost the mother who hugged the son she never got to raise, and we became grandparents many times over, and then one autumn day, I dug up the old pictures, and a question started to haunt me.

What became of Antonia, the mother of my husband's birth mother? My husband's grandmother? There was no one to ask; even Google seemed hampered in its search. It was almost like she disappeared after 1920. The startling thing about this lady is that when my son saw her picture which was taken in Nebraska when she married in 1912, he said he felt like he knew her. She looked like his guardian angel.

He was a grown man by then. He was thinking of naming his daughter after her. That's when this mysterious Antonia began to take hold in my soul. Somehow, this grandmother has a connection with a family she never met. Our family is now scattered throughout the country. I set her picture by my bed, and my heart was set on finding her. Searching for her death record has turned up nothing. Yet.

I had a dream that I was to move to Nebraska, and we sold our stuff, packed up, and moved here in April of 2015. Nebraska was where Antonia married and had several children before moving back to Brooklyn, New York, where she was raised as a child and where we assumed *her* mother Pauline stayed. Then the trail went cold. Where are these people?

Fast-forward to a few months after moving to Nebraska when a grave is found, not of Antonia the grandmother, but of *Antonia's* mother, my husband's great-grandmother, Pauline Korn who died in 1916. The grave was found by accident, while searching online for Antonia, a grave not ten miles from where we settled here in Ord.

We took a drive on a September day to a small cemetery on a hill. My breath was taken from me with the view. There was farmland in every direction, great sky above, a place well-taken care of, and a gravestone in the corner, broken, but beautiful. *Fell asleep in Jesus*, it reads. Our minds cannot comprehend how unreal this all is, and I snap a picture of our great-grandson with his great-grandmother. The circle is reconnected. The gaps are filled in. The past is reunited with the future.

A little boy's assignment — I remember it well. How has one poster taken us this far?

> *"If you don't know history, you're a leaf that doesn't
> know it's part of a tree."*
>
> Michael Crichton

So, a dream brought us to Nebraska? You could say that. Or you could say that people just know they're being driven or called or awakened to something, and they do it. And tough as it may sound, sometimes, you have to let go of things in order to make room for new opportunities. It was not the first time I'd done something crazy like move for no reason other than I wanted to. I never thought I'd ever leave Philadelphia, but one day, when I was twenty-two, my husband got the itch to see the west, and we packed up our two small children, sold our car, bought an old truck and a trailer, sold everything we couldn't cook with or wear, and moved to Washington state.

Yup. We did that. I had just seen the movie *The Wilderness Family*, a not-so-glamorous but rather adventuresome look at packing up and leaving everything you know and moving as a family, and though there were times when I thought how is that lady in the movie keeping their clothes so clean and getting such a meal on the table while living so primitively? I was young and full of hope, and there was a scary kind of excitement in trying something so courageous.

We were heading west. We knew exactly two adults in the place we would move to. I knew them, barely, but my husband, Wes, knew them well enough to trust our future to their good words. Oh, we would start out simple and back to nature, but in the space of eight

years we would build a house, start two businesses, have two more
children, and then leave it all and move three thousand miles back to
Pennsylvania.

We would bury a child there, too, next door to the house we built,
in an old cemetery, and it would break my heart.

I wrote a book about it.* I write a lot of things, journals, letters,
notes, and grocery lists, because when you look back at your life,
you can't believe you did the things you did, unless you wrote them
down. Nobody would believe this spoiled little girl, the woman who
spends hours in the bathroom primping and powder-puffing, once
lived in a bus without running water. Although she didn't move west
in a covered wagon, she would read other women's journals about
those days in the late 1800s and think to herself, no way, was she tough
enough to have made it back then. Little did she know, one day, she
would explore her husband's past and learn he had a great-grandma
who did that very thing.

.   .   .

"Chapter One: When I'm Rich and Famous

*"What fascinates me," Dodie wrote during one of her
long delvings into the past, "is how long I have been
obsessed with getting my own life down on paper. I had
thought I only began attempting that when I started this
journal... do I need to write my woes out of my system?
Or does it stem from something deeper? I am constantly
trying to possess life, to save it up, to bring the then into
now, and make it available for ever."*

— Dodie Smith

When I passed through Nebraska the first time, I had no inkling
we would move here. Seven years later, we passed through, again, on
our way to a wedding. On the way home from the wedding, we took

a detour off I-80 and drove through Ord, the town that showed up
as the burial place of my husband's birth mother's father's parents.
Whew. People who I knew nothing of had no photos, nothing except
an email from a distant relative named Don, who had done some
research once he learned my husband's birth mother passed away.

Some people are into family lineage. Don sent us pages and pages
of names and dates and birthplaces and gravesites. I brought them
with me in the rental car, and as we drove north off the Interstate, the
sky darkened, the rain let loose, hordes of frogs leaped back and forth
and under our tires, the wind blew like I'd never seen wind blow, as
the thunder boomed and the lightning cracked open the sky. It was
mid-June, and I was seeing the wrath of God. We made a quick run
through Ord, and I said, *"Huh."*

I still have the photos on my phone of the movie theater and the
stained glass of a church window. Night looked precarious, so we
never looked for a cemetery but stopped for a soda at the Pump and
Pantry, and Wes asked the man at the counter if he'd ever heard of the
Albers family.

Oh, yeah, the old Albers place. Sure.

Wes' eyes lit up. I made a mental note. We knew we couldn't stay
the night and look, because the rent was due, and we had miles and
miles to go before we slept. Seventeen hundred to be exact. We were
younger then and could do that driving to exhaustion thing.

That was June 2010. The trip from Washington state to Pennsylvania
I dreamed of — -our youngest son's wedding, enabled us time to see
my mother in a nursing home where I cried and cried, and she patted
my back and said no words. I think she knew who I was. Maybe, she
was just comforting someone crying on her chest. My father just died;
we were reconnecting across the East, meeting grandchildren we'd
never met, holding babies, stopping off at Wes' stepmother's house.
The mother who raised him was overjoyed for a time with so many
of her loved ones gathered together to celebrate a wedding. A happy
occasion. It was bad enough we only get together at funerals.

The old ones were getting older, and the babies were growing fast. We tucked away the family emotions of a Pennsylvania summer trip with all its hugs and kisses and drove home through Ord, Nebraska. A few frogs came home with us in the tread of our tires, and when I unpacked my suitcases, I wrote to the town of Ord and asked if they could send me a newspaper. One day, the *Ord Quiz* showed up in my mailbox. I was hoping if I wrote to the editor, someone in Ord would look for the grave of my husband's people, but I knew in my heart, or hoped in my heart, that one day we could get back there and do it ourselves.

"Freedom of the press ensures that the abuse of every other freedom can be known, can be challenged and even defeated."

KOFI ANNAN

Can't Read

NANCY GENEVIEVE

"Can't do it," his hulking frame belied the gentle tone. "Can't read 'em words you ask me to," he said, as his eyes skittered off my gaze and settled on the corner behind me.

"Well," I stalled for words. "Well, we'll learn them." His black eyes leaped from the hiding corner to my eyes for less than a blink's time.

"I've tried and tried, but they don't form meanings. They play games with my efforts." His shoulders wilted, and I could see the old man he could become if he never learned to read, the phony sun-bright "Yes — mam's" of the forever poor, the brim clutching hopeful of a menial job, the desperately snatched trinkets for the cornered hopes.

This child deserves better. I gritted my teeth so hard in thought my jaw was aching as I started to talk, "Every morning before homeroom, you come to my classroom. You can learn to read."

"But-t," he stammered, and I knew that the best-selling job of my life approached. "But, what if?"

"Look, I can't promise you straight "A" s or even that you'll get the scores you need to get for your football scholarship. I promise you my best teaching. All I ask is that you give me your best learning for fifteen minutes a day."

"OK," he said, but his voice sounded more like he was humoring me than resolved.

But so we began. Fifteen minutes — every day — he never missed — neither did I — through the falling leaves, mounting snows, and into the blooming spring.

We read first the comic strips in the paper — they were short and understandable. We progressed to the sports page, where he explained to me more than I'll ever understand about quarterback sneaks, broken plays, or off-side kicks.

One day, slightly wilted carnations lay on my desk — I was pleased at a gift from my "unknown" student. I did notice that the flowers appeared the day after someone had been buried in the graveyard next to the school. But I kept the observation to myself, as I placed my chosen flowers in a vase on my desk.

Reading every day cost my scholar a lot of ribbing — some not so gentle. The Uncle Toming calls had to hurt, but the power of unlocking words gave him strength to pull away from the group who thought failing was cool. He grew quieter in class, but he listened and gripped his book firmly, mouthing each word, unscrambling for himself homework assignments.

Years later, I saw his home; nine of them had lived in three rooms, and through the cracked linoleum on the living room floor, the ground could be seen beneath the floor. No place to read could have existed there, or then.

But read he did. And graduate from high school, he did. I saw him at college a few years later. He'd grown even more; perhaps, I'd shrunk. He only needed another semester to graduate. He'd come a long way in his reading. He thought he'd lined up a job as a safety inspector, but in his soft, ever gentle voice, he apologized, "It only offered $21,000 beginning pay." I told him that's what I made my first year. He looked at me in disbelief; then in the middle of the bustling student union building, he gave me a hug. We both walked a little taller when we left that building that day. It started with his trust, so many years before, that somehow he *could* learn to read, and I remembered for a golden moment why I had entered this profession.

P. S. — I was paid $0.015 a word and was sent a check for $9.06. It was the first time I had been paid for a piece of my creative writing. I carried that check until where it had been folded was nearly worn through.

....

First Published: *Just Write: A Quarterly Magazine Offering Instruction, Motivation & Markets for Writers.* Ed. Gloria J. Urch (Spring 1996): 40. Print.

The Best Possible Childhood

ELIZABETH GREUNKE

Children *need* time to be creative, to explore. Many famous people were told they were not good enough, while in the process of becoming great. Now, they are well known and are recognized geniuses who broke through barriers when they were told, "You're not smart." We should not monitor kids' activities so much and let them make mistakes while growing up.

It breaks my heart that not every little boy and little girl had an opportunity to explore and be creative as a child. I was, and still am, extremely blessed to have had the childhood I did. I was such an explorer. I was one of the few kids in my elementary school who had direct ties to a grandparent and parent who farmed, so I spent much of my time exploring. I had adventures in a "forest" of trees and looked for rabbits. I ran around in a field of grass with my childhood best friend, and we climbed on hay bales. We played in a "playhouse" and cooked with old spices and dirt. My grandma would take my cousins and me on a ride in the trailer attached to a garden tractor, and we would drive down dirt roads in the summertime, get off, and go play in the irrigation pipes' sprinkler. I would find "gold" in the gravel. I collected hundreds of rocks that had "gold" in it. I later found out it was just pyrite, but that didn't stop me from walking back and forth for hours on end with a little basket to collect my treasures.

In the midst of my grandparents building a new building, we had a pile of dirt. That was my mountain. I found a lot of things in there, actually. It was dirt from ditches, so you can imagine all of the bottles and colored glass pebbles I found there. I had the time of my life on my mountain. I would spend hours in the sun digging and finding "ancient artifacts," I told my grandma. Growing up with ties to a farm has been one of the biggest blessings in my life. I look back on it now, and I wouldn't trade that for any life in the world.

I was also a science girl. Every Christmas, I asked for some science item from the Toys R Us store. One year, I got a microscope and some slides, and they were the greatest things ever. I looked at so many things under those lenses. One year, I got a telescope, and every time I went out to the country to see family, I took it with me. I loved looking at the moon. My dad said it was the best garage sale purchase he ever made. I will forever cherish the childhood my parents and family gave me. I hope I will give my child, someday, the best possible childhood, too.

"Desert Southwest," Sagauro National Park, Tucson, Arizona
photo by Derek Burdeny
derekburdenyphotography.com

Am I Supposed to Feel Guilty?

SARAH GUYER

They stand me here, dictate my deeds to a governing crowd, but what's the point? Ain't no way to take back what I'd done. I'd done what I'd done, time to move on. But they all seem so set on parading me for some sort of entertainment, some sick show masquerading as justice. My actions were my choice; don't seem to be much sense in proving me guilty.

The man beside me doesn't seem to get that.

He blubbers on and on, sometimes audible, sometimes not, sometimes coherent, mostly not. Something about his wife, maybe kids. Second cousin? Sister? I dunno. It's not important who he's leaving behind. If it was, he'd articulate.

The man in power steps onto the platform, hugging the edge, as if his pastoral shoes have never touched such sinful ground as this. He mops the sheen adorning his forehead and adjusts the intersecting medallion adorning his chest. His mouth opens; words spill from his nervously coated lips. He must be new. This isn't so rare an event.

Pulling out his little blue book, he lays his hand on the cover, eyes fluttering closed, reverent rhymes crawling from under his fuzz of an upper lip. Addressing the crowd, his arms rise, hundreds of lips mimicking his own.

The man beside me chokes back a sob.

Another powerful figure rises beside the first, announces to the crowd again, and begins by pointing an official-looking finger at my compatriot. With each recounted tally against him, the tears fall a little quicker down his sunken cheeks, desperate eyes widening as the gravity of his fate befalls him. I stand still, staring out into the crowd.

The people stare stonily back.

Before long, the finger migrates to point south, drawing an accusatory line through the middle of my chest. My list is much shorter than the crying man's, but apparently worthy of the same show. After a pause, the judicial leader states our obvious consequence. The crowd's silence is almost enough to make a man falter. He doesn't.

Another bout of formality before the first man clambers quickly to the ground, patriarchal robes fluttering in his haste to abandon the souls engraved in the wood grain. The pointing finger follows, and shortly after the crisp echo of a snare rolls across the dewy lawn. The sun has come up hours ago, but still shines almost gently on the square, avoiding the platform beneath the oak like it, too, is wary of the eternity of the place. The man wearing the cross moves to stand in the light. The sun shines a mite brighter for him.

The platform rattles with the weight of the sorrowful gentleman who mounts it. I nod as he passes, hobbling on bones and leather, a grandfather deprived of any offspring. He refuses eye contact. I'm not surprised. His milky eyes seem devoted to naught but his job.

With well-rehearsed steps, he shambles behind my line of sight and fiddles with his pulleys, checks his knots, tightens his grip. My companion is bestowed upon first; I don't turn to watch, but his broken sob filters through my mounting concern. Seven shuffled steps, before I feel my own gift.

The shadow of a man does his job well and despite my feigned indifference I begin to hate him for it. My searching eyes move quicker, scouring face after face with no sign of my goal, and for the first time I start to doubt my promised savior.

Nah. Doubt ain't got a home in my seasoned mind. I've seen enough — hell, I've done enough to know what to expect. According to the public, I'd done enough to warrant punishment. The man who'd found me — he's good people. I can trust him to prevent this disaster.

So why, then, if I am so certain, why then do my palms bleed salt from their pores?

A sharper wind whistles through the leaves above me, shaking the branches and their rotten fruit, the creaking of wood and thread seeping through my front of steely calm. I muster the courage to swallow; my feet shuffle momentarily on the fragile planks below them. Suddenly, I am aware of their temporary nature. My gaze flickers to the lever on my right, to the shivering harbingers, skeletal digits splayed obediently atop it.

Ain't nothing to worry 'bout. I'd did what I'd done, but I don't deserve what's to come. They surely will recognize it.

The pastoral head raises his arms again, the gargantuan sleeves of his robe unfurling at his sides like great wings, and the company bows their heads, folding their hands. I scan the horizon, and then the buildings surrounding the plaza. He's still not here. He promised he'd be here, where is he?

The proctor steps forward, a comforting presence to the crowd, again lifting his finger to punctuate the markings in his speech, and as he continues to highlight the wrongs I and my fellow prisoner have done, the people's lowered lips move in unison to continue the chant their winged guardian began. The gnarled bones of the barren grandfather creak to attention when the proctor's finger flies up, and as if attached to strings, the crowd's eyes soar skyward, basking in the half-shadowed light shining through the great tree. Panic surges in my skin from their hollow stares, and my own nose points to the sun.

Directly above, an empty branch, sturdy and bare except for two knotted ropes dangling to rest on the platform. But this barren branch is an oddity on this tree, for swaying gently in the chilling breeze are the leftovers of those who shattered the law before me, porcelain spines and off-white skulls missing jaws and arms, rags stained with bird droppings, and mildew clinging desperately to the shells of what once were men, some still dropping pockets of oozing flesh to the speckled ground where crows gather in flocks to pick at the ripened treats before them. Leaves flash verdant in the wind, knocking against the strings holding souls tight to this world, fluttering down to blanket the ground where savaged ghosts will trod. Several threads have frayed and dropped their luggage down to the soiled earth, but still others are looped again through each building block of humanity, leaving bones hanging like beads from a knotted bracelet, branches adorned again after the long death of those they carried. Frozen, here, on this raised dais like a lamb brought to the slaughter, I stand, staring up at my future, my eternity, cursed to spend tasting the wind as it whistles through my teeth, watching the lives of those who condemned me through eye sockets empty of reason or rhyme. That high, I am sure, the whole town can be seen spread before this tree. My death, it seems, is to be hung above for a perfect view of life.

Back my head falls, until the crown of my skull bumps the knot on the joining of my necklace, until the rope tied to the branch above me shifts from the motion, and suddenly my chin hits my chest, again, and I'm staring back at the crowd, grasping for anything I can say to stop this. What need have I to stop it, however, if my savior is on his way? Is it not better to stay silent and let the professionals handle this?

I gulp in breath after breath, as Proctor continues, storing oxygen as if it can help me when the boards beneath my feet hit the tainted floor and the pulleys on the deck crank my body up, up, up, until my neck can't survive the pressure, and it snaps, dripping saliva like essence from my slackened jaw. Unlike Mary, my body will not be lying exposed in the front room of a speechless little house; my sins won't be buried under the blame of a mourning husband. The man, who found me first, told me I was different, that most would not deem a broken spine as a suitable response for welcoming another man. What I'd done was rash and ill-thought-out, but I'd done what I'd done, and now was time to move on. I see what I have done wrong. I see that my wife's sentence was not one I had the right of discerning. If I had exposed her as she lived, it would be her neck cracking under the deadly pressure of this damn rope, not me. It is not I who should be reduced to this gasping mess atop a platform, shown to the masses that all who live in this plucky town shall abide by the law, or the law will punish all. It ain't the law who pulls the lever but the shadowed hangman resting beside the latch, as if he'd ordered his Sunday pie, so it is truly he who has done the murdering, not I. Not I.

My lips pull into a smile, triumphant; my logic sound, my reasoning exact, for surely, this will save me from this wretched fate, but as the words sink in from that deadly, deadly finger, I realize that I have not said my piece, that the logic I moments ago was so proud of did not leave my cursed head, and thus, I am resigned to this slaughter.

A twitch of that finger and the latch on the lever falls to the side, the slack on my puppet's string pulling taught, and I rise to my toes to keep from dancing so soon. I refuse to simply go quietly into the leaves, but my lungs are preoccupied with filling with enough oxygen to satisfy my raging heart, so no refusal moves past the fear gathering in the corners of my eyes. Chafing wrists pull tighter, closer together, shaking fingers dripping sweat to the deck, and suddenly, my desperation is coupled by a fury so complete it scorches the wood beneath my toes. How *dare* they assume they have the right to condemn me. How *dare* they believe that they can exact this justice. No man can decree the death of another, for if it is done, the death will simply outweigh the life. But through my shadowed eyes, I can see no accusatory fingers pointed back at the judicial decree, only the finger stabbing blame into my soul like a stamp for all of Heaven to see how he deemed me unworthy.

That finger opens, and the gremlin shifts at his post, and the fury is replaced by terror, white-hot against the backs of my eyes and burning down the length of my spine. My lips stutter into motion, hoping to plea for a change of heart, a shift in moral belief, a bloody heart attack to distract from this, anything at all — but my wheezing breaths are cut from my lungs, and they flop languidly on the floor like fish, as the man behind the finger calls for any last words.

For once, the man beside me is silent.

Attention shifts to me, and I scan the crowd again and again, desperate to see an unfamiliar face, for a chance at my salvation, but none appears, and as the seconds drag on, I come to the realization that I have wasted precious time, time better spent explaining my logic, pleading, crying, begging on my knees for any possibility of survival, time that should be devoted to demanding to be released, time deprived from the fragrance of this massive tree. Suddenly, I find the words to say. Suddenly, I know just how to explain to their empty faces that I was like them, and I can continue to be, convincing them that the very last thing I wish in this world is to dance in the sky as the crows scavenge their food from my rotting skin, to show them that by doing this to me they are deserving of the same fate they decided I was.

The words trip over my tongue, and the only thing I can say is a low, guttural whine.

A pause.

In this pause, I see the outline of every hair, hear the chirp of the birds nestled beside the carcasses of those outlaws long gone from this time. In this pause, I see with unlimited length, watch the clock chime in the town across the river, taste the baking bread left in the ovens of the farmhouses too far away for a visit, and for this instant, a moment encompassed by this pause, I wait and breathe, as they make their final decision.

The moment ends. The world resumes. The preacher man moans a final prayer about dust and belonging to it, his bejeweled cross shimmering in the sun's favorable shine. The judge closes his powerful, lethal fingers into an angry fist, punctuating the end of his talk. The shadow-man's bones curl around the wooden stake and crank backward. The man beside me closes his eyes, tears like sunken rivers on his cheeks, as he stands resolute in this darkness. With a snap, the crowd's faces all turn to see me at once, see me naked, as I sway on a braided string, my sins and deeds spread open over the dirt and decidedly not enough. The pulleys creak, wood shifts, the wind blows fiercely through the people, steals the cry of anguish from my teeth, and tosses it to the lackluster chorus above me.

The lever hits the back of the platform.

My feet touch air.

Freshman Year: April 30, 2017

AMANDA B HANSEN-WEIGNER

High school ruined
any chance she had
to move on
and leave the past in
the past
Her bucket list
was filling up
of things she could
have lived without.
Peer pressure
rocked her world

///

"When a man has pity on all living creatures, then only is he noble."

BUDDHA

///

Meet Me in Moscow

JEAN HART

The flight from London was the only thing moving at Sheremetyevo that dark afternoon. Men in suits and fancy eyewear carrying briefcases and fur-trimmed coats filled the British Airways cabin. I was the only woman. Two cannibalized Aeroflot planes sat on the edge of the tarmac, their big bellies open to the icy wind. Metal parts and hoses were strewn around in the snow like animal entrails. It was February of 1992, and the world had descended on Russia like a flock of vultures. Everyone wanted a piece.

When the USSR dissolved three months earlier, my European colleagues at a big California computer company scrambled to get to Moscow and clean up before the rest of us noticed. The English and Germans got there first. The French heard the food was bad and stayed home. We Americans waited for permission.

That free-for-all didn't last. In January, my division was given responsibility for all the former Soviet Union and central Europe. We already managed most of the developing economies in the world, including Canada, to their profound dismay. They didn't like being lumped in with South Korea and Chile, but the metric was revenue, and they didn't make the cut.

Hobson, a man I worked with in other dicey countries, was promoted to country manager for Russia. This was a chance for him, and me, to redeem ourselves. The year before, we had lost a deal with PDVSA, the state-owned oil company in Venezuela, worth tens of millions. We'd gotten sloppy after winning the Petrobras account in Brazil and overbid the contract.

Hob's reputation would survive; he was a star, but my future was less certain. For months, I stewed about that mess, the revenue and jobs lost, the recognition. Now Hob had another chance. Gazprom, Russia's monster natural gas company, was a make or break opportunity. Capturing that account would mean a two-year stint in Moscow for a simulation expert, someone with my skills. Modeling is cheaper and more efficient than actually drilling or blowing things up. The position was made for me, and I was keen, but so were others. Hob asked me to survey the situation at Gazprom, and while that was a good sign, it didn't mean the job was mine. If this didn't work out, I was finished, and I knew it.

My first task was to find out what I could from colleagues who had been to Moscow. Our UK guys didn't like it when the new territory wasn't given to them, but they didn't howl. When I asked them about Gazprom, they were no help. The Germans had bet proximity would influence the decision, never mind organizational integrity. When they didn't get the new region, they threw a fit, then sulked.

My German contact, Gunter A., had an iffy reputation all the way to California. I wanted to arm myself before approaching him. The company was fifteen thousand strong by then, but I'd been around since the early days and knew where the bodies were buried. If I didn't know, I knew who did.

I asked a trusted colleague for the low down, off the record. She called me one night, when I was still at work. "Fiona, this Gunter guy is power hungry," she said. "You know that killer deal with Euracoal a couple of years back? That was his. He's been milking it ever since and says his next conquest is Gazprom. He laughs at the Russians. Calls them Neanderthals. He's arrogant but plenty smart, fancy degree from Karlsruhe, an expert in your field. So good luck, and be careful." The report was worse than I'd feared. I thanked her and drove home in a bleak mood.

Early the next morning, I sent a dry e-mail to Gunter. It was customary and good form to do a hand-off when organizations shifted. If Gunter played it straight, I might learn a lot from his answers, not only about Gazprom but how much he knew and what work he'd done. An in-person meeting would tell me more, but the truth is I didn't want to face the guy. I was betting he didn't see me as any kind of threat. Just some flunky of Hob's.

Gunter replied within hours. "Why don't I meet you in Moscow? Go to the meetings with you and Hob."

I hadn't mentioned any meetings, and I didn't tell him Hob would not be in Moscow that week. "It would be easy to meet in Frankfurt, since I'll already be in Europe," I wrote back.

"There are some things I need to take care of in Moscow," he replied. "I may bring a colleague, Dieter. He knows about our next generation processors. That will be important."

I tried one more time. "Why don't you just send me a summary? That would probably be enough."

"Too complicated. I'll arrive on the Sunday afternoon Lufthansa flight and spend the week." Gunter figured a week with Hob ought to seal the deal.

"I'll be at the Penta," I wrote. "Call me when you check in. We can have a drink, compare notes."

"We are staying at the Penta, too." That did not comfort me.

• • •

The Sheremetyevo terminal building was cold and dank, as if water was seeping through the walls. I clomped down the dirty wet floors toward baggage claim wearing rubber boots I'd been advised to buy for the trip. There wasn't much to choose from in Palo Alto, short of pea-green waders at Smith & Hawken. I finally found a pair at Macy's that fit my narrow, bony feet. Shiny black rubber cowboy boots. Silly, rubber cowboy boots with my red Chanel suit. Great.

A bored looking woman at the taxi kiosk took my US dollars and waved to an old man with a ruined face. He hustled over, grabbed my bag, and with a jerky nod led me to an ancient Lada that reeked of cigarette smoke. Hugging my briefcase to my chest in the back seat, I willed myself to relax as the car crept down dark, empty streets. I craned my neck to read the street signs in Cyrillic. There were almost no other cars. I longed for a stiff drink and a warm bed. A good night's sleep.

Thirty minutes later, the driver parked in front of a square building with the brightest lights I'd seen since leaving home. He jabbered and pointed. "Penta." I lifted one hand in thanks. *Spasebo.* That was the only Russian word I knew besides *Piva.* Beer. I tipped him too much.

An hour later, I found my way to the bar. The place was jammed with men in ties and bottle-blonde Russian girls dressed in tight black clothes and tall boots. I ordered a whiskey and listened to the banter around me, the shrieking, giggling girls, British English, German, and viscous languages I couldn't identify. Tomorrow was Sunday. Ruslan Sokolov would pick me up after breakfast for a few hours of sight-seeing and then work. Ruslan had connections at Moscow University and the massive Academy of Sciences, both potential customers, and he'd spent several years at Gazprom. He was a kind of ambassador for us. I didn't know if he was compensated on or off the books, but Hob trusted Ruslan, and asked me to work with him.

At 10 o'clock the next morning, he met me in the hotel lobby. He was a tallish, full-faced man in his mid-forties. His impish blue eyes radiated good humor and intelligence.

We shook hands. "I'm Fiona," I said. "Thank you for giving up your Sunday. I'm jazzed to see everything."

"You have a warm coat." He nodded, approvingly. "It's quite cold today."

Outside on the sloppy sidewalk, he said, "Fiona, what means this word 'jazzed'?"

"Sorry, Ruslan. American slang. It means excited."

"I must learn everything. You must help me."

"Okay. For every English word I teach you, I want to learn a Russian word." I looked up at him.

"That is a good plan." He narrowed his eyes. "*Zdravstvujtye.* It means hello if you just met someone. You must know that word."

Zdravstvujte. Zdravstvujte. Zdravstvujte. Christ.

Ruslan's car was another faded old Lada. He opened the back door and gestured. "You must sit here. The front seat does not work." His face had turned pink. "I have put rugs for you. The back seat is also broken."

I reassured him that was fine and climbed onto a pile of rugs that covered springs poking through split upholstery. For the rest of the drive, I sat with my arms flung over the broken front seat so I could hear him talk over the clatter of the engine. I bounced between fear and Christmas-morning excitement. I was a million miles from home in a country unaccustomed to foreigners where I spoke exactly three words of the language with a man I'd known one hour in a car that might or might not make it back to Moscow. There were no seat belts, and I didn't want to know how long Ruslan had been driving.

Inside the famous old 17th century Russian Orthodox Church, Ruslan explained important icons, the curved apse, the splendid gold dome and lacy cross. It was a vision from the past. In the parking lot, people from the countryside had set up tables, selling hats from the Soviet era, cloth dolls with pigtails and aprons, green bottles of vodka, and Matryoshka dolls. I fell in love with a crudely carved troika.

"Ruslan, should I pay in rubles or dollars?" I whispered. I was ready to whip out a twenty and feel guilty about paying too little. Taking dollars was against the law for most citizens, but everyone did it, including the customs guys at the airport. I'd been told that two one dollar bills tucked under a pack of Marlboros cut off five minutes processing time and guaranteed fewer questions about what one had been up to.

Ruslan ducked his chin. "Possibly dollars. Ten is good."

"Ten?" I mimed surprise.

"It is a lot," he said. With our backs turned, he showed me how to fold the bill so I could slip it to the eager old man who was wrapping the toy in wads of newsprint, mumbling and smiling. When he was finished, he handed it to me with a small bow. I didn't know how I'd get the thing home, but I'd worry about that later.

After a while, Ruslan said we must leave, because he wanted to show me the Kremlin. And Red Square. And Lenin's tomb. If there was time, a museum he thought I'd like.

"Can we do all that?" It sounded like a lot.

"Possibly so." Possibly was one of his favorite words.

Walking around the Kremlin, Ruslan pointed and told me who had signed what or who shot whom in which rooms. The museum wasn't crowded, and we got through in an hour. Red Square looked like it does in the movies, only vastly bigger. St. Basil's Cathedral looked smaller. Lenin looked like an old wax doll left out in the rain.

By four o'clock, I was cold and hungry. We went back to the Penta bar and ordered Heinekens and snacks. The place was less crowded than the night before, but it was still early. When I'd warmed up, I pulled out a small notebook and pen. "You talk first."

In the middle of explaining the pent-up demand for technology at Gazprom, Ruslan asked endless questions about how our company was organized, our processes and procedures, and were most US companies possibly like that? He wanted to understand thirty years of technology and half a century of organizational development in a single afternoon, as if I were the right person to explain. I was chastened by my limitations, how much I took for granted. Jet lag had fuzzed my brain, but he was quick, and he forgot nothing.

Then, I mapped out my approach to Gazprom. The big picture. "This is good," he said. "You have thought about this."

Ruslan's approval made me light. "We'll talk more. But before you go, have you met Gunter A., my co-worker from Frankfurt? Hob says he's been talking to people at Gazprom the last two months. He arrives this afternoon. He wants to go to our meetings with them this week. Some engineering weenie is coming with him. I'm fairly certain what Gunter really wants is to meet Hob, lobby for a position here."

Ruslan frowned. "Sorry." I'd fallen into slang again. "Weenie is an insult, but not very bad. Lobby means he wants to talk to Hob about a job. He wants to manage the Gazprom account. If we win it."

He wiped the moisture off his glass. "But Hob is in California."

"He's still here. He leaves in the morning." I tapped my pen on my notebook. "He said he'd go with me to meet them tonight."

"I do not know this Gunter." Ruslan's voice was soft, apologetic.

I was speechless. There were only a handful of company people floating around Moscow, and the tech community was still embryonic. Ruslan knew all of us. It was inconceivable they hadn't met.

He shook his head. "I can tell you the people from your company I've talked to." He held up three fingers. "And you." I believed him.

I didn't know what to say. I closed my notebook and asked Ruslan brainless questions about his family, about perestroika and Yeltsin. We finished our beer, and I walked him to the lobby.

Back in my room I unwrapped the troika which was bigger than it had looked in the church parking lot. Maybe, the hotel had a discarded box I could use to get it home. I'd paint it in bright colors, the sledge red, the harnesses green, and the horses brown and white before giving it to my sister for Christmas. I hoped I'd given the old man enough money. I tried to read *The English Patient* but couldn't concentrate. My mind kept racing ahead to the meeting with Gunter and what I'd do if this job fell through. Plums like this didn't come along every day. After tonight, I'd know more, and if Gunter impressed Hob, I'd muddle through the week, fly home, and start over. I was overdue for a change.

At 7:30 that night, I still had not heard from Gunter. I dreaded telling Hob the meeting was off after I'd encouraged him to join me. "I haven't heard from them. I don't know what to say."

He was going to bed. "I've been working all day, and I gotta get up at 4:30 to catch the 7:00. Carry on, find out what you can." I wished him safe travels and went downstairs. The front desk wouldn't tell me if Gunter had checked in, but they confirmed the flight had landed on time. The Lufthansa pilots and attendants all stayed at the Penta. I went to the dining room, but it was closed on Sunday nights. I was stuck with bar food.

I was upset that Gunter had blown us off, after I'd showered and put on makeup, and I wasn't in the mood for a smoky, loud scene. At the entrance to the bar, I looked for a quiet place to sit. Directly in front of me, two men who could have been from anywhere snuggled with young Russian women wearing black clothes and make up applied with a trowel. I beat down my instinct to gawk, as I walked by them.

I ordered a wurst with spicy mustard and from across the room watched the foursome. I thought about my earlier conversation with Ruslan. It was telling that he'd not seen or heard of Gunter in all his trips.

The girls in the booth waved their cigarettes around theatrically, and they giggled and clinked glasses. One of them straddled the lap of the man next to her, gave him a long kiss, then climbed off, and laughed maniacally. I wondered what language they were speaking. Not that it mattered.

I signed the bill and went to the front desk to check for messages one last time. When I heard the elevator behind me ping, I raced across the lobby to get in before the door closed. The men I'd watched in the bar and the two Russian girls were braced against the back wall swallowing each other's tongues. For half a second, I hesitated but looked away and turned my back. I pushed the button for the fifth floor and tried to be invisible. They paid no attention to me.

The next morning at 7:30, the phone in my room rang. It was Gunter. "Why don't we meet for breakfast at 8:30? We were delayed last night." No apology.

I hesitated, then made my voice chilly. "I'm wearing a red suit." At the last minute, I took off my rubber boots and put on high heels. I checked my hair in the mirror again.

At 8:30, I was in line at the dining room. A few yards away, a man lifted his hand. It was Gunter. He was one of the men from the bar and the elevator. At the table was another man. I assumed he was Dieter.

Disgust and fury nearly choked me. I wanted to pretend I hadn't seen them and go back to my room. Not answer the phone. But it was too late. I took a ragged breath and made my way through the crowded tables.

There was so much I wanted to say that I didn't know where to start, but decency helped me keep quiet. "Fiona Gibson." I offered my hand.

His smile was more of a grimace. Purple crescents rimmed his eyes; his skin was pasty, and his fair hair was limp against his head. "Good morning, Fee." Familiar twit. I'd set him straight later. "Will Hob join us?" he asked.

I introduced myself to the second man, a middle-aged guy in glasses who didn't look much better. "And you're Dieter?"

A waiter offered coffee. Using my best German, I ordered a small pitcher of hot milk, a three-minute egg and dry wheat toast. Gunter slid his eyes at Dieter. Now, they wouldn't shut me out by not speaking English. Dieter refolded his napkin and brushed the tops of his legs. I gave them a weary look. If they remembered me from the bar and the elevator the night before, they hid it well. The distraction of thinking in another language had calmed me, and I was back in control, at least for now.

"Hob and I waited for you last night." I held Gunter's eyes, in no hurry. "He left for California this morning. He tried to call you. He thought he'd gotten the date wrong." That was a lie but not one they could prove.

Gunter turned another shade of pale, then shot a mournful look at Dieter.

"Well," I said brightly. "Let's have breakfast."

With Dieter on his heels, Gunter hurried toward a buffet table loaded with trays of food. I stirred my coffee and considered my next move, my breathing almost back to normal. I wanted these guys to fall into a trap of their own making. My job was to trip them without being obvious. It helped that they had hangovers, but food might make them feel better. I didn't have all day. The waiter brought my egg and toast, and we ate in near silence. I asked Gunter if he'd been to the famous old Metropole Hotel and if he usually stayed at the Penta, knowing the answer. He said he did. Then, he complained that there weren't any restaurants in Moscow he'd patronize. "The food here is for pigs!" he said.

When our table was clear, I pulled out my notebook. "We have an advocate in Moscow, a man who used to work at Gazprom. Gunter, you've met him I trust? On one of your trips? He's been helping us for several weeks."

"Who are you speaking of?" he asked.

"Ruslan Sokolov. Dr. Sokolov. Hob says he's an expert on our products." I waited for that to sink in. That Ruslan knew so much should have prompted questions and made them curious if not uneasy, but I got no sense of that. Gunter was counting on his past successes to smooth over a minor bump.

Gunter shook his head. "I have not met him." He looked at his watch, already planning his exit now that Hob wasn't expected.

"Do you have to be somewhere?" I did not smile. I wondered how he'd engineer getting away, what excuses he'd make. He had no interest in talking to me, because I was not useful. Smart money would have checked me out when I sent that first e-mail asking for information, on the outside chance something interesting turned up. Gunter didn't need to be smart.

He smoothed the table cloth. "We have time."

"So, tell me who you've met at Gazprom, what you think." I wouldn't play dumb, but neither would I show my hand. The men exchanged looks again. Dieter moved his butter knife.

Gunter leaned back in his chair, pleased to have the floor. "They are not well informed about simulation. This is my field. I specialized in absorption isotherms and density profiles in cylindrical forms. Pipes, in other words." He sniffed. "I matriculated at Karlsruhe Technical University."

Matriculated. If there's a more pretentious, fussy word in the English language, I want to hear it. With effort, I kept a straight face.

"I understand very well Gazprom's requirements," he went on, then launched into a discussion meant to dazzle me. It was basic stuff, nothing innovative or unique, but I listened attentively, pitching him a softball from time to time just to confuse him, wondering how long he'd be entertained by the sound of his own voice. Then, he launched into how he'd beaten the competition at Euracoal. For three minutes, he babbled on about how he'd evaluated their needs and how he'd methodically met them. And then some. He was animated and the color had come back to his cheeks. Dieter nodded and made encouraging noises from time to time. I kept my questions and comments to a minimum, hoping he'd wind down.

In the middle of this mini-lecture, Ruslan appeared at the table. We'd planned to meet in the lobby at 9:30 that morning. When I didn't answer my phone, he looked for me in the dining room. I was ridiculously glad to see him. "I was just telling Gunter and Dieter about you," I motioned to the empty chair.

Ruslan beamed happily at them. "How was your meeting with Hob last night?"

My mean streak said I should make Gunter answer, but throwing him a bone might seduce him into relaxing. He was showing signs of impatience, his narrowed eyes, and the lowered chin. Maybe, my questions had been too obvious.

"Hob couldn't make it," I said. "He worked all day and had to get up early."

Ruslan nodded. "That's unfortunate. Fiona tells me you've met with people at Gazprom."

"Coffee?" I signaled the waiter.

"This is good, because I am from there. Perhaps, you know people I have worked with." He spooned sugar into his cup. "Did you meet Anatoly Kuznetsov? The platform choice will be his decision. I know Anatoly well."

Gunter moved his water glass. "I have not heard that name."

Ruslan stirred his coffee and was quiet for a moment. "Dr. Kuznetsov is head of all simulation applications, in all operational areas. I am surprised you have not met him."

"Do you want breakfast?" I asked him. "The pastries look good."

He lifted one hand. "No, *spasebo.*"

"What do you think of Gazprom's plans?" Ruslan asked. "Have you seen other examples of this approach, perhaps, in Germany?" He was playing it straight, still believing they knew something useful. I hadn't coached him, and it showed. His sincerity was obvious. Gunter mumbled something I didn't catch.

Ruslan went on. "They plan to begin with improved predictive maintenance, they can realize many savings there, then work on operational efficiencies and pipeline integrity using dynamic and stochastic processes." He stroked his chin, thoughtful. "To begin."

I wanted to applaud. Ruslan had practiced the English terms, and he'd gotten them exactly right.

Gunter sat up straight, then gave a watered-down version of the Euracoal lecture I'd just heard, as if Ruslan were dim. "I'm not worried about Gazprom. They will be easy compared to Euracoal." He was about to launch into the entire monologue again, but he checked himself.

Then he changed the subject. "Our next generation processors will be important." We weren't talking about processors. "We have a non-disclosure agreement. Dieter is prepared to give them an update." He nodded to his companion. "Intertek is porting their software to our hardware. Their traceability and corrosion analysis capabilities are key. Beta tests start next month. This will be good news for them." He babbled on a few minutes about how critical Intertek was to Gazprom.

Ruslan frowned. "Dr. Kuznetsov decided against Intertek a month ago. It will be too difficult to integrate. They're looking at other software. Did they not tell you?"

"On my last trip, we had an appointment. I have the name in my papers, but I had to cancel."

Ruslan scribbled something in his notebook. "Maybe, you met one of Dr. Kuznetsov's staff?"

His tone was resigned, almost sorrowful. For seventeen minutes, we'd listened to Gunter preen and strut and he, like I, had learned nothing.

When Gunter didn't answer, Ruslan closed his folder, a signal he was ready to leave. I was silly with relief. Next week, he would discreetly tell Hob that Gunter was not someone he could count on. That was death to Hob. Someday, over some very old scotch, his treat, I might tell him the story about the bar and the girls. I could hear him now. "Those dumb turkeys!" He'd laugh and shake his head, but not yet. I had to earn this job the right way, by knowing more than anyone else and out-maneuvering them. Today was a start.

Ruslan looked at his watch and then at me. I nodded. "Fiona and I must go." His voice was quiet but firm. "I hope you have a good week in Moscow. Have you been to the Kremlin museum?"

He pulled out my chair, waved cheerfully to the stunned Germans, and followed me out of the dining room.

Man vs Nature
photo by Nia Karmann

LADIES OF THE ISLAND

Several years ago ten creative women, all loosely connected with Camano Island, Washington, began a conversation over dinner about life, creativity, and art. The conversation has continued over many more meals and gatherings. Powerful bonds have been forged between these friends, inspiring stronger work by each.

Early in 2018, the ladies decided to write about their lives based on the poem *Where I'm From,* written by Kentucky's 2015–2016 poet laureate, George Ella Lyon. The poem lends itself to imitation and has been used in classrooms and writing groups throughout the United States. For the ladies it turned out to be a powerful, insightful exercise.

The poems were used as companion pieces for their second show in September 2018 at Scott Milo Gallery in Anacortes, Washington. The exhibition was called "I Am From."

> Indy Behrendt: *jewelry*
> Marguerite Goff: *clay*
> Janet Hamilton: *paintings*
> Elizabeth Hamlin: *watercolors*
> Kathy Hasting: *photo encaustics*
> Lynne Nielsen: *watercolors*
> Patricia Resseguie: *fiber embroidery*
> Jackie Roberts: *photography*
> Susan Cohen Thompson: *oils*
> Renate Trapkowski: *acrylics*

Their "I Am From" poems follow.

I Am From

INDY BEHRENDT

I am from Walter and Hannah's Midsummer Night's Dream,
    I join the world amidst the crocus, daffodils and dandelions of
        spring.
I am from black-and-white TV and film, silver spirals and horse
        liniment.
I am from the view of Puget Sound reflected sunsets,
    mmmm, the smell of sea air!

I am from cedar trees and horses, late night art projects,
    Saturday morning sleeping in.
I am from classical music, slide rules, potters wheels, silver, and
    glass beads.

I am from children should be seen and not heard
    from promises of "maybe" and "we'll see."

I am from self-reliant resiliency, affirmations of self-talk.
I trust God. I am from fear of dark, I recite yeah though I walk
    through the valley of the shadow of death I will fear no
        evil.

I am from family knowing from intuition and trust.
    from a grandmother who "knew things." Some might call
        "esp."
I sometimes know things too.

I am from East Coast snows and sandy beaches,
    long U-Haul and Jeeps to new land out west.
I am from bric-a-brac, brooches and handmade earthenware,
    fine china, silver utensils and silver coins, a heritage of
        sentiment

and the value of family passed to future families.
Collage of photos and art on the fridge held fast
    with the magnets of many places.

I am from little bits of brightly colored paper, far away and exotic
    places,
    postmarked over decades of dreams and aspirations.
I am from two continents, old world treats and new.
I am from cold cuts on New Year's Eve.
I am from driftwood fires on the beach, hot dogs
    and late summer plum kuchen.

I Am From

MARGUERITE GOFF

I am from the hope of parents
    who believe the world can be a better place,
intertwined with the despair
    of flying lamps crashing as a family disintegrates

I am from twin outfits;
    sisters practicing courage in fringed vests and cowgirl boots

I am from the tragedy of early death,
    the aching void and empty crib
    when baby Billy doesn't come home

I am from the little childhood suitcase
    holding doll and book and patent leather shoes,
    necessities for running away to a better place

I am from the miracle of books,
    and "the house could fall down and you wouldn't notice"
  I am from the glass beads counting decades of ritual,
    a rosary pleading "for okay"

I am from the persistence of generations rising each morning
    to catch the fish and build the roads

I am from the scent of Lily of the Valley
    and the refuge of Nana's love

I am from Grampa Guy dollars,
    every Wednesday's windfall
    of allowance, abundance, and penny candy

I am from the chips littering the attic floor as Bill carves the wood
　　from the perfect clay heart cradled in my hands

I am from the chaotic strands of hope and despair,
　　shaded by love, terror, and peace,
　　colored with beauty and humanity,
　　that weave the container of my soul

I Am From

JANET HAMILTON

I am from the land of hot, sticky summers and mosquitos that feasted
    on my pale, white skin.
I am from the land of shyness and solitude, enclosed in my stifling
    room
        Drawing pictures of horses, fairies and swimming pools.
        Nighttime dreams — I am flying over the landscape,
        flapping my arms like a bird
        seeing trees, fields, and water that I would someday paint.
        But those were the good dreams.
I am from the smell of frying bacon, white bread and BLT's.
        Jumping over creeks and crawdads, hanging from trees
        Do your chores every day
        Blaring Motown music with sisters while sewing clothes —
        "Make it yourself" was the motto.
I am from the tradition of being a good girl —
        My sisters fought, but I didn't.
        I learned to stay out of trouble
        – but also learned to stay apart.
I am from April — the cruelest month —
        Turbulent storms and Kansas twisters
        Such heavy rain — full of potential
        Some days — in the undertow, just
            dragging along
        Until finally, a sight of land to inspire
        Bringing me back up to Grandma's fun —
        Happy voices and creating stuff.
I am from the land of doing what you need to do —
        And if you're lucky or smart,
        What you wish to do.

I Am From

ELIZABETH HAMLIN

I am from sand and sea and earth.
>Feet bare and dirty

I am from the family farm.
>Depression and the whole family worked
>Picking strawberries and beans and potatoes.

I am from father knows best.

I am from go out and play and be home for dinner.

I am from three siblings.
>Our playground was the farm, the woods, a stream, ponds,
>>the bay
>
>And even occasionally the railroad tracks.
>We were free range kids.

I am from Maple trees marching down both sides of Main Street.
>A Maple in my yard — a perch high up for reading.

I am from a small town.
>Knew everyone on my two mile route to grade school.
>Visited indiscriminately on my walk home.
>Loved to visit Mary Wells. Her Civil War veteran brother
>with dripping rheumy nose — sat unseeing in the corner.
>Here my drink of water came from a well in the back room where
>Mary needed to lower the bucket and crank up the water.
>>I watched.

I am from music.
>Fiddle, mandolin, piano and voice.
>Milton Cross and the Metropolitan Opera on radio Saturday
>>afternoons.

I am from parents in the church choir and a brother Off Broadway
>The Messiah with mother and brother soloing every Holiday
>>Season.

I am from German immigrants and speak their language.
    I am from WWII.
Bullied in school and called "Nazi"
    I grieved for Grandmother and Aunt. Bombed.
I was from rationing and blackout curtains
    and U-boats sinking ships just off the Coast.
    I didn't know which side I was on.
I was also from the city. NYC. Visits only. Experience the "culture"
    mother said.
    Plays and operas and museums and baseball games in Yankee
        Stadium.
I look back at the life my parents provided
    The farm and the work ethic. The coast with boating and
        swimming.
    The best of the city. The foreign language. All now tucked away
    in the black crumbling photo album.

I Am From

KATHY HASTINGS

I am from salt and chlorine —
    the taste on my skin after a day at the beach;
        cloudy, hazy vision after hours in the neighborhood pool.
I am from The Little Mermaid (before the movie)
    bedroom walls painted aquamarine to mimic the sea
        fish and seahorses in bubbling, aquarium homes
           a Jacques Cousteau wanna-be.
I am from hours running through California sprinklers,
    summer play ending sprawled on short, mown grass
        gazing into an out-of-focus fairy world
           of twinkling, rainbow water droplets.
I am from fog lifting,
    early morning fishing off Redondo Pier
        puddle mirrors on the way to school
           a backyard pretend lake when it rained.
I am from scuba diving,
    weightless in the ocean's embrace
        the sway of kelp, coral reefs
           sea glass mornings on Caribbean shores
              wakes of boats, crests of waves, spindrift.
    I am from tide charts and ebbs and flows,
        undulating colors, rusty, algaed, oxidized surfaces
           my red kayak floating in a grand canyon of boats.
I am from the mysteries of water
    the surface of
        what floats upon
           what lies beneath

what's reflected in
my first home —
what is mostly me.

I Am From

LYNNE NIELSEN

I am from the seas and the rainforests
    and the California Redwoods my great grandfather saved
    for me and mine and yours.
I am from a surrounding and gentle love; parents who kissed.
    Mother's Saturday bread baking,
Dad's white shirts being stirred in melted starch,
    the radio blaring operas I know to this day.
I come from strong women: my mother who blew the whistle

and my grandmother who threw him
out that very day.
I come from Cowboys and Indians
and the smell of cap guns smoking,
strutting all-powerful and beautiful
in my Dale Evans fringed skirt and
cowgirl boots.
I'm from "Don't dawdle, Martha
Lynne" and "Clean your plate"
and "God goes before you"
I come from woodpile forts
and hopscotch and a pet skunk
(deodorized)
from swinging higher than all the
boys,
    and waiting an hour before swimming again,
from Christmas pageants and trick-or-treating for UNICEF,
church potlucks, being nice to Old Hazel even though she
    smelled bad.
I come from running naked in the dark through our drafty old
    parsonage

to dive into almost-too-hot flannel pajamas Daddy warmed by
    the fire,
I come from Family Sings late into the night,
    harmonies forming, rising and falling,
    the vibrations of my father's baritone passing straight into my
        heart
    from my cheek against his chest, until embers smoldered
        and spit
    and we children were carried off to bed.
I am from salt air blowing our sailboat to Turn Island,
    our Robinson Crusoe paradise, whittled cedar utensils,
    mounds of the softest moss under our tent,
    bathing in the saltwater with floating Ivory Soap,
    lying on warm pebbles to dry,
    the fragrance of sun on our skin
    singing Deep blue sea, baby, deep blue sea;
    we pray for peace in all the land, and o'er the deep blue sea.
I come from Saturday classes at the Frye Art Museum,
    having my father all to myself,
    hanging out in the galleries after,
    speaking quietly about paint and flesh and wonder.
I come from seeing and seeing and seeing —
    amazement at how a fir bough bends the light,
    my fingers finding the touchstone agate in my pocket,
    the very cells of my body storing up knowings for those days of
        loss
    when I'd have to Cope.
I come from mercies that are new every morning,
    the very mystery of Beauty that births my paintings
    and saves my life!

I Am From

PATRICIA RESSEGUIE

I am from bleached gloves
    from Ivory soap and mothballs.

I am towering Dutch elms over quiet lawns.
    (Sunlight dancing between clouds and leaves.)

I'm pink peonies on white linens
    spilling ants into the butter
    from Clyde Felton and Dorothy
        (never Dotty!)

I'm from pinched pennies
    and great expectations,
    from "You're Better Than That!"
    and "Get Busy!"

I'm from silent afternoons,
    watching insects trek mountains of
        moss, and vast plains of lichen.
    Under a magnifier, their ropey struggles
    but fragile threads in my benevolent vision.
    (Do the gods see us so?)

I am from molten resentments
    Mom and Dad's mom hissing over
    dinner plans, crockery or bone china.

I am crested French aristocrat
    and small beer German folk.
    In a drawer deep beneath my parents' closet,
    yellowed lace and forgotten ancestors
    whisper of secrets unspoken.

I am shooed away and told to live in future tense.

I Am From

JACKIE ROBERTS

I come from Calderwood
    a long ox train and Indians
    heading west around the Civil War
    strong
    one woman, sewing and farming
    but that was long ago
    a memory in the breeze

I come from the end of a hall
    where my mother sang a hymn
    left there in her moment
    alone
    singing How Great Thou Art
    to no one there
    but her belly full of me

I come from the pulpit
    where my dad would tell a joke
    before he preached the
    cross
    my grandmother deaf and
    reading his notes
    he'd bring you to your knees

I come from the fourth grade
    they called me giggle pants
    headstones beyond the play field
    ghosts
    where we'd kick the ball too far
    and Larry promised me a kiss

the whole class there to see

I come from an apricot tree
 in the heat of summer
 until the fruit dropped
 jam
 on the lawn beside the roses
 and we had to scoop it up
 a gooey mess filled with bees

I come from love
 a lucky one, Jackson
 my dad would call me;
 daughter
 fishing in the Sierras
 horseshoes on the lawn
 potluck cold chicken in the heat

I Am From

SUSAN COHEN THOMPSON

I am from the dreams of my ancestors.
     Their difficult journeys
     across unknown seas
     hoping for the future to find freedom
     so that I might find happiness.

Mother was a Feng Shui Master in a past
          life.
She carried the skills of object placement
into her life as my mother.
I learned these skills with my own rhythms
and they inform the flow of my art.

Father was born in a distant country from which he had to flee.
At five he traveled across the world holding his mother's hand.
Injustice made his heart ache.
Ethics ruled his mind.

I am from the city but my heart is from a slower greener place.
I was an adult before I learned to walk on unpaved earth.

In a past life, I was a cedar tree in an ancient forest.
Rooted in one place for many hundreds of years
has had an effect on me.

I've dreamt of freeing golden birds into the forest.
The birds flow out of my hands
and sing about their connections with the natural world.
In this I find my happiness.

I Am From

RENATE TRAPKOWSKI

I am from love
       a seaport town in the German north,
       with loving parents, one of four children — Daddy's Girl
       my first years in a warm home filled with music and
           laughter.
I am from tragedy, a Kriegskind (war child),
       my father killed on the Russian front
       his pillow the only comfort for my three-year-old self
       the music and laughter changing to deadly quiet.
I am from fear,
       my mother crying alone in her room,
       air raids, sirens, darkened homes, black-papered windows,
       sleeping in daywear, always ready,
       roaring attack bombers overhead,
       no room in the shelter, my baby sister with Whooping
           Cough,
       beautiful lights in the sky when a target was hit.
I am from devastation,
       coming out of the shelter and seeing the entire city ablaze
       followed by an hysterical screaming, pushing mob.
       ninety-five percent of the industrial city
       where most of the people lived destroyed.
I am from hunger,
       returning after the bombing to our only slightly damaged
           home
       ordered to give up parts of our tiny living area to the now
           homeless,
       to share our belongings until the government found ways
           to feed us

eating rare bits from the fishery harbor,
raising vegetables on a cemetery plot of land.
I am from responsibility,
always Mutti's little helper
cooking my first bean soup at age five for my ill mother,
(my brother grudgingly lifting the pot)
Mutti placing me in charge.
growing up fast, smiling rarely.
I am from fantasy,
writing poems for no one's eyes but my own,
picking bouquets of dandelions for Mutti,
inventing plays to perform with the neighbor kids,
cooking make-believe food from crumbled bricks,
unraveling old sweaters to knit new ones,
learning to play music on an old, shared accordion,
always longing to be free, to sing, to fly…

Nebraska City

ANNA M. HENG

Nebraska City,
The small town of 7000.
Smiles from everyone you see,
So kind and generous to those in need.
The feeling of happiness is everywhere,
Trees and beauty from end to end.
The more you look around,
The more amazing things you see.
A quiet place to clear your thoughts,
With no traffic or loud sounds.
A perfect place for a young family,
Full of fun parks and places to go.
The history goes back way before me,
Including J. Sterling Morton and ten museums.
The oldest fire department in the state of Nebraska,
With volunteers responding since 1867.
Every year is an eventful time,
Applejack and Arbor Day bringing visitors from all around.
Amazing, quiet, and perfect for me,
Nebraska City is the place I love.

Teachers Affect Students' Lives

KATIE HERNANDEZ

Many teachers do not realize that students' futures depend on how they treat them. The way a teacher expresses herself towards students can either help them improve and help their mindset or feel like they have no hope that there will be a better tomorrow. The smallest actions or words will either help or break a student's decisions for their future. Not everyone has the same support system or has an easy situation going on in their life. Teachers should be more cautious in the way they treat and talk to their students. Teachers change student's lives either in a good or bad way, and they are not always aware of that.

Teachers do not always realize they may be the only hope or support system a student has. Children come from all kinds of broken homes, and graduating from high school and attending college may be the last things on their minds. Those around them may not encourage them or believe they can achieve big things, because no one else has before or because their full potential is not shown. When teachers start believing that those students can do big things and encourage them, then it can completely change their lives. All those students need is a push to get them doing something they never imagined. Teachers also do not realize that what they might say to a student can also destroy their dreams. Such as saying something rude to them so often that they actually start believing in what they were told, and completely crush their dreams. More teachers need to understand that part of being a teacher is teaching broken people.

In the book and movie *Freedom Writers,* a teacher helped pursue what her students only dreamed about doing. Most of her students came from broken families, whether it was drug, gang, or violence related. Her students slacked off and never did any work, but she completely changed them around. The teacher, Mrs. Gruwell, made her students keep a journal for class where they would write any type of event that happened in their lives. After Mrs. Gruwell read her student's journals, she realized why they acted and did the things they were doing. Mrs. Gruwell started interacting more with them this way and with one another as well. She would make activities in class, so the students would be able to get their mind off things, including field trips. Mrs. Gruwell made sure all her students graduated from high school, and some of them even made it to college and earned degrees. She made them do what they never thought they would be able to do. She made a big change in their lives, and more teachers need to understand this important opportunity.

I have been in both situations where one of my teachers was the worst and put me down, but another supported me so much and pushed me to do better. My worst experience was in second grade. I was in ESL at the time, and my English was not the best. I stuttered a lot when I spoke. My teacher used to call on people to read out loud, and she happened to pick on me that day. As I started to try to read, she stopped me and told me that at the rate that I was speaking I was never going to be able to speak English fluently. She did not just tell me once, but multiple times. It put me down, because for the longest time, I believed what she told me. My English has improved, but to this day I cannot help but wonder if it is good enough. It is teachers like this who need to realize that what they say can and will affect their students. It is eleven years later, and I am still traumatized that what she said may be true. It did not stop me from going after my dreams, but it is the reason why I get so nervous talking in front of a group of people.

I have also had teachers who showed they really cared and pushed their students to be the best they can be. It was with the smallest things that showed they wanted the best for their students. Some were with a simple greeting and asking if everything was going well, while others would have a serious conversation of how successful I could be. One of my teachers in my junior year of high school saw the potential in me that no one else was able to see. It was during a dark part in my life, and he did everything in his power to push me through it and helped me reach my senior year. Teachers like these should be appreciated more. They are the ones who go out of their way and truly change students for the better. He always checked up on most of his students and that is what made him such a unique person. He made sure that no one in his class ever felt small. Many times, in class we would discuss hard patches we have been through, and it would always help get it off one's chest. His class turned into something I actually looked forward to. He pushed all of his students to their full potential and made sure we were always doing well.

It takes another level to be this kind of teacher. Not only did he have to worry about himself and his own family, but he made time for all his students. All he could have done was just support us and see the potential, but he went above and beyond. He would stay late after school to help and would always have a one on one conversation on his own time with us. It must have been hard to balance everything, but because of him students were able to achieve things they only ever dreamed about doing.

Some teachers are quick to lose their tempers because of the way their students behave towards them. They do so without realizing those are the students who do not know any better, and this is the only education they know. It is a topic that is not brought up a lot, because not many realize it is an issue. It is believed they are rude children and are uneducated. When teachers behave this way, it only makes their students feel worse. In my situation, it was not my fault. I was not fluent in English, and when I realized it, criticism only made me feel like I was behind everyone else. So, when these students are treated poorly, it makes them feel terrible. Teachers do not realize, sometimes, they are the only positive role models students see.

Teachers change students' lives all the time, whether in good or bad ways, and they are not always aware of that. More teachers need to take into consideration they are the only person a student has, and when teachers act harsh towards them, students start losing the small hope they had. Teachers can help students succeed when they have no one else. There needs to be more awareness of these situations, because now this is not a priority. Simply by seeing potential in students can change their lives. Children do not have satisfactory guidance or enough hope, but good teachers can change young people for the better.

T.J. Cheese: The Talent Is Passed On

ROWAN F. HILL

5th grade, Alice Buffett Middle School, Omaha, NE

How much trouble could two innocent (not) little boys cause on one normal summer afternoon? T.J. Cheese was in his room, when his little brother Jeff came in.

"Oh, hi, Jeff," T.J. muttered.

Jeff had a water balloon in his hand. He walked over to the window and pointed it at the elderly man's house across the street.

"Oh, ya!" T.J. Cheese agreed, with an evil smile.

They opened the window and put the balloon into the launcher.

Ten minutes later, T.J. announced, "Wow, it's hard work causing trouble. I think I need a snack."

Once they got back upstairs, they saw him! They shot the blue overfilled water balloon through the air and watched as it smashed on the poor old man's head.

SPLAT!

All the balloon bits went everywhere, as the old man cried, "Why meeeee?"

T.J. and Jeff laughed so hard! Then, they went outside with another water balloon. Once the old man came out with dry clothes, they launched the hugely filled red water balloon through the air but missed the old man. They ran before the old man saw them.

"Whew!" the old man said.

Later that day, when the old man was watering his flowers, they launched their last, green, overfilled water balloon and hit him right on the head.

Splat!

They started to laugh as the little green balloon bits went everywhere, but this time, the dripping, wet, old man sprayed them with his blue hose, and they all got all wet. Their faces turned as red as a tomato!

"Karma!" the old man yelled.

Now, every time T.J. Cheese and Jeff are outside together, their neighbor throws water balloons at them or soaks them with his blue hose of shame.

Dehli Guide
Photo by Kim McNealy Sosin

All I Need

EMMANUEL HUFFMAN

A sanctuary could be as close as two inches or hundreds of miles away. Humans have two impulses in life, to fight or flee. Staying to fight helps get closer to our roots. Instead of running away from problems, it helps to write them down on paper and stick them into our unconscious. Most problems dwell in our hearts. Writing is a good tool for bringing inner situations to conscious levels. People deal with them and take charge of their lives.

I never thought of writing as a tool to bring thoughts to conscious levels. I looked back at my personal journal and realized these issues are bad in my life, and every time after I write, it feels like these issues cannot sneak up on me. My notebook is helping me become a wiser and stronger person, and I always knew that aspect of writing. I just never knew that seeing the words on paper brings them to my conscious levels. My personal journal is starting to look like a history book about my life, something I can show my kids and their kids, and something that could teach them about how powerful writing can be. I know there is someone else out there who is going through some of the same things I go through. I thought it would be nice to share a writing from my journal.

My Life

Nowadays my thoughts really got me tripping
Pouring up I swear I never stop sipping
I've been thinking 'bout that girl I've been missing
And the reason why Dad doesn't listen

Why Momma is always in her bed
Is the depression really getting to her head?
I'm regretting all the things I ever did
Go to college, make Momma proud instead

I'm recalling all the pain that I caused you
I remember all the good times we had, too.
Now I'm asking for a chance, and it is past due
Should've taken a step back to get another view

Grandma's stressed, and she's crying
I've been buying all the treats that she loves, too
But she can't escape the pain she goes through
I've been loving Grandma, since I was a young dude

You took my brother, and you put him in a cell
Now I've got demons telling me to go to hell
It's not magic, and it's surely not a spell
I've got way too many wishes for the well

Cash is not the answer to serenity
I couldn't find the answer in some Hennessey
Little did I know they were the enemy
I really wanted love — It's all I need

On the Moors of Omaha

TREBBE JOHNSON

I stepped outside and shut the door behind me, and the moors swept me into their updraft.

Space opens before her, resolute and uncontested under the sky. The wind slaps at her cheeks, whips the long cape against her legs. All around the grasses bend and recover with the gusts.

Just across Western Avenue at 60th Street, the neighborhood made a quick transition from small ranch-style houses on small lots to larger ranch-style houses boasting lawns more spacious than garages and shaded by large trees.

If she were to turn around now, the ramshackle old house would look minuscule. She will not turn. At last she is alone with the land and sky. Without slowing her pace, she heads up the nearest hill. It is not the summit she craves, though, it's this movement of attaining it. She is cold, out of breath, but she is not tired. Instead, she finds the harassment of the wind, the demand of the slope exhilarating. The moors join forces with her body and push her to keep going, for the more energy she puts into matching nature's rhythm, the more she forgets the restlessness burning in her heart.

There were several options for turning right off 60th Street, and all of them led through Dundee, the stately neighborhood where the houses were brick with two or even three stories, big lawns, gardens, walls that made you wish to peek behind them, and windows into rooms where, now and then, you could gauge a personality from a glimpse of chair, a vase, a toy.

No matter how far she walks or how many summits she crests, the moors beckon her, even as they back away. She knows the land is teasing her, knows that it wants her just as much as she wants it. It wants to be chased, and she's more than willing to give it that. She strides toward the peak of the next hill.

That was me at fifteen, walking the flat, tree-lined sidewalks of Omaha on my way to school. Since we had moved two years earlier to the duplex, where I lived with my mother, my grandparents, and my younger brother, I had loved my walk to and from school, for it offered a cradle of time and space where I could be alone without being an outcast and where I could indulge in imagining myself as someone other than who I was. I had several favorite houses on the route to school, and up until September of my sophomore year, I had amused myself by making up stories about the families who lived in them, and pretending that life was mine. But in recent weeks, my mind, if not my feet, had been covering new ground. Now, what I walked was the Yorkshire moors and with them some inkling of transcendence I could scarcely have put into words but was just beginning to glean. By the time I got to my school twenty minutes after leaving home, I was dazed, vague, elsewhere. The locker room, the bustle, the gossip of girls popped the spell. But, once again, I had found something on that walk, and it was all because of *Wuthering Heights*.

We had a new English teacher that year, a young woman named Miss Hansen, Lonnie Hansen. She was in her early twenties, a graduate of the University of Omaha, who returned after spending a year in Europe. On the first day of school, she told us what to expect in her class during the coming year. We would be reading some of the great classics of world literature. Twice a year, we would each be assigned a book on which we would write a term paper. And every week, we would also be required to write an essay — she called it a "theme" — to be turned in on Friday. It felt scary and alluring. I couldn't wait.

All my life, I had been a reader. My mother used to say that when I was a baby, I would wake up early and start to cry, and she could get a little extra sleep and keep me happy if she just put a few picture books in my crib. She read to me when I was small, and by the time I was in kindergarten, I couldn't wait to learn how to read myself. The pace of the lessons in first grade frustrated me. On the first day of second grade, I had read the entire volume of our new Dick-Jane-and-Sally book by the time the bell rang.

It wasn't long before I realized that stories did not exist independently; they had makers: Laura Ingalls Wilder, C.S. Lewis, Rumer Godden, Frances Hodgson Burnett, Beverly Cleary, Noel Streatfield, Elizabeth Headley, Rosamund du Jardin, and Janet Lambert. The presence of the author accompanied me throughout the reading of every book I checked out of the library. Just as the scenes of a book materialized in my imagination, sketchily detailed in the center, fuzzy at the edges, so an even fuzzier, but larger image of the author hovered over all the pages, looking critically down at them as if, even now, she were conjuring them, sentence by paragraph, into being. I began writing myself when I was about eight. Using the Aetna Insurance note pads my father brought home from the office, I wrote and illustrated little books about happy families and the things they did to move closer to some culminating happy event like Christmas day or a summer vacation in Sweden or Death Valley, places I studied wistfully in *The World Book Encyclopedia* and fantasized fleeing to, far from Omaha. Now that I was in high school, I often pretended, while doing my homework, that I was an adult living in New York and working on a feature story for *Newsweek*.

The first novel Miss Hansen assigned was *Wuthering Heights* by Emily Brontë, published in 1847 when its author was twenty-nine. I still have that Airmont Books paperback. In the middle of an ochre-colored border an oval contains what is meant to be a portrait of Cathy and Heathcliff. Behind Heathcliff, the sky is dark and stormy, while the backdrop for Cathy, who sits demurely at his feet with her legs tucked under her, is a wash of greens and yellows, a summery lawn, flat as Omaha, leading up to a large gray house. Both the man and the woman gaze off to their right, as if watching something that he is more engrossed in than she. His expression could be described as "brooding"; hers is merely pleasant, as if she knew her portrait was

being painted and wished to look pretty for it. The more I looked at
that illustration, the more convinced I became that the artist had no
idea what the book was about. Catherine Earnshaw would never sit
at anyone's feet. Neither of them would treat the land that held them
as a mere backdrop or a view to gaze at. The landscape of Cathy and
Heathcliff was no nice lawn; it was the moors, and they were the incar-
nate with wild, unimpeded, gale-force winds.

Wuthering Heights is the story of a few thornily interconnected people
who inflict love and punishment on one another. The cuts begin
when a dour householder brings into his home an orphaned boy
named Heathcliff. Catherine, the man's daughter, and Heathcliff form
a close bond, while the son, Hindley, resents the interloper. Growing
up, Cathy and Heathcliff are rude, daring, careless, and critical of
others, but when, as adolescents, they peek into the windows of the
upper class manse of Thrushcross Grange, everything changes. Cathy
eventually marries the heir, Edgar Linton, and Heathcliff, choked by
grief and rage, flees, only to return three years later, with money and
determination to wreak revenge. Cathy dies giving birth to a daughter
named after her, Heathcliff marries Edgar's sister Isabelle, who bears
a child called Linton, and then Heathcliff plots to force the second
generation Cathy into a marriage with Hindley's child, Hareton. It
all takes place on the Yorkshire moors, whose wind, briars, crags,
and desolate expanses chart the fate of the characters and twist their
yearnings.

The moors pervade Emily Brontë's one novel. The author does not
describe her landscape all at once, as if to position it in the background before concentrating on what another author might consider
the more important actions of the characters; she makes the moors
a character, too. Rather than writing detailed passages of that land,
moreover, she injects frequent, brief encounters between it and the
people who abide with it: a lapwing "wheeling over our heads in the
middle of the moor," "the wind sounding in the firs," "hazels and

stunted oaks." Wuthering Heights, the Earnshaw house, is exposed to the weathers, and "one may guess the power of the north wind, blowing over the edge, by the excessive slant of a few, stunted firs ... and by a range of gaunt thorns all stretching their limbs one way, as if craving alms of the sun." "There was no moon, and everything beneath lay in misty darkness." The crags were "bare masses of stone with hardly enough earth in their clefts to nourish a stunted tree." It's as if Brontë was so attuned to this land that she took its presence for granted, even as she marked its temperamental shifts.

In the introduction to the novel Emily's sister Charlotte compared the author herself to a sculptor who, finding "a granite block on a solitary moor," worked it into the shape of a human head. "With time and labour, the crag took human shape; and there it stands colossal, dark, and frowning, half statue, half rock: in the former sense, terrible and goblin-like; in the latter, almost beautiful, for its colouring is of mellow grey, and the moorland moss clothes it." Charlotte, whose own novel, *Jane Eyre*, had been published just two months before *Wuthering Heights*, was calling attention to what readers for a hundred and seventy years have perceived in this rugged, rough-edged book: that it is inseparable from its landscape.

Once, in the middle of perhaps my third reading of *Wuthering Heights*, when I was in my forties, I decided to count the number of scenes that actually take place between Catherine and Heathcliff on the moors. I assumed there would be too many to discern, that the peaks and vales, entrances and exits would roll into one another like the hills themselves. But imagination contrives its own plots. Since the story is told from the point of view of the housekeeper, Nelly Dean, those scenes turn out to be few indeed, and the ones we readers are privy to are but reports and gossip: Catherine recalling how she and Heathcliff dared each other as children to stand in the grave-yard and call to the ghosts to come up; Joseph, the gnarly servant, tattling that he's seen the pair up in the moors late at night, even as Cathy is courting Edgar Linton; young Heathcliff explaining why, after a walk with Catherine, he has returned to Wuthering Heights alone. That's about it. In the second half of the book, there's more action on the moors, for Nelly accompanies the overly protected second-generation Cathy on many of her ramblings. I preferred the first part, the first Cathy, even though Brontë's style became more sophisticated as she worked her way through her novel. The Cathy-and-Heathcliff half scraped, bit, screamed, and spat; the second half strolled leisurely. How could a dreamy fifteen-year-old girl for whom the yearning to escape and the ache to belong were at constant odds not love a book whose heroine declares, "My love for Heathcliff is like the eternal rocks beneath — a source of little visible delight, but necessary. Nelly, I *am* Heathcliff." For me, the plot, the characters, the setting, and the author herself crystalized all I secretly wrestled with and could never admit.

There was an image I had of myself at that time. No crag of human shape, I felt like a rag doll whose stuffing was coming out at the seams. I hated being that way and wished I could be unruffled and contained, like the popular girls in my class. I had known most of them since I started attending this small private girls' school in seventh grade, after my parents got divorced, and they seemed to have been born into smoothness. Their hair, parted on the side, swung neatly around their chins as they bent over their books in class. Although we wore school uniforms, they had a dress code of their own, which shifted in subtle ways that they either instigated or began following together with the attentive immediacy of pigeons in flight. One year they wore flats and panty hose. For a while they sported circle pins on their blazers. There was a camel hair coat phase, a pink lipstick phase. There was the phase of White Shoulders cologne. No matter what the accouterments, they had a knack for keeping their skirts neat and their white shirts crisp, so they looked the same at the end of the school day as they had when they arrived in the morning. Nothing unpredictable seemed to issue from them. "Oh, God!" they would sigh as they rolled their eyes at one another when something was beneath their consideration. Even their alarm was calculated. Whenever a bee flew in the classroom window, they would scream and jump out of their seats.

I, to the contrary, got rumpled. My shirt came untucked, ink from my cartridge pen stained my fingers, and my hair was curly and unmanageable. I couldn't keep up with the fashion trends, not only because my mother's job as a secretary at the University of Omaha didn't pay enough to afford such luxuries, but also because I disdained them as much as I coveted them. I longed to be one of the smooth girls and despised the adherence it demanded to their secret rules. I didn't get invited to parties. Often, when I spoke up, the words burst out of me in a sudden gush of revelation, and when that happened, the other girls sighed or pretended not to hear. Every now and then, I tried to imitate them, as if I could act my way into their world. Once, when a bee flew in the window of the biology classroom on a warm spring day, I, too, shrieked and leaped up from my seat. When we all sat back down after a mild chastising by our teacher, I felt a fool.

Restlessness, fury, and desire burned so hot in me that I felt at times it would erupt like a rash on my skin. My parents' divorce had solved one big problem, but I soon found out that it had created others. For years I'd begged my mother to get a divorce. My father was an alcoholic who, when he drank, discovered all kinds of reasons to resent my mother and beat her up for them, and I was the one who had to pull him off, call the police, and wake up my little brother so we could flee for the rest of the night to a neighbor's house. After the divorce, I had been excited to move with my grandparents into a new apartment, where there was a swimming pool and built-in air conditioning, even though I would now have to share a bedroom with my mother. Shortly after starting at my new school, however, I began to understand class and wealth and how thoroughly they can exclude, for all my classmates had two parents and lived in big homes. Two years after we moved into the apartment, my mother could no longer afford the rent, so, when I was fourteen, we moved into a two-bedroom

duplex. Now my brother had his room in the basement, and my
mother and I crammed into an even smaller bedroom. She was under
the impression that we were both happy with this arrangement. She
liked to think of us as best friends, and she often told me that she
knew me better than I knew myself. Because she had suffered a lot and
was vulnerable, I didn't correct her.

What I was quite sure she had no inkling of were the florid con-
tents of the inner life I was actively conjuring. In the afternoons after
school, before my mother got home from work, I would crouch on
my bed and peek between the curtains at Johnny Miloni, the handsome law student who lived with his mother in the front part of the
duplex, as he shot baskets in the driveway. Johnny was tall and lanky,
with black curly hair, and he wore shorts and t-shirts that pulled, when
he dribbled and jumped, to reveal olive-colored skin above his shorts.
The muscles on his arms rippled when he moved and his skin glis-
tened with sweat. Sometimes I glimpsed his armpits, furred with dark
hair. At night, as my mother slept in the twin bed just inches away,
I contrived epic fantasies of being swept up in Johnny's arms as he
rescued me from tornadoes and school bullies or navigated us to the
safety of a desert island after a storm at sea. What I craved was both
privacy and liberation. From the library I checked out books about
distant places and made detailed itineraries of imaginary journeys that
I unfurled on the walk to and from school. That brick house with the
circular driveway curving around a garden, for example, was Piccadilly
Circus, which I was just now passing on my way to see my publisher
about my new book. The intersection of Western Avenue and 60th
Street might one day be the gateway to Temple of the Golden Buddha
in Bangkok and another day a lane winding through a fishing village in
France. After we started reading *Wuthering Heights*, however, all other
lands faded. Now it was the moors I crossed to and from school.

Wuthering Heights gave me the inkling that being contained was not so
advantageous after all. In fact, studying that book, I encountered not

only characters who seemed to have the same kind of unscratchable itch I did, but a new grasp of how an author could throw herself into things like longing, rage, jealousy, and madness as if into a "range of gaunt thorns" and emerge, yes, of course, stung, but with a tale that she had created in the process. The book itself, not the author and certainly not the characters, became the thing contained. The writing had the power to contain all manner of old rags spilling messily out of seams. Without the mess, in fact, the writing could not exist.

As we read the novel, Miss Hansen taught us about the Brontës — the whole family, not just Emily, since you could not talk about one Brontë without talking about all of them. By the time Emily was seven, her mother and two older sisters had died of tuberculosis. Barely four years separated the remaining four siblings, Charlotte, Branwell, Emily, and Anne. The family lived in a two-story building of gray brick at the edge of the village of Haworth in southeastern Yorkshire. Right outside their door rushed the moors. The children's father, Parson Patrick Brontë, was a grim, self-exiled man who pre-ferred to dine alone in his own room. He did have a good library, and he encouraged his children to use it. The young Brontës read eagerly and soon began to create their own imaginary worlds, which they called Angria and Gondol. They wrote the stories of the inhabitants in tiny books they made by cutting pieces of paper into two-inch strips and binding the pages together with thread. Of all the children, tall, thin Emily was the most strong-willed. She refused to attend Sunday school; she was not good at needlework, and she daydreamed. Sometimes she got her way by self-destructive means. At seventeen she enrolled as a pupil at Roe Head School in Mirfield, where Char-lotte was working as a teacher, but she was miserable there and, after starving herself for two months, she was sent home. Two years later she herself worked briefly as a teacher in Halifax, eight miles from Haworth, but the work was odious to her, and again she returned to Haworth. As they grew up, the three daughters continued to devote their creative energies to writing, while Branwell became a painter.

Emily and Charlotte contrived a plan to start a school of their own and traveled to Brussels to improve their French, but after nine months, they changed their minds. Again the moors and the parsonage took them back. By then, Branwell was in the throes of alcoholism and drug addiction. Charlotte, Emily, and Anne devoted themselves to writing books and in 1847, calling themselves Currer, Ellis, and Acton Bell to disguise the fact that they were women. They sent their three novels to a publisher, who accepted all of them. Emily died a year later, at the age of thirty, of tuberculosis. "We are quite confident that the writer of *Wuthering Heights* wants but the practiced skill to make a great artist," read a review of the book found in Emily's desk after she died.

Emily Brontë's novel is rough. Her writing can be excessively passionate. Even at fifteen I could discern that. But compared to *Wuthering Heights*, other books, both of her time and my own, seemed superficial in their depiction of yearning, an ache that the writers I was familiar with tended to portray as a mild hankering for a sweet, but which, as Emily and I recognized, was actually more like a monster with teeth and claws and a thirst for blood. She knew how to reveal, maybe even revel in, not only cruelty's manifestations, but the drive to commit them. Emily Brontë tortures her characters: a bulldog grabs Cathy's ankle and won't let go, Heathcliff hurls a pot of hot applesauce at taunting Edgar, the narrator of the book scrapes Cathy Linton's wrist back and forth against the jagged edge of a broken window, and Hindley hangs a spaniel by a kerchief on a fence. Love and rage get all tangled up together in this book. One is either proof of the other or a pike right through the middle of it. "Well, if I cannot keep Heathcliff for my friend — if Edgar will be mean and jealous, I'll try to break their hearts by breaking my own," vows Cathy. Did expressing all this violence relieve the author, no stranger to her own brand of self-harm, of a drive for more outward forms of savagery?

In my own life, rage and desire were forces that wracked in ways I would never admit. How could I tell anyone that, even after the divorce, I sometimes still wished my father would die? I'd wither up from shame if anyone found out how, when I watched Johnny Miloni play basketball on the driveway, I wished he would jump, bend, or twist in such a way that I could get a glimpse of the mystery inside his shorts. I knew, too, that I was, to my core, a selfish person. Ever since I was small, my mother had gotten periodic migraines, and when that happened, she had to lie in bed for two or three days with the curtains drawn. In the afternoon, when I got home from school and went into the darkened bedroom, the room smelled of sweaty, stale sweetness. My mother moaned as she greeted me, which I knew was no greeting at all, but a message of her desperation and a plea, aimed at me, for help. "Could you rub my head?" she'd ask. I could. I did. I sat on the edge of the bed beside her and worked my fingers back and forth in her thin, soft hair. Her neck was moist with perspiration, her skull and the pain inside it resisted my hand. In those moments, the prospects for freedom seemed as unreachable as fresh air, untrodden snow, the dunes of the Sahara Desert, a boyfriend, a room of my own. I never could make my mother's headache go away, and I hated both my own powerlessness and her sickness. I hated her for expecting me to make her better, and more than anything I hated myself for so despising this small thing she wanted. So, I punished myself for my wickedness. With my right hand, I kept rubbing gently, just the right pressure she liked, back and forth, back and forth, while at the same time I pressed my left wrist into my mouth, and I bit down as hard as I could.

In the end, Emily Brontë brings all her characters with the exception of Nelly Dean to ruin. She has them torturing one another's psyches until they either die or just manage to hang on, clinging to what we assume will be a life of misery. Even the names of these characters harass and grab: Cathy Earnshaw Linton, Linton Heathcliff, Heathcliff, Hindley Earnshaw, Edgar Linton, Cathy Linton Heathcliff, Hareton Earnshaw — all that C and L and H and E, like cries from hell. What taught this strange, solitary writer so much about passion, cruelty, and suffering? What did she really yearn for? What was it that so enraged her? Whatever it was that got inside her mind and ate away at it like an earwig, she was not afraid to scratch so hard that her very soul poured out into her work. To me, at fifteen, it was all immensely startling and satisfying. *Wuthering Heights* hinted that, one of these days, I would be able to shape my own disorderly outrage and wanting into words.

I had gotten a C on our first essay assignment, a description of my summer vacation. Miss Hansen pointed out that I had written two endings for it and ought to pick just one. However, she had also circled a part of the essay that she liked. The next week, I made sure to write one clear and precise ending, and I studied what I had done in that one paragraph, so I could cadge some style from it. I got an A. And in that moment of looking at the paper she'd handed back and seeing that red mark of excellence inked at the top, something opened up. I got a glimpse of a thing I could do, possibly quite well, and the long path — one whole school year — in which to get better and better at it. In the weeks that followed, I wrote about the Brontës, I wrote a memoir from the point of view of a giant in a laundry soap commercial who lives in the washing machine, about the pop-up place on the outskirts of Omaha that opened only in December to sell Christmas trees, about a statue in front of a Chinese restaurant. After the Beatles came to America, and I fell in love with them, I found a way to write about them a few times. Every week I got an A. An A– was a disappointment. Sometimes I got an A+ and once an A++. On one essay Miss Hansen wrote, "You are becoming one of my favorite writers."

In those essays, I never exposed the details of our embarrassing duplex or my mother sleeping naively in the bed beside mine as I conjured epics that always ended with my being swept up into Johnny Miloni's arms. I didn't write about my own experience with the violence of alcoholism or the torque of envy and contempt I nursed for the girls who never got rumpled. I knew, however, that one of these days, it would be permissible to do so. Emily Brontë and the weekly essays taught me that, no matter how weird or broken your family, or how wild your own cravings, none of it mattered if you could write. That was the great revelation. Anything at all could be written, and when it was written — or even before that, even while you were in the act of writing it — you had power over the stuff of your life. It could get you down, but it couldn't conquer you.

"Nelly, I *am* Emily!" I practiced the moves of my own possible self each day, autumn, winter, and spring of that year, on my twenty-minute walk to and from school. What united us — Emily, Cathy, and me — was the moors. I walked the straight, flat sidewalks of Omaha as if I were striding over the moors. To walk on the moors was to move with purpose and without restraint. On the moors you could go in any direction. Sidewalks did not limit you, stop signs did not require you to look left and right, people were absent and so did not judge. On the moors you could run away and run toward at the same time. The moors were waves, they were the stratosphere, they were magnets, and they were the physical manifestation of your own inner drive. They were wild, and they wanted to eke the wildness out of you. The moors wanted you out of breath, drenched with the experience of keeping up with their rhythm. And you were glad to comply, because in that breathless state, you were of their making. You were filled with moor and sky, self and purpose, drive and solitude. As I walked each day down the suburban streets on my way to school, I was out walking my old idea of myself. The girl with the stuffing seeping from her seams was ripping it all clean out.

I finally visited Haworth Parsonage when I was in my mid-thirties, more than twenty years after we read *Wuthering Heights* in Miss Hansen's class. I went there with the man I would be marrying in a few weeks, along with his son, who was spending his junior year abroad at the University of Edinburgh, and his son's new girlfriend. The Brontës' old home is a large house built of gray stone, not high on a hill like Wuthering Heights, but standing rather snugly at the edge of the village. It's a museum now, with some rooms devoted to exhibitions of Brontë memorabilia and some staged to make it seem that the family still lives there. On the second floor, in one of the bedrooms, a glass case contains the children's tiny books about Angria and Gondol, along with maps and floorplans for those imaginary lands. Downstairs in the dining room, you can stare at the long table where the women wrote their books, as you imagine all the brilliant strokes of the pen that fortunate piece of furniture bore. Near the table stands the black horsehair sofa where Emily died. One of her shawls is draped over the arm. The sofa faces the window and the moors on which Emily must have gazed for sustenance in her last days, even as her body weakened. "I'm sure I should be myself were I once among the heather on those hills," the dying Cathy Earnshaw entreats Nelly. "Open the window again wide: fasten it open!" Next door to the house, the old gravestones in the churchyard heave out of the ground, as if the dead themselves cannot bear their confinement.

When we arrived at the Brontë house, it was late in the afternoon, much later than we had intended. We had gotten delayed in London, and the young people had to be back at the university the following day, so we couldn't stay overnight, as I had hoped. We hurried through the museum and then, because I had expressed my wish to walk on the moors, we all set out together. It was not a gratifying experience. My fantasies of attunement with this landscape had never included others and, to make matters worse, it was apparent that the other three were just indulging me, and their hearts were not in this venture. We strolled, we did not stride. The young woman held back, while father and son kept up a running conversation. I experimented with gunning out ahead of them, but that make-believe rendezvous with my fantasy felt awkward and silly, as unconvincing to the moors as to myself. We turned back after half an hour or so and settled down for tea in one of the shops in town that cater to Brontë tourism, and then we got in the car and headed north. I was excessively disappointed. It wasn't until years later that it occurred to me that I had already made that walk on the Yorkshire moors many times and many years before, when I strode over the moors of Omaha, practicing wildness, freedom, and a writer's life.

A Love Story

PSAWPAW KASUH

I fell in love with the game of soccer when I was in sixth grade. At first, it was just to fill in spaces for teams because there weren't enough players. After playing more and more and having fun playing with my Karen community team, I fell in love. I hate to run, but it was running with the ball, helping out teammates, making assists, and scoring goals that made running so much fun. My prime time with soccer was when I was in high school. I played for the high school team. I had a team that I played with in my community. My days in high school consisted of school, work, and soccer. When things were stressful during school or at home, I would grab a ball and walk to the field. Soccer was my stress reliever.

My senior year of high school was when I loved it the most. My high school coach, Kyle, had a lot to do with this. Before Kyle, I just played, and there was nothing more to it. He taught me to love the game. He taught us different ways to play. He would tell us to play with style and flavor. When the season was over at school, we would have indoor soccer, which I enjoyed and still miss. He taught us that it was okay to make mistakes and mess up; that is how we grew to be better players. He helped us create meaningful friendships with team members. Soccer was more than just a game; it was a lifestyle and a connection for all of us.

Throughout the years during high school, I knew that once I graduated, my relationship with soccer wouldn't be the same. I dreaded the day I graduated. I knew that once I started college, I wouldn't be able to play soccer the same way I did my senior year of high school. It was worse than I thought, because I had multiple knee injuries, but I wasn't patient enough for them to heal. My first year of college, I tried hard to keep playing. I joined a club team, but the team consisted of 40 boys and 5 girls. It wasn't fun playing with them, so I stopped. Since then, I slowly stopped playing soccer, to the point where I'm ashamed to go back and play.

I'm in my second year of college, now, and I thought things would be different. I thought I would come back to Minnesota from Nebraska, and things would be just as I left them. However, that wasn't the case. Summer is another prime time for soccer, and last summer I was gone the whole summer, so I wasn't available to play in tournaments, which led to further distance from my relationship with soccer. I was upset because I saw my community team playing and having fun, and I wasn't there to play with them.

I thought I would start playing indoor soccer with all my high school friends, but I realized something. When I stopped playing, they continued to play, and each day they would improve and be better players than they were before. Because of that, I was embarrassed to play. I'm a rusty player, and they are now better than me. I would get invited to play, but I make excuses not to go. I'm working on gaining more confidence. It doesn't matter if I play well or not, I'm just there to have fun.

It is not too late to go back. It's never too late. I have to stop feeling insecure about myself. I need to consider the fact that my knee is still not better, and I should start my physical therapy, again. Writing about this makes me miss the sport and my high school days. Soccer helped me connect with my friends, and now that I stopped, I haven't been as close to my friends as I would like. I should take chances, like playing intramural or club soccer at school. I need to suck it up. I hope with that class I learn it is okay to feel what I'm feeling. I want to have fun.

Proposal
Photo by Sarah Cortina

Somehow, Someday

MADELEINE-ROSE RAWLINSON KNOWLES

My name is Maddie. I am a lot of things. I am an artist. I am a friend. I am a feminist. I am a listener. I am a traveler. I am a first-generation American and a dual citizen. I love Jesus more than anything. I am so much more than any piece of writing could explain. A person can never just be one thing. I love people because of that. Every single human is a galaxy, a soul, a story no one else can tell. I love to draw faces. Each face is a constellation of emotion, beauty, and complexity. I never get tired of looking into another person. That is something I love about myself.

It is so hard for me to find something to love inside of me. I speak before I think. I speak too loudly. I hurt people. I am so afraid that I am too much and overwhelming to be around. I never learned to be anyone except myself, and I cannot adapt to other people. I am so angry, all the time. I feel helpless to create the change I want to see, and that fills me with rage. So many people I meet do not care. Sometimes, I wish I could be like them. It is exhausting to care so much, about everything.

When I was much smaller, I wanted to be a scientist and stop global warming. I wanted to be one of those activists who stop people from chopping down trees. I wanted to save the world. I still want to save the world. I have not stopped caring about the environment. I care about the refugee crisis, about Syrians, about starving Sudanese children, and about the millions of infants aborted in China simply because they are female. I care about all the women in my own country who are trying to survive in a world that attacks them and refuses to believe them. I care about all the students killing themselves and those who are killed in their own schools.

I care *so much,* about *everything.* It is *exhausting.* My mom tells me that I can't help everybody, so there is no point in making myself sick over it. She cares about me, but I think *someone* has to care about everyone. Even if I cannot help everyone. At least, I can hurt along with them, as if somehow my pain could lighten theirs, all the way across the world. I refuse to stop. I refuse to accept, "That's just how it is." As a woman, I can vote, own property, and learn, because of the people who came before me and who refused to accept things just the way they were then. I have to believe that I can make a difference, somehow, someday, for others who come after me.

I am stubborn like that. I love that about me. I do not really know how to write an affirmation, but I know that I am not perfect, and I am still beautiful. My heart is a fire, and even though it sometimes burns me, someday it can be warmth for someone who needs it. My kindness and affection are weapons in a world of loneliness. My God has a plan for me. My art makes the world a lovelier place. My perspective is unique and valuable. My inability to be anyone else but me might, someday, inspire others to want to only live life as themselves. I hope so.

I grew up wanting to be a superhero, and that never changed. I will not be able to save the world, but I can be a sign pointing to the one who can. I am an artist who can paint the stars in a person's eyes. I am a girl whose heart overflows. I am a warrior. My name is Maddie, and I am a lot of things.

At Last, I Rest

ELIZABETH KOPETZKY

Five-colon-zero-five-A-M. The characters stare judgingly at me
from the corner of my screen. I've been awake for so long now that
their meaning is indecipherable to my caffeine-fueled mind. My
fingers insist on typing unnecessarily lengthy words and sentences
that my future self will think of as pretentious. Five fifteen AM. Four
sentences took ten minutes to write. I don't know if that's an aspect
of my autism or my personality. I don't know if there's a difference.
Five eighteen — my internal clock is ticking, ticking, constantly
ticking away, reminding me that *it's far too late, no one should be
awake, you haven't even gotten any work done, you're a failure, you're a
failure* — I think this would work better as poetry. But then I'd have
to perform it, and I've always had horrible stage fright. Ironic how
my biggest dream is to perform. Or is that just the cruel humor of
existence? Five twenty-seven, and I've long forgotten what my point
was. My vision is blurring and my body has been aching for an indef-
inite amount of time — has it been days or weeks? Months, maybe?
I'm numb with cold, past the point where I shiver so violently I'm
sore from it; my body knows when to stop fighting a losing battle. I
wish I could say the same.

Fifty-three minutes past, and I'm thinking a million wordless
thoughts. I think of how I wish the ink on the page could match the
pure *feeling* in my mind, and how badly I wish I could see past that
gap and create despite it. I think of the seemingly endless list of things
the doctors say are wrong with me; I think of how desperate my eyes
look in the mirror when I wish that I could just be *normal* for once. I
don't know who I would be if I was normal. I think of the boy I saw
once, whose beautiful hair and enchanting smile caught my heart

instantly — how it is entirely possible that in an alternate universe, I captured his heart as well. I think of how much time I spend dwelling on alternate universes and forgetting to live in this one.

Six twelve in the morning, and I hope to finally sleep. Whereas most people rise and set with the sun, I have always preferred the gentler glow of the moon. Sadly, our love affair is doomed to fail in a largely diurnal society. But at least I know that on nights like these, her soft light will be there to guide my nocturnal muse in whatever outlet strikes her fancy. Six twenty-three AM. At last, I rest.

Marty Pierson and Summer Writing Campers

Invisible Wounds

JACKIE LE

What would a boss do if an employee called out because he or she just got out of a break up? How would that conversation go down from an employee to a supervisor? A likely story would be that the said employee receives a written warning for allowing his personal problems to interfere with his job. Now, I do not believe a break up is really a serious crisis for a person, and I hope one would not need to miss school due to this. This is a less severe example of what would cause an employee emotional distress, but the employee would have to cope in order to get through school or work the following day. Now, imagine a more emotional example; a beloved has passed in our family, whether it would be our furry friend, sibling, parent, or grandparent; the loss is significant. The loss impacts the way we function, concentrate, perform, and operate on a daily basis. Perhaps, I should speak for myself. However, I can confidently say that unless people were part robot or some other unknown type of human incapable of feeling emotions, losing someone we care about is never going to be easy. The sad truth is mental illness is stigmatized, and while there are certain times of the year when we attempt to "recognize it" as "Suicide Awareness," our society still does not take it as seriously as we do for visible conditions.

Is it acceptable to not do our homework assignments, since our instructors have the responsibility to keep their courses moving? Is it typically acceptable to not show up at our jobs or else our employers can always decide to find replacements? The answer still appears to be "no," because we are required to push on through these hard times, since our bodies can physically make it. Yet, taking time off is understandable when a life-threatening physical injury occurs. An employer

seems more likely to accept that their employees cannot make it to
work if they get into an auto accident that prevented the employee
from walking. Imagine if someone were to get a limb amputated, a
more serious, severe life-threatening physical injury. There is no way
a student or an employee can perform under these circumstances.
These are life-threatening emergency situations and will require
immediate medical care. Our society has perceived mental illness as a
less severe condition due to the fact that it does not inhibit our ability
to perform physically. Society has taught us to believe that mental
illness is something that can be dealt with, and it will get better on
its own. When I was sixteen, starting my first job as a movie theater
cashier, an orientation video said, "A good employee does not bring
his or her personal problems to work. We all deal with stress in one
way or another. Choose to come to work in a good mood, leave whatever personal problems you have at the door." Based off this video
alone, I can see how society indoctrinates us to think that mental
illness is no issue that should be taken care of first. This is what I call
the "double-standard" on medical conditions. I would be interested
to hear a supervisor tell an employee, "Oh? Bob got his leg chopped
off in a highway accident on his way to work this morning? Tell Bob
to leave his severed leg at the door," but of course, it is appropriate to
teach video orientations about not dealing with our mental issues.

What if I said that mental health can be as serious as an amputated limb? The typical responses I have heard include: laughter,
accusations of exaggeration, and the most likely; "Yeah, right." Dr.
Omar Latif, a professional Psychiatrist who has been treating military active duty personnel, and veterans, stated that, "Depression,
Post-Traumatic Stress Disorder, and all similar conditions of mental
health is the same as having cancer. There is no cure, there is only
ways to manage the symptoms, and treatment has to be continuous,"
this adds evidence that medical professionals who specialize in
treating patients with mental health believe the severity mental
health. Another veteran named Demetrius Maxwell, who is also

an intern at the VA Medical Center, stated "The fight never stops. You can never just wake up one morning and be completely recovered from your condition. I don't care if it is a combat related case, a sexual assault, or the feeling of being alone. The battle is always happening, and it is up to all of us to reach out and take care of one another as we did when we were deployed."

From testimony, I have acquired by talking to professionals, it is bothersome that the majority of adults feel many people should "just get over it." Suicide should never be taken lightly, and as much as people try to acknowledge it, I can say without a doubt that mental health is taken lighter than more common conditions. Would we consider telling someone who just broke is legs to "Walk it off?" Well, I suppose we can, if we really detested that individual, but typically that is not possible. If a person's legs are broken, he needs to get medical care. A broken leg may not be a life-threatening emergency; however, if it were to remain untreated for an extended period of time, I am fairly certain that we can all agree that a broken leg, or any limb for that matter, can result in a possible death. How this relates to mental health is in the same fashion for a person who is having a rough time, horrible days, feeling low, and not getting the proper care for their symptoms, suicide becomes a much more viable option for them.

The way the majority of Americans feels about mental health has been even more detrimental to our military and veterans. Movies that exaggerate a military lifestyle dramatize a very tough-love mindset. We hear words like "Suck it up, soldier!" and "Feelings? What the heck are those? The Army would issue you feelings if we needed you to have them, private!" Imagine combining that with how society already sees mental health as a form of weakness. As a veteran who served six years in the United States Air Force, four years active duty, and two years as a reservist, I attest to how the stressful military lifestyle, in addition to the barriers to seeking help, have caused the suicide statistics in all branches of our military to be greater than those who died in combat. According to Military.com, for every one death in combat, seven more die from suicide. This report was generated by both the Department of Defense and the Department of Veteran Affairs. This report shows that the barriers to seeking help and treatment for one of the most stressful occupations in America has caused a larger number of deaths by suicide.

Mental health is as important as physical health, and it has taken more lives of our military members by suicide. We need to realize that we have more barriers than encouragement to seeking help. Stress and distress is a part of all lives, and getting help is the courageous thing to do. It can never be stressed enough; have the courage to care. Taking care of ourselves and saying, "I cannot manage this anymore, so I am going to talk to someone before this takes over me," is not a sign of weakness; it is a sign of strength. Being able to shed tears and let out emotions, once we have kept them inside for so long, is a way to not allow the emotions to spiral out of control.

> *To cry is not to be less of a man. It is because you have tried to 'man up' and be strong for much too long.*

> — Major Zimmerman, Matthew
> Lt. Col, USAFR 439 AMDS.

The Blaring

WATERS LLOYD
Elementary student, Massachusetts

My name is Sarah. Sarah is a pretty common name, I think. I mean there are three Sarahs in my grade, two on my soccer team, and I've met at least twenty, so it couldn't have been me, right?

You're probably really confused right now. Why am I pondering over if my name is common or unique? Well, yesterday evening, my eyes had drifted to the blaring TV screen in the corner of our house.

There was a man, who was wearing a maroon suit and a gold tie. He had brown eyes and blaring white hair. His skin was an olive green color, and he seemed to be on a sugar high, for his movements seemed hesitant and jerky.

I stared at the man closely, and then I heard my name.

"Sarah, Sarah" he repeated.

His tone held amusement but a touch of revenge. His voice shot into my soul like a bullet, and my mind stumbled with questions and concerns. My heart started racing, and my arms were shaking. Sound from the TV started fading out, and my arms felt heavy.

I refocused. I was overreacting. This was probably nothing.

That's when I heard, "Go get Conner."

My brother! His voice was filled with anger and rage. Conner was at baseball, and my mom was going to pick him up. I lunged for the phone and dialed my mom's number. She didn't pick up. Conner didn't have a phone, yet, so reaching him was almost impossible. I ran to the door. It was locked. It wouldn't budge. I raced around the house, panicked, and started slamming every window but nothing moved. I was locked in my small, white house. Everything was spinning.

I looked out the window and saw a man with a maroon suit, a gold tie, and blaring white hair. He was coming to my house.

I Am Thankful

BRENDA LOPEZ

We, as a society, underestimate the capacity that any individual holds. Most people overlook most people, not realizing the potential skills they have and can acquire. Most people pass up the opportunity to help transform the lives of students like my classmates and open doors to their creativity. I find it inspirational that certain teachers take the opportunity to grant their students a chance to learn and live positive lives.

I am grateful to have had educational and spiritual teachers in my life who believed in me, who helped me realize my own abilities. These wonderful people challenged me to think beyond the limits I thought I had. If it weren't for their efforts and care for my education and overall well-being, I would not be as mentally equipped in strength of will and depth of love, as I am now. I would not have grown into the flower I am today.

Those teachers demonstrated what it is to be true leaders. They represent love, dedication, and patience. They instilled a strong sense of inspiration in me that led me to follow in their footsteps and help any person I can. I am infinitely thankful to all of my teachers for teaching me valuable lessons and helping me recognize my place in this world. I am thankful for their powerful impact on me.

Homesteading: How Paragons Prevail

DESHAE E. LOTT

I.
Attentively adapting in
the triple-digit heat,
the unmistakable flutter of red
perched
then dipped his bill
into the one tilting planter
with water resting
in its ridged blue rim
where you had just watered
the burgeoning porch tomatoes.

II.
You plant, fertilize, and
again and again and again
irrigate by hand
pepper, herb, and tomato plants
to pick and present to me
bearing your comforting smile
meal by meal
much like the cardinal
seeks, finds, and brings
its mate and fledglings
sunflower seeds and berries.

III.
She who designed the nest
Now sits and sings,

and it is enough.
Chicks come,
and we hear
her whistles and notes.

Sandhill Cranes Dancing, Lincoln County Nebraska
photo by Ron Boerner

Memory

JENNIFER LUCZYNSKI

What shame memories are.
We're never able to fully trust them.
When we remember memories,
We create new ones.

What about those we can't remember?
Do we simply forget them,
Or can we remember lost memories,
Bringing back past lives of love and sorrow?

When we were young and playing in trees,
We built castles out of forts and stuffed animals as friends.
The first time we kissed was under the slide at the park,
Or was it the monkey bars?

Memories are treacherous things, anyway,
Ruining lives of make believe images.
We believe, but did it happen?

I've lost you so long ago that I don't see your face anymore.
Your name is just a whisper on my tongue.
I never speak again.
I know I once loved you,
but now I wish to forget you.

Maybe, life would be better,
If we could never remember at all.

Friendship

NORMAN LUND

As I reach the age of reflection — early 70s, I have been doing some thinking about the importance of friendship. The writing process helped crystalize my thinking. I have come to the conclusion that health and friendship are all that really matter. You might say, what about family? For me, the benefits of family are the friendships I have with each of them.

Definitions of friendship: (1) "The mutual feelings of trust and affection and the behavior that typify relationships between friends." (2) "A relationship between people, organizations, or countries that is characterized by mutual assistance, approval, and support." (*Encarta Dictionary*)

- Friendship is ethereal, delicate, light, airy, highly refined, and fragile.
- Friendship is reciprocal, and if not, it won't last.
- Friendships can deteriorate and become broken and painful.
- Friendship means participating, sometimes, in things that seem hokey but are meaningful to the other party.
- Marital partners are often friends.

In the end, we are on this Earth alone, or at least, sometimes, it feels that way. No matter how good a friend or marital partner we may have, in the end, we each have to take responsibility for ourselves, and at least in marriage, the partnership is as sacred as the individualism. This is a dichotomy for both friendships and marital partnerships.

There is much written about massive losses of jobs as robotics and artificial intelligence become more widespread. Many people will essentially have nothing to do with their time, and friendship will be more important than ever. Various leaders have suggested that our society will have a "basic income" for everyone who is displaced, which will be different from welfare, because it will be more for those who won't or can't work. In other words, jobs, even ones we may not like, have social value beyond the wages earned.

The harshest term I have heard for this phenomena is the "useless class." Assuming robotics and artificial intelligence come to the fore as predicted, it makes me wonder how smart the human species is. Why invent technology that will make most people less happy? This will be an essay for another day.

Thus, it may come to pass that camaraderie, friendship, will become more important than ever before, else many may feel they are on Earth alone, with no usefulness.

Does friendship have limits or no limits? It sounds "cool" to say real friendship has no limits, but is that true? Would you give your life for your friend or your partner? Soldiers have. Would your friend or partner do the same? Or would your friend/partner say, "I know that you can save me, but don't do it, because the price is too high"?

Like everything, the answer is complicated and depends on the situation. I doubt any human being can say there are no limits to friendship; however, I believe there are marital partners/friendships that will give to each other with no limits. Even that has constraints, if it becomes too unbalanced.

Here is an interesting study:

"A full three-quarters of all study participants reported moderate to high levels of loneliness," said Dr. Dilip Jeste, senior author of the study and a professor of psychiatry and neurosciences at the University of California, San Diego.

"One thing to remember is that loneliness is subjective. Loneliness does not mean being alone; loneliness does not mean not having friends," said Jeste, who is also director of UC San Diego's Center for Healthy Aging. "Loneliness is defined as 'subjective distress.' It is the discrepancy between the social relationships you want and the social relationships you have," he said.

Friendship happens in many different ways and at many different levels. It is the hardest and most valuable thing there is to come by, and it is more necessary to happiness than any other commodity.

MAIL

Dear *Fine Lines* and Seth DePriter:

A short time ago I received a message from *Fine Lines* that you had written a letter to me regarding my poem "secrets in the soil." It moved me to tears that someone took the time to analyze my work, let alone let me know how they felt when reading it. When I learned you are a college freshman, I was shocked at your analytical mind and desire to write.

In college, as an English major, I was and still am much like you when it comes to analyzing works of literature. I used to dive into famous pieces and pick them apart for papers. I had no problem writing multiple pages about something for an assignment. So, to read what you thought about my work made me feel honored. Perhaps, someday, other students will be reading my work and wondering what went through my mind. Perhaps, it will inspire them to write.

I often wished I could talk to some of the famous authors and ask them what was going through their minds when they created a piece, such as poetry. So, I will share a bit of insight below about when I wrote this poem and what went through my mind. I will also share here that "secrets in the soil" just appeared in the current online edition of *Another Chicago Magazine*. It's my first appearance in a major Chicago literary magazine. In the world of publishing, some-times the window of time from acceptance of a piece to when it is printed can take a year or more. You will learn this as you try to submit your work over the years. *Another Chicago Magazine* took nearly two years to publish this piece from the time it was accepted. You can see the piece here and view other literary works. https://anotherchicago-magazine.net/2018/12/05/five-poems-by-tracy-ahrens/

Sometimes, I think I have a bit of a dark side, but I am a realist and I tend to crawl inside of a subject to explore it and then tell a story about it, like focusing on tree bark, but needing to crawl inside of the crevices and see and feel the world from inside of it in order to describe it. This shines light on a subject in a completely different way.

Poetry, for me, is a time to play with words and etch a lasting impression. I do hope you can see some of my other poems, especially about nature. I have a book of my early nature poems through *Finishing Line Press*. It is titled "Nature Will Heal." The link to that site to order my work is https://www.finishinglinepress.com/product/nature-will-heal-by-tracy-ahrens/#reviews

When I wrote "secrets in the soil" I was sitting in my car at the cemetery where my grandmother, great grandmother and grandfather are buried. I was actually eating lunch in my car. I find cemeteries peaceful.

I started thinking about how many bodies lie deep within the soil. How many stories there are below. Libraries of stories. All entombed.

The words to this poem rushed forward. Six feet under is how deep people are buried. Roots drill downward around the caskets and try to enter them. Granite headstones are paperweights to these stories six feet below. Caskets are slid into earthen notches. The dead all gather in a silent social (lying side by side over many acres). The living try to keep their loved ones alive even when dead — adorning them with fine clothing and jewels and placing loving trinkets beside them. In the darkness below the soil surface, they are all different. But at the surface (what we see), they are all the same: a grave marker, soil, grass. Likewise, we are all the same in the eyes of God. People still try to defy this when loved ones die — sealing them up in coffins with their style of clothing and personal items.

Above ground we still seek to hear the voices of the deceased ("muddled whispers"). Above ground we are in the light — always surrounded by "white noise" that drowns out those whispers.

The dead are six feet under where it is cold — "icy" — and it's ironic they are all facing/saluting a warm sun no longer seen. From what I have learned about burials, most people are buried facing east, where the sun rises. The sun, represents God returning to raise the dead. If you wish to think deeper, my poem says "a rising sun no longer seen" — and that "sun" could stand for Jesus (the Son of God). In death, people finally face their Maker.

I hope to catch something you have written, perhaps in a future edition of *Fine Lines*.

I posted your letter on my website, and the link is here: https://tracyahrens.weebly.com/poetry.html

Again, thank you so much for writing. You are the first person I've explained my poem's creation/thought process to.

— *Tracy Ahrens, Illinois*

Dear *Fine Lines* and Miracle Olawuyi,

I appreciate your kind note about my PTSD story. David Martin asked me if I would try to do this. As it turned out, this topic was among my list of possible topics. I am doing well, thanks for asking. Therapy and medication are managing the PTSD/depression. Biofeedback was effective for reducing anxiety. I have sessions with my VA psychiatrist, periodically. Working to help other veterans and writing to give me something to look forward is a big plus for me.

I truly appreciate your thoughts. I will walk through life more easily, for certain. However, I don't want to be like it never happened. My Marine experiences are an important part of who I am. I will always grieve for all my military brothers and sisters whose lives were cut too short. And that's all right by me.

— Best regards,
Joe Benson, Hiawatha, KS

Dear *Fine Lines* and Anna Heng,

Your sweet note in regard to my PTSD piece was forwarded to me. Thank you for taking the time to let me know you enjoyed the essay. I am doing very well, thank you. Since beginning treatment, I have better defined goals and look forward to my future more than before. I am "giving back" by helping other veterans get the benefits and services they earned from serving our country. Additionally, my daughter helped me find writing. We are in the initial stages of writing a memoir of my military experiences. In the meantime, I've been doing some pleasure writing. Please watch for future issues of *Fine Lines*. I have a story that will be in the next issue, and I have submitted a poem, too.

I will always be a work in progress, as I deal with my emotional issues. I anticipate continuing to use a mild antidepressant and work through anxiety issues. I have the tools to do this, now. I will always grieve for my fellow service members, and that's as it should be.

Keep reading and writing.

— Best regards,

Joe Benson, Hiawatha, KS

Dear *Fine Lines*,

Hi! What a nice issue you put out this winter! It is a lovely collection of people and work. I am honored to be included. Thanks.

— *Dr. Dottie Bossman*

English instructor, University of Nebraska at Omaha

Dear *Fine Lines*,

I finally re-subscribed to *Fine Lines* today. It was sad to hear about our friend Mary Oliver. I was actually rereading "Blue Pastures" when I heard the bad news. "Of Power and Time" has to be one of the best "Write On!" essays ever written. Has any other writer ever selected words more deliberately? (Or successfully, I'd like to add) Sometimes, I think I cannot read her slowly enough, and she constantly confirms the theme that runs throughout that "Working Habits of Creative People" article you sent to us: active devotion. Forgive me, if I'm repeating myself, but many times, she made clear her daily dedication to the craft she loved. See her "A Poetry Handbook." Listen to her delightful "On Being" interview. Once at a Fine Lines Summer Writing Camp you asked me if I knew what I would speak about, and I promise you, if I'm ever around for another camp, I'm certain I could

at least give a mini-presentation (which I believe would appeal to all ages) on Mary Oliver's writing journey.Thanks again for pointing her out to me. She may have passed, but her gift and spirit will remain with us forever.
— *Take care,*
Bret Brokaw, Rice, MN

Dear *Fine Lines,*
   Good luck with *Fine Lines* in the coming year. Glad it's still going!
— *Dr. Robert Brooke*
Director, Nebraska Writing Project, University of Nebraska at Lincoln

Dear Miracle Olawuyi,
   I am writing to express my admiration of your poem "I Am from a Blooming Meadow," which was published in the winter 2018 *Fine Lines* issue. I don't know whether or not English is your first language. Either way, I love the way you use metaphor! Nigeria is "a blooming meadow" "the thunderclap of Africa." It is clear that you love your homeland and it is a source of joy and pride to you. You make me want to jump on a plane and visit that wonderful country of fertile land and great men and women. Thank you for sharing your country and your skillful poetry!
— Write on,
Mary Campbell, editor, Omaha, NE

Dear *Fine Lines,*
   Thank you for all that you are doing to enrich our community.
— *Dorie Gebhard, Omaha World Herald*

Dear *Fine Lines,*
   Love the new FL! While I haven't read everything, I had to write to tell you how much I've been enjoying it. Yes, we all must laugh more and invite all we can meet to share in the joy of being!
— *Nancy Genevieve, Reading, MA*

Dear *Fine Lines,*

What a fine line that was. Thanks.

— *Steve Gehring, Omaha, NE*

Dear *Fine Lines,*

Thanks! This is another beautiful issue. The cover is stunning! I enjoyed both Yolie Martin's poem and Ed Connolly's lunch box story. I am thankful for your commitment to publishing the creative works of incredible writers and artists.

Have a blessed weekend!

— Joy in Jesus,
Cindy Goeller, photographer, Wisner, NE

Dear *Fine Lines,*

While we don't get a lot of writers here (most of our students are visual artists, not word artists), I will definitely send those student submissions that we do get. If you are ever in the market to hire a graphic designer, please, let me know; I'd love to help with that as well.

While I have you, I want to thank you for your creative writing camp and your publication. My daughter, Sarah, loves to participate in both, and it has done her a world of good — both in experience and in confidence. You are doing great things.

Have a great holiday!

— *Kim Guyer, Omaha, NE*

Dear *Fine Lines,*

The passing of candlelight. That's what you've started with *Fine Lines.* Shine on!

— *Maria Harding*
First chair flutist, Omaha Symphony

Dear *Fine Lines,*

My writing coaches here in Oregon have put nice things about your journal on Facebook. You are getting lots of attention. I don't have a FB account, but many do, so the exposure should generate some submissions from Portland and this area. I hope so. I was thrilled, too, that your editorial staff will publish my piece on Moscow in the spring journal. I think that's the plan, anyway.

I'm thrilled you took "Dreaming of Eboli" in the winter issue. That makes my month. Thanks for sending the digital copy. I will order print copies for my brother and a couple of friends who know the story. I'm also encouraging a couple of fine writers here in PDX to submit to you.

I'll keep writing. Focus! That's the trick. Who cares if the floor needs vacuuming?!

I hope you are well and thriving.

—*Jean Hart, Portland, OR*

Dear *Fine Lines* and Deshae Lott,

My name is Maddie Knowles. I read your poem, "Aspects of Love," in *Fine Lines*. It is beautiful. Your writing is full of air and light and the words are like wildflowers dancing. I feel like they are fireflies. I want to run and hold one in my hands, because they seem so alive. I do not know you at all, but I do know that you really know how to make some *magic*, and you must be stunningly lovely. Only a stunningly lovely person could write a poem like the one I just read.

The third part of your poem is my favorite. I read the words, and I can *feel* the movement. When I watch the Olympics and I see the figure skaters or the gymnasts, I find myself wishing that my life had turned out very differently, just so I could move in that way. When I see such a dazzling performance of grace, I feel like all the sacrifices the athletes make must be worth it. That is how this poem makes me feel. A dazzling performance of grace. The verbs have color and life, and I want to join the dance.

I have never been in love. At least not with a person, but when I read poetry or listen to music or look up at the autumn sky, I fall in love with being alive. Sylvia Plath talks about the tired old boast of her heart, "I am, I am, I am." Sometimes, heartbeats can feel tired, but poetry makes me thankful for every single beat.

Thank you for creating, and thank you for loving. I hope that when I do eventually fall for a human, it feels like your poem.

— Sincerely,
Maddie Knowles

Dear *Fine Lines*,

I am grateful for your friendship and for all *Fine Lines* does to advance the cause of writing. Your teaching touches the heart, and that makes all the difference. God bless you!

— *Loren Logsdon*
Retired English professor, Eureka College, Eureka, IL

Good night, *Fine Lines*,

I submit "Our Antique Nightstand" for consideration as a publication in *Fine Lines*. It is a variation on the theme in the poem submitted this morning — about how I tend to what is mine but also how I use it, knowing that brings about the markers of cohabitation (sometimes more extreme than others, not particularly desired but worth the joy from the "thing" living a vital life).

Some of us envision the ideal and wish to help bring embodiment to that, but my soul resonates best with those who are both aware of the ideal and, yet, lovingly engaged with brokenness.

How beautiful is the latest issue — like the others. Your positive contributions and vibes are a welcome, cherished marvel. Congratulations on and thank you for 27 years of *Fine Lines*. What noble work! I watched the trailer for the film about Mr. Rogers; wherein, he says the most important things are to show others they are loved and capable of loving. How well you embody that credo!

— *Angels on your pillow,*
Deshae Lott, Bossier City, LA

Dear *Fine Lines,*

That "Happy Holidays" card is just beautiful! I am singing silent night in German on Christmas Eve at 5 and 11. Franz Gruber wrote the music 200 years ago. His descendent is our children's pastor. Dan Gruber is going to play the guitar, and we are going to sing. His relative is going to talk about the backstory. It should be interesting. Merry Christmas to you and your entire family.

— *Wendy Lundeen*
Spanish teacher, Omaha, NE

Dear *Fine Lines,*

It is a pleasure working with you.

— *Jerome McAllister, New Richmond, WI*

Dear *Fine Lines,*

I just wanted you to know that I always buy copies of *Fine Lines* through Amazon. I already bought 5 of the latest issue and may buy more for the family who, hopefully, will be interested in my essay.

— My best to your editors,
Jeri McIntyre, Salt Lake City, UT

Dear *Fine Lines,*

The spirit and the essence of what you generate for others in your publication is amazing.

— *Kent Nielsen*
English instructor, Metropolitan Community College, Omaha, NE

Dear *Fine Lines,*

I am honoring the spirit of that lady who always took the time to read to me, help me edit papers, and most of all listen! I am wishing you and yours a peaceful time in this holiday season! Here's to helping one another through it all.

— Fondly and in Hope,
Kristen Norman, Edgartown, MA

Dear *Fine Lines* and Mary Campbell,

I really appreciate your feedback on my poem. It means a lot to me. Thank you so much. Also, English is my first language. It is the official language in Nigeria. The difference between the American English and the Nigerian English is the accent; most of our spellings and pronunciation are British, as we were colonized by them. It would be great if you come to my country and visit one day.

— Best Wishes,

Miracle Olawuyi

Native of Nigeria, student at the University of Nebraska at Omaha

Dear *Fine Lines*,

I appreciated seeing the latest edition of *Fine Lines*. You are doing wonderful work with your team of editors and contributors to support the art of writing. My current role is supervising student teachers for UNL and finishing a term on the Secondary Section Steering Committee for NCTE representing CEL (Conference on English Leadership). I will take the opportunity to remind writers about the opportunity to submit to *Fine Lines* — a remarkable publication!

— *Ann Quinlan, Lincoln, NE*

CEL Nebraska State Liaison, NCTE

Dear *Fine Lines*,

Thank you for accepting my poem. Winter came early for us this year. Already, we've had one light dusting and lower than average temps. I put together my Granberg Mill, although, I think I'll wait until spring to cut. I still need to learn a little more.

Have a good weekend.

— Write on!

John Robinson, PhD, Huntington, WV

Dear *Fine Lines*,

It is no coincidence that you just emailed me. While on a plane this morning I remembered our conversation while flying a while back. I realized I do have something to write about and want to submit it to you soon. When this will happen I'm not sure, but I haven't forgotten our conversation and the spark I have to write.

Thank you for the email!

— Peace to you,

Alex Rodriguez, Omaha, NE

Dear *Fine Lines,*

(I sent the following and more to Amazon.com as a book review of the 2018 Fine Lines winter issue. I suggest more Fine Lines members send their own reviews also.)

If you acquire this quarterly journal, you will be inspired to study metaphor, imagery, scene setting, and much more to advance your self-healing and creativity. You will be exposed to traditional and experimental writing at all levels. The intergenerational nature of these writers provides excellent evidence of the development of writing skills from young children through adulthood, which is found inside of each issue.

There could be no better book to place on your Christmas gift list or coffee table. It will provide unexpected moments of pleasure and joy to both children and adults alike. It is a rich anthology of expressive essays, poems, stories, illustrations, and more.

When I was recently hospitalized following a cancer diagnosis and chemotherapy, this book provided the diversity, light-heartedness, and inspiration that lifted my spirit from self-pity to larger worlds of hope and future promise!

— Best of good writing to you,

Robert Runyon

Head librarian, retired from the University of Nebraska at Omaha

Dear *Fine Lines,*

Fine Lines just keeps getting better and better. I don't know how you do that! The 2018 winter *Fine Lines* is a beautiful edition! Thank you for including my photos!

— *Kim McNealy Sosin*
Retired Department Chair of Economics
University of Nebraska at Omaha

Dear *Fine Lines,*

Thank you. I will mail in my payment check tomorrow to renew my *Fine Lines* membership and to buy two books. I am excited to become a member of *Fine Lines* and continue my passion for writing!
Sincerely,

— *Lillie L. Weatherall, Bellevue, NE*

Dear *Fine Lines,*

I mailed my subscription check. Keep up the great work, *Fine Lines*!

— *Barbara Widman, Lisa Shulman's mom, Omaha, NE*

Fine Lines Summer Campers: Dr. John McKenna,
Barbara McKenna, and Mason McKenna

Let Your Light Shine

DAVID MARTIN

My best friend has always been Bubba, my journal. He listens to me, when no one else will. If I ignore him, he comes to me in my dreams and asks, "Where have you been? Are you coming back? I miss you." He listens to me write about Mozart in the jungle, a high school junior offensive tackle who wanted to play fullback but was too slow for the backfield, how I got over my fear of facing the blank page, why I hunger for discovering how the drive for increased creativity affects some people and not others, why I laugh out loud when my personal muse finds me, the psychological differences between poetry and prose, introverts and extroverts, young authors and mature ones, why all forms of creativity are spiritual expressions, why certain people I meet become important to me, and why my interpretation of the American dream matters.

Bubba taught me to make time for what is important every day of my life. I use the precious moments of each twenty-four hour window for causes that matter. This searching has shown me that the most important answers to life's questions lie inside us, and all we must do is let them surface. I write first and edit later. Wisdom windows appear between the lines of Bubba's words. Each journal page is a marriage of whimsy and dreams with logical thinking and creative composition in the church of Standard English. All he asks is to be fed regularly. He is a work in progress, and he accepts this position. His job is to create a state of mind, remain open to new ideas, and make them visible. At times, he sounds like Leonard Nemoy in *Star Trek*: Write. Learn. Prosper.

True artists live lives of purpose. They live each day as a verb. They let their lights shine into the future. They are full of stories and must tell them or die. After every great sorrow is a great joy, but when we cut out all the dragons from our lives, our angels disappear. Art does not capture. It interprets. I want to live like this.

There are 3,000 possible expressions in the human face. Should we be surprised that 93% of all communication is nonverbal? The difficulty for writers appears when we try to use our 26 letters in the English alphabet to persuade, entertain, and argue on paper in that 7% of communication. Growing our vocabulary helps to accomplish these goals. Incorporating style, grammar, metaphors, research, proof, facts, and knowledge of cultures come to our aid. All languages are instruments. Writers must learn to play them, not let them play us. What goes onto the page is an image, just the way an artist paints a canvas. Effective communication comes down to the use of creativity, as in all art.

Fareed Zakaria said, "Every year, 100 million children around the world never go to school." What might happen to this civilization if everyone who wanted to was able to attend school every day? Writing is a living bridge that connects us all. Only 1% of the people on this planet have a four-year college degree.

Don't fight. Create. To grow requires relinquishing control. Let moments happen. Give all gifts with joy to help others through their lives. Be a spiritual warrior with art. The spirit is in us. Perfection is not necessary. We are enough. Do our best. That will do. With hope and good editing, the best in writers will reveal itself.

Before the beginning of brilliance, there must be chaos. Before people begin something great, they must look foolish. Go ahead. Make mistakes. From these errors, learning begins.

Words matter. Look up the unfamiliar ones. Use the right word, in the right way, at the right time, to convey the right meaning. Eskimos have 40 words for "snow." What is stopping you? Learn a lot about one thing. Learn a little about many things. Vocabulary is the best item in the writers' toolbox. When I was writing about the lack of love in the world, Bubba pointed me to Cornell West, "Justice is what love looks like in public."

If we want to achieve, we must believe. Life is waiting. Be ready. See it. Touch it. Hear it. Taste it. Feel it. Smell it. Write it.

• • •

A few years ago, my son and I went to Fontenelle Forest in Bellevue, NE, and walked through the beautiful, changing colors that nature provides each year. In that peaceful atmosphere, as so often happens when I least expect it, an epiphany occurred.

While enjoying that moment for its own beauty, I noticed two ants, one large and one small. Possibly, they were a father and son duo, too. As I sat on a fallen log, I found them inside a hole in the bark. I spent twenty minutes watching them work and just be ants.

In the distance, an auto horn trumpeted, announcing my newfound discovery. As I peered deeper into the ants' world, I saw much more: their relatives, family, and concerns. It seemed their entire world was inside this log.

How like these ants, we are. Imprisoned by our bodies, values, and the inability of our minds to dream, our lives bordered by barriers stopping the growth of our spirits and developing our human potential.

I wondered if Mr. Ant noticed the tree tops of the forest where he lived. He could not know much about the world outside of his small existence. Was there a spiritual presence for him? Could a larger being and his son, greater than my son and me, as we are greater than the ants, look down through their hole in the sky and watch us, our world, relatives, family, and work?

Am I stuck in my place, in this body, and set of circumstances like that ant, hurrying to and fro, never bothering to look up? I was too high above the ants for a presence of closeness to affect them. I wonder if Mr. Ant would look up and wonder more often about things outside of his world, if he could imagine a totally different circle of existence around his log. Can we imagine a larger circle of existence around us?

This new year, let us use our words to reflect our tolerance of others and let our families and friends risk being themselves. Let them look up or inwardly to find the spirit, warmth, and love they need to feel good about themselves and their passions. Let us take time to look through a hole in our own "hollow logs" to rejoice in the lives we live, to stand in awe of life's immensity, mystery, complexity, and simplicity. Let us read between the lines of our lives, notice more than the words, and discover the wisdom that lies inside each of us.

This year, many things will happen to us, our country, and our world. Whatever occurs, let's hold onto each other, be tolerant in our opinions, try to see the big picture of things, and remain open to the possibility there is a larger world that we do not comprehend at this time.

Like the ants, work hard and do what needs to be done; however, don't forget to look up. You might see the tops of the trees in your forest and beyond. Let your light shine.

"Scribo, ergo sum."

MARCIA C. FORECKI

Nebraska – 1980

YOLIE MARTIN

A lone deer silhouettes against the early sky,
Hoofs planted firmly in the rich soil of the Platte River basin.
Awake, Nebraska, to a new morn!

On the horizon, emerald bluffs call to the wildlife,
"Come feed on my bountifulness. The rains have fed the Earth well.
    Come. Eat."
The pilgrimage begins.

> The noose of Interstate highway weaves between Omaha and
>   Lincoln.
> Fifty miles of manmade asphalt. Caution: Slippery when wet.
> The Great Plains has its barrier, its hangman, its rope of highway.
> Semis, cars, cycles speed by — 50, 60, 75, 80 mph.
> Pass, honk, get out of the way; deadlines, highway lines,
>   headlines.
> Watch out! Beware of Man.

Apollo races his steeds across the gentle horizon.
His golden trail ignites the prairieland skies.
Fingers of fire caress the living.

The crimson flames shimmer on the young doe's cinnamon coat.
She hungers for the luscious leaves of life. The bluffs sing.
Glancing to the East, the eager deer faces her doom.

> The saber-toothed tiger could have killed more cleanly,
>   compassionately.
> The semi-trailer truck viciously, vindictively, severed the doe's
>   flesh in two.
> Alone, the upper torso spews along the side of I-80.

The wild daisies wistfully whisper to the wind, "Who loves me? Who
    loves me not?"
Pluck, you live. Pluck, you die.
The heavens cry, and the rains come.

Veil
photo by Tracy Ahrens

Discovering Jim Crow

JEROME McALLISTER

On a May morning in 1955, my sister Julie and I were seated in the middle live oak. A low rumble came up Avenue J from the south, from the other side of the railroad tracks. The incline grade concealed the rumble's source. Soon, a team of horses, followed by a second, and a wagon appeared on the tracks. As the wagon drew closer to us, the rumble grew louder, and the staccato of horseshoes on the blacktop emerged. On the wagon was an old, colored man whose white hair was in sharp contrast to his dark skin. Firm hands held the reins and controlled the four horses. With jet coats and flat-black manes and tails, the horses stepped high and lightly. The wagon's box was empty, although the horses and driver were, of necessity, deliberate in taking it somewhere. As the wagon reached our tree, the rumble became a roar. It came from steel rims on wooden spokes, rolling on hard asphalt and reverberating through the empty wagon box. The old man was careful not to take his gaze from the horses and the road ahead, and he gave no recognition of passing within an arm's length of our feet. The morning sun at our backs caused the oiled-leather leads to glisten.

The wagon and four horses and the colored man driving them were exotic on Avenue J in 1955. Our usual morning fare was two-toned cars with high rear fins, white children like us on bicycles, and colored maids walking to work. Later, during supper, Daddy explained that the man lived in a part of town called Southend, the same place as Bobbie, our maid. He came to our neighborhood with his wagon and horses to pick up junk white people didn't want. He took it back to Southend to sell. Many colored folks couldn't afford cars or trucks, and a few of them still used wagons pulled by horses.

The front of our house in south Texas was separated from Avenue J by three live oak trees which grew branches big enough for seven and eight-year-olds to climb almost to the top. The spacing between the branches was so perfect that we were up there every day. The only problem was that the lowest branch on all three was several inches beyond reach. To get up, we had to jump, grab a branch, and swing our bodies up violently, all in one motion. The coarse, hard bark was initially painful on a bare throw-over leg; however, after two years of living there we had mastered technique for painless entry. We frequented the middle tree most because its lower branches made a seat for two people to sit comfortably with limb support for back, butt, and feet. Julie and I scanned the neighborhood, the street in both directions, and our yard from this vantage. The live oak leaves stayed green year-round and concealed us from everyone, except Mother who always knew where we were. If we had been in the same room at school, people would have thought us twins — bright hazel eyes surrounded by the same round face with prominent cheekbones, even though her light hair stood in contrast to my brown.

Mother said the live oak trees were part of what brought us all here in the first place. Along the coast, creeks and rivers created a rich prairie that brought white, cotton planters and slaves over a hundred years ago. They turned the prairie to cotton and sugar cane. This only lasted a short time. After the War Between the States, the prairie re-appeared with cattle. The live oaks were always the same though, marking the watercourses for everyone who came.

There were more things to do than watching the neighborhood from our oak tree. Our garage was away from the house and had an attached storeroom with windows on three sides. Very little was stored there. We appropriated it for a pretend place. It was a fire station with our wagons as fire trucks, an overland stage stop with horses boarded in the garage — bicycles for harnessing the same wagons, and a home where we were the adults and Julie's dolls the children. It was also a magnet for our neighborhood friends.

Our most regular friend was Harriet West. She lived south, down the alley, across a side street, then down the alley some more, right next to the railroad tracks. Mother didn't let us play near the tracks and strictly forbade crossing them — ever. Harriet's house was concealed by overgrown bushes. Julie and I were uncertain about its status as part of the forbidden zone; however, it didn't matter because Harriet never asked us over. We lived the closest to her. All our other friends lived in the opposite direction, even farther away from the tracks. Harriet wore the same clothes most of the time and got to go barefoot a lot. She was never called home for lunch. She didn't talk much and followed along with everything we did.

Julie and I liked to play a trick on new friends from the neighborhood. Our house on Avenue J was among the oldest in town. Soon after moving there, we found that the previous owner left wonderful plants distributed about the yard for us to discover. Our favorites were kumquat, pomegranate, dewberry, and chili petite. The first three were for eating when ripe; the chilies were for tricking. The red berries were smaller than a pea, and a hundred or more would grow on a little bush no higher than our knees. A first testing had caused our mouths to catch on fire and run to the house for help. Julie devised a strategy for sharing this experience with friends: plunk a chili into your mouth, pretend to chew, and then swallow it whole, exclaiming how good it tasted. The victim would do the same, then scream, clutch his cheeks, and get us in trouble with Mother.

On Harriet's first visit, Julie and I showed her about the yard. We picked and ate a ripe pink pomegranate. Harriet enjoyed the little molar shaped seedpods. Proceeding to the chili petite, Julie said, "And these are our favorite food."

Upon completion of our act, Julie continued, "My, that was good. Wanna try one?"

Harriet did as suggested. Her face turned red. A tear appeared. She took a deep breath and said, "Yes, that was really good. Can I use your faucet?" After a drink, she gave us a smile that said, *let's play some more.* Although the trick disappointed for the first time, Harriet impressed us.

Bobbie took care of our little brother while Mother taught school. She cleaned the house and did the washing and ironing, too. Bobbie cooked noon dinner for all of us when there was no school. Daddy would even come home from his auditor's job at the courthouse. My favorite dish was her okra gumbo. Julie and I liked it better than Mother's shrimp gumbo. She paid Bobbie a $20 bill every Friday. Sometimes, if I had been good, she let me give her the money. On the days with no school, Bobbie and Mother would do big jobs together, like washing the windows. This day was one of those times! Julie and I were excited because Bobbie was bringing her little boy, Sessia, over to play with us. He was in the same grade as Julie but didn't go to our school. He went in Southend.

Harriet, Julie, and I were in the storeroom with the bicycles tied to the wagons when he arrived. The cap pistols were at the ready, as we went from window to window expecting an imminent Indian attack. They wanted the horses.

"Jimmy and Julie, I'm here," Sessia announced from the horse garage.

"Do you wanna play cowboys and Indians with us?" I asked. "You can be an Indian. We can't because we're the white people they're trying to get. At school, the Mexicans are the Indians. Here, it's okay if you're one of them."

Julie interrupted, "He can't be an Indian. He's the wrong color. He oughta be in here with us, helping to fight them off." She turned to Harriet." What do you think?"

"Well, he oughta be out there with the Indians. He's not white like us. Daddy don't want me playing with people like him anyway," Harriet said, as a frown crossed her face.

"Sessia, just get in here and close the door. Help us," I said and pushed my cap pistol into his hand.

After a couple of hours, victory over the Indians was declared. Harriet disappeared when Mother called us for lunch. Bobbie served the food, while Sessia stayed in the kitchen. Bobbie and Mother cleared the dishes and went back to cleaning the windows, while Julie and I went into the kitchen to watch Sessia eat a lunch from our leftovers, standing at the counter.

"Too bad Bobbie won't let you eat with us. We'd already be back outside," I said.

"Mama says that colored folks are just as good as white people. We have our own places and don't do anything together except for work. I'm helping Mama with her work," he said and dug back into his food.

We watched him finish. Harriet reappeared, and all three of us took turns teaching Sessia the techniques for climbing the three live oaks. Later, around four o'clock, I rode my bicycle five blocks to the *Daily Tribune* building on Avenue G, where I picked up newspapers for delivery in the neighborhood. When I got back home after folding and delivering my seventy-eight papers, Bobbie and Sessia were gone.

Three days later, Harriet, Julie, and I went back to school at Jefferson Davis Elementary. Sessia was at his school in Southend. The whites and Mexicans went to Jeff Davis. It was five blocks from home using the bridge over Cottonwood Creek, three if we high-wired the creek using the water pipe. This was difficult with shoes. However, it was May, and Mother had been letting us go barefoot for several days, so we used the water pipe. Luckily, the Mexicans all lived in the other direction from school and didn't share the pipe. If they had, someone would get pushed off. There was big trouble at school and at home, if we got wet in the creek. At morning recess, all the boys had triangular shaped pistols folded from notebook paper and stuck in paper holsters dangling from our belts. The whites gathered by the front steps, while the Mexicans assembled a hundred feet away under two huge oak trees. At the proper time, by some signal, we'd draw our pistols and start swirling around the playground firing at each other. Occasionally, someone was pushed down and got skinned knees. Mainly, everyone got out of breath and sweaty. We never talked to the Mexicans at recess, because on the playground, they talked in Spanish. In homeroom, they knew us and spoke English.

By noon, it was too hot to run around shooting pistols. Lunch was from brown grocery sacks, outside with everybody, girls and boys, Mexicans and whites, mixed together. Julie found me and said something was wrong with Harriet. We met her behind the building underneath the fire escapes. Jeff Davis Elementary was an ancient brick building. It had the only basement in town. Above that were two stories of classrooms. The windows were so large that a first grader could stand on the sill and not touch his head to the open window above. Emerging from the rear windows on the second story were long, high-walled metal slides reaching to the ground, used only for fire drills. Underneath these was the only noontime shade except from the oak trees out front.

"Hi, Harriet! I brought Jimmy. Tell him what your Daddy did," Julie said with a small quiver in her voice.

Harriet was alone, sitting in the shade from a fire escape, with her lunch spread out on a flattened paper sack. She looked up for a moment, then back down. The cheekbone beneath her left eye had a yellowish cast. She spoke quietly to the lunch laid before her, "Daddy said I can't play with y'all no more. He says I can't ever go over to your house again." Harriet seemed to be disappearing into the fire slide's darkness.

My throat got smaller, and my stomach jumped up. "Does that mean here at school, too?"

"I dunno. He didn't say about that," she said, still looking downward.

"Well, why'd he say you can't play anymore?" I asked.

"He says he don't want me playing with n —, and he don't want me playing with kids who like them. He said he warned me before not to go over to your house when that little n — boy was there."

Julie's eyes met mine. Her look said, *this is bad, and there's nothing we can do.* She asked, "Can Jimmy and I still be your friends?"

"Yes. Please don't stop."

The shade held us quietly until Harriet finished her sack lunch. She stood, folded the wrinkled-soft bag into her dress pocket, looked at us momentarily, and walked into the sunlight, disappearing around the corner toward the side door. Everyone lined up there for the bell ending lunch break.

The next day was Tuesday, May 31, 1955. As this day began, it seemed important only because there were only four days of school left. This was to look forward to, even if there was something else pressing down on my chest because Harriet wouldn't be around. *Why can't we play with Sessia? Mother told us to! Maybe Harriet should have gone home when he first stood in the doorway and said, "I'm here."*

When I got home from school, Mother said Daddy had called and wanted me to bring a *Tribune* to him at the courthouse, before I started my paper route. This was curious; he always read it at home. The courthouse occupied a whole block in the town's center and was surrounded by a high curb and then a sidewalk. Between these two was a boulevard, a block-size square of green carpet grass and pecan trees, broken only on the south side by a high marble statue of a Confederate soldier, with the inscription, "Lest We Forget." The building was a large white frame two-story. The first floor contained wide hallways with polished, dark hardwood floors, laid out in a giant plus sign. Daddy was the County Auditor. He was a slight man with a far back forehead and a very inviting presence. His office was off the plus sign's northern arm. If I wore shoes and clomped my feet, echoes ran up and down the corridors and the stairway to the second floor courtroom. It was a place where I saw lots of colored people. At the hallway intersection, there stood two large white porcelain water fountains with stools in front for small children.

I stopped for a drink, and Daddy's voice came from down the hallway, "Jimmy, are you blind? Read me that sign above your head." Before he finished, I had released the water fountain's handle.

"Colored," I answered.

He came closer and spoke in a low voice. "Son, we expect them not to use our water fountain. Least we can do is leave theirs alone. Come on down to my office."

I reached across his desk, handing over the paper. Daddy went right to something on the front page, paused a moment, then gave it back to me. "Jimmy, your mother told me about Harriet and Mr. West. I want you to read me the headline at the top of the front page." He waited for us to go somewhere new.

"High Court Orders Segregation in Schools Ended Soon as Possible," I read.

Daddy leaned toward me, clasped his hands, and placed them on the desk directly in front of me. "Lots of white people, like Harriet's father, don't like colored people. In a way, they're afraid of them. They're human beings, too, and God wants us to love everybody. That's an unpopular idea here. You don't have to talk about it with anyone else, not your sister, and not Harriet."

He reached to get the paper back. "The headline you'll be delivering this afternoon tells us that someday we'll have to live side-by-side with colored people. That it's against the law to make them stay in a place like Southend and come out only when we let them. They call our way of separating the races *segregation* or *Jim Crow*, and the Supreme Court said today, in Topeka, Kansas, that it's against the law. It'll be years before anything happens, before colored children are in Jeff Davis, but after today, it is coming. We may not like it, but it's the law of the land now."

The papers were ready, folded, and put in saddle bags stretched across the pump seat on my bicycle. It took about an hour-and-a-half to drive up and down Avenues H, I, J, and K throwing each paper up close to the front door. Even with a late start, it was easy to finish before supper, a little after six o'clock. When I got to the end of Avenue J by the railroad, I was hoping to wave hello to Harriet. Instead, Mr. West was sitting on the front porch. He was short, thin, and very fair complected. His white scalp stood out through a thinning pompadour. Beneath that was an intense gaze aimed directly at me. His look was that of a person who had not achieved his place. He stood and came off the porch as a man who had been waiting for me. His eyes never left me while my bike quickly cut the distance between us. The weeds along the sidewalk concealed him from the knees down until I was almost even.

He continued staring at me from the curb. I made ready to say hello and toss a paper to his feet. "Boy, what took you so long today. Get off that bike and hand me the paper."

I did as asked. He unfolded the paper and looked at the headline, the same one I had read to Daddy. He turned the paper a little, so I could see it, too. "Do you know what this means? You'll be going to school with n — . Those black bucks will be with my Harriet all day long, every day. What do you think of that?"

"I don't know, Mr. West." My eyes wanted to take me into the earth at a spot just in front of my toes.

"You better start knowing! And look at me when I'm talking to you! It's people like your family that caused this to happen. N — have a place, and it's not with white folks. This is awful! I think I'll cancel the *Tribune*. They shouldn't even print this kind of stuff. Now get on out of here!"

I felt sent to a place with no escape, where nobody else would go. For a few days, I was quiet. I didn't tell Mother, Daddy, or Julie what was wrong with me. I never told them about Mr. West.

Six days later, in the morning while it was still cool, Julie and I were in the middle live oak tree surveying the neighborhood again. The wagon rumble came up the street from the railroad. The colored man with the empty wagon bed was going to pick up junk. This time, when the wagon drew even with us, the old man turned to our tree, looked up, and smiled a little.

The Economy of Grace: To Bob

VINCE McANDREW

Blindsided by nerves jangling out of control,
    By irritating skin eruptions,
By pain that would not go away during long nights nor in the light of
        day,
        He, my friend, an ordinary man with extraordinary compassion,
Leapt with his heart to the heart of another he will never meet
But who like him was in pain different from his but pain nonetheless,
        The pain perhaps from both loss and fear,
Perhaps from hunger in a desperate search for food or water for his
        child,
Or safe shelter if only for a day from the madness of bombs falling
        from the sky.

My friend knows there are so many in this kind of pain that offering
        up his
        To lessen that of another, a stranger out in the world,
is to cast wide his net of unquenchable love,
is to help in a way he can never prove yet knows to be real in the web
        of life,
in the interconnectedness of our world in a cosmic-wide field of
        energy encompassing all,
        he can in fact alleviate and help an unknown other,
living as he does within the economy of grace

Lost in the Wilderness: Finding Our Way

BRETT MCLAUGHLIN

In the summer of 2011, I went on a trip to The Boundary Waters on the northern border of Minnesota and Canada. At that time, I was a part of a Boy Scout troop in Bellevue, NE and this was our high adventure trip for the summer. The idea was to take a team of eight members into the wilderness in canoes, travel 50 miles for a week, and canoe back. It was going to be a great experience. On the fifth day, it was my turn to navigate with the map. We were on schedule and coming up to our last portage for the day, until I sent us down the wrong trail.

We arrived at base camp on Monday morning excited to prepare ourselves for the adventure that lay ahead. That first day was quite uneventful and full of signing papers, triple checking our bags to make sure we had everything we needed to survive a full week in the wilderness. As the day rolled on, we all started to get more and more eager to start our trip. Before we knew it, the night had descended upon us. It was time to rest, as tomorrow would start our long journey.

The first day started out great. It was a nice, calm day, the sun shining brightly, and birds chirping delightfully. The next few days went just as well with not a single bump in the road. We were about to hit our 25-mile mark to turn around, then it all happened. I was in charge of navigation that day. I could see on the map the trail we needed to take to get to the next lake to turn around. We got out of our canoes and began to help one another load our gear to start our quarter mile trek across the rugged landscape. Once we walked for about 30 minutes, we began to notice we had been hiking along the wrong trail.

We sat down and looked at the map. It was clear to us that I sent us on the winter trail meant for snowmobiles. The longer we looked at the map and followed the trail we knew it would be all right, so we thought. The rugged trail slowly turned into a marsh that was dense and thick with weeds and deep mud that was hard to navigate. All of a sudden, the trail ended. We had no idea where to go. Panic began to sink in, and my stomach started to twirl at the thought of being lost in the wilderness.

After sitting down and taking a breath, we were able to collect our thoughts and come up with a solution. When we looked at the map, we figured if we kept heading west, we would eventually hit the lake we were looking for. The only problem we had was we needed to carry three canoes across a marsh. Each step taken would cause the person to sink into the mud about a foot, and it was too rocky on the surface to drag the canoes, as the rocks might damage the canoes. After many hours of trekking through a nasty marsh, we could see the lake we were desperately searching for. The fear of being lost was over.

To many people, this story may not seem intense. I believe it was. I do not know if I am biased or I feel this way because I witnessed it firsthand. One thing that came out of this experience that I can list as positive is I learned to keep calm, use my skills, and trust others, but I don't think any of my fellow scouts will trust me with the map anytime soon.

Cross the Line

BARB MOTES

As an educator and coach, I have spent endless hours trying to teach my students that they could run faster, jump higher, and lift more. I want my students to understand that stopping short of one's ability isn't what living is about. It's about doing one's best, then just a little more. We tend to avoid trying to cross the line. Maybe, it's the fear of pain and failure, or maybe, they feel they need to save a little of themselves in reserve.

I have come to realize that crossing the line and not holding back is about more than just athletics. If we live our lives as spectators and never cross the line, we will lose out on what life can be, sharing our hearts and souls at the highest level, having a passion for who we are, and realizing that crossing the line is worth the risk.

Be brave. Cross the line.

"If you don't have time to read, you don't have the time (or the tools) to write. Simple as that."

STEPHEN KING

In a Heart's Tick

KRISTEN NORMAN

Forsaken love — eternal mystery
Of timing.
A chained watch we mortals
May never mend a pocket for
Hindsight and heartache
All we white knuckle, for eternity.
Until God's gentle shepherds
By glowing window panes,
Press fingers to warped glass
Call us home, allegedly greeted
Evading shame or judgment.

Casual reference to formed religion
Saved; I recall the times painfully
Where there lay quiet moments,
Like empty tombs; I felt
Compelled to fill. Like stones from
The ground, back to the bottom of
That hole bore into the Earth.
As if I scratch to itch, I would sorely
Attempt to slake them with
Clever quotes or anecdotes.
Nature observations of cloud formations,
Stories dug up from my past
Bitter berries I'd sweeten,
Lightheartedly and poor.

Pouring myself to empty,
So you'd adore me.
Love me the way I begged for,

In silent yearnings — when you'd
Leave a room.
Unsure of deserving — all for naught.
The trueness of the unmated soul
Will remain always impermeable.

A skipped step, a missed glance
A wrong turn — if only —
A solitary frame from a film could
Be rewound or repeated.
But alas, alas — you're gone.
I am back here, a bit aged and
On some days, scorned.
Dropping stones in that well —
Hollow, where only its echo remains —
Deafening to my burning lobe.
While your bones, your bones
Grow colder with years, feeling a
Chill — to my touch alone.

A state of unrest by both our graves
A prayer rests; a prayer for all those
Who stand behind me, who will
Look away — and for posted
Letters that will arrive
A day too late.

Nigeria: The Giant of Africa

MIRACLE OLAWUYI

The name "Nigeria" was taken from the Niger River running through the country. It was coined by a British Journalist, Flora Shaw, in the late 19th century for the British protectorate on the Niger River. Nigeria became a British protectorate in 1901. Colonization lasted until 1960, when Nigeria gained its independence. Nigeria first became a republic in 1963 but succumbed to military rule three years later after a bloody coup d'état. Over 500 languages are spoken in Nigeria, but its official language is English. It also comprises 36 states, including its Federal Capital Territory, Abuja. Nigeria is in West Africa and shares land borders with the Republic of Benin in the west, Chad and Cameroon in the east, and Niger in the north. Its coast in the south lies on the Gulf of Guinea on the Atlantic Ocean. Nigeria is often referred to as the "Giant of Africa," because of its population, wealth, and political influence. It is a country of resilience, and regardless of the various catastrophic events and acts of history, Nigeria and its citizens have gone through much and endured it.

The flag of Nigeria designed by Taiwo Akinwunmi in 1959, consists of three equal sized vertical stripes — the left and right stripes are green, and the middle stripe is white. The Nigerian flag was adopted the same day Nigeria gained independence from Britain. The coat of arms of Nigeria has a black shield with two white stripes that come together, like the letter Y. These represent the two main rivers flowing through Nigeria: the Benue River and the Niger River. The black shield represents Nigeria's good earth while the two horses on each side represent dignity. The eagle represents strength, while the green and white bands on the top of the shield represent the rich soil. The red flowers at the base are Costus Spectabilis, Nigeria's national flower.

Nigeria is a country full of people of different races and ethnicities. It is the most populous country in Africa, the seventh most populous country in the world, and has the largest diversity of butterflies. This is because Nigeria has the best favorable microclimate for butterflies. It is a country of friendly people. As a visitor, one is bound to receive the best hospitality and respect, because respect is the most vital key in Nigeria, and hospitality knows no boundaries.

Nigeria is also a country packed with an abundance of valuable possessions and wealth. It is mostly known for petroleum. Nigeria remains the largest oil producer in Africa. Nigeria's petroleum is classified mostly as "light" and "sweet," as the oil is largely free of Sulfur. Oil plays a major role in Nigeria's economy, accounting for about 70 percent of government revenue and 95 percent of the foreign exchange income.

Nigeria is also famous for cocoa production. It is currently the world's fourth largest producer of cocoa and the third largest exporter of cocoa. Cocoa production is important to the economy of Nigeria, as it is the leading agricultural export. In Nigeria, cocoa production is traditionally for export, with less than 10% utilized for cocoa products like cocoa butter, cocoa biscuit, cocoa liquor, chocolates, and many other products.

There are thousands of reasons why a non-Nigerian should visit Nigeria. Nigerians are very optimistic and happy people. Life can be cruel, but this does not have anything to do with what we believe in. We are very optimistic, which is why we can translate every negative situation into something positive. We see the good in every situation. We do not let difficult situations define us, instead we define the situation in a positive way.

Another reason to visit Nigeria is the food, which has some of the healthiest and most appetizing food combinations on the planet. In addition, it is a smorgasbord, and there are lots of dishes to delight everyone's taste buds. Starting at the local eateries to the continental and intercontinental ones, they reach some of the nicest hotels and cafeterias.

The mark-downs and cheap prices for goods provide a lot of reasons a non-Nigerian should visit my country. In Nigeria, I go shopping every day, and I can change my hair and nails every weekend without worrying about being broke because they have me covered. Bargaining in Nigeria is even more possible, and the clothing and costumes are durable.

The stunning fashion and style are things anyone cannot afford to miss in Nigeria. Nigeria stands as the second most fashionable country in Africa. The average Nigerian was born with a sense of style and creativity. The Nigerian fashion industry is booming across the world with its indigenous designs. On any given day in the streets of Nigeria, advanced new designs and styles are everywhere.

Leaving Nigeria to come study in the United States was not easy, but it has been fascinating. Thinking about the memories I had to leave behind, including my friends, family and the aroma of the food I perceive every day, but I had to challenge myself to think about the future because I know the best is yet to come. I decided to come to the United States for so many reasons. I wanted to get out of my comfort zone because it is accessible, we learn the most in uncomfortable, bizarre situations. In our daily routines, we know how to act and respond to people in our surroundings. Being in a new place, with different people, who hold different values and go about life differently strips all that familiarity away.

I also wanted to learn about other people's cultures; to be able to develop cultural awareness. I believe cultural awareness is a key to our world's development. Being mindful of cultural values and norms is not only appealing but can also help us understand international issues and conflicts, or even relate to the cultural norms of a foreign business partner. Cultural awareness is a vital skill to be able to modify perspectives and recognize the point of view of someone else's opinion. Cultural awareness can especially help students with their communication skills.

As time passes, things change, both good and bad. Every so often, there are moments that define a nation. We face our own defining moments. Caught in the history of Nigeria, great challenges exist, but greater opportunities also exist. As a nation, we faced hard days and our own share of failure, but we learned then that no matter how great the challenge, or how difficult the circumstances, people who love their country can still move it up to the desired state of nationhood, a course in which we are currently advancing in Nigeria.

There are 54 countries in Africa, but I am very proud of being a Nigerian and have never regretted being a Nigerian because Nigeria is a country full of amazing and talented people. Regardless of race, religion, and ethnicity, they welcome visitors wholeheartedly without animosity. Nigerians are also happy people, it doesn't matter if we are living in floating slums or the government of the day is not living up to our expectations. Hardship can never take away our happiness. Amid fear, challenges, difficulties, pains, frustrations, and anger, we still find reasons to be happy.

Be Careful of Your Dreams

I.V. OLOKITA

You have a dream, for years since you were a young boy it has been nesting in thee. You want to be something when you are big, and unlike the rest of your peers, you already know what it will be. That talent you have, the one considered as God's gift, you must develop, through which you will tell the world the beautiful stories you write. The truth is that your fantastic writing ability is just an excuse you can share with others, when they ask why you write. You answer everyone that being a writer is respectable, and there is not much of a living to make from it, but you'll manage. You are sparing them the simple truth that only someone who has been writing all his life knows, writing is a necessity. If you stop writing, you will die.

The first time you decided to share a story you wrote with someone besides your parents and friends, you expected enthusiasm. Always when your mother or father read your stories, they were enthusiastic and with an excited look, they told you that your writing was terrific. Now that your words hang on the Internet, no one responds to it, and you choke on the inside. Again, you find an excuse that maybe it's just a short story, and your great success, the breakthrough you expect so much, will come when you publish a book.

Days and nights of writing, considerable financial investment for your age and your book are finally in stores. You're waiting, excited by every word you read about your book on Facebook posts, and literary reviews annoy you. People who don't know you and dare to criticize the book you wrote, others annoy you by not writing a word about the book, even though you know they enjoyed it. You wait for the money to come from the shops, but the check is late to arrive. The agent and bookstores cluck their tongues. The book did not sell enough copies for you to have anything left of the profits.

Again, you return to old excuses: the book is too short, it's not the right genre, and in general, you didn't invest in marketing. Then you do something about it and write a thicker book, one that will surely succeed — if not in your country of origin, then abroad. Then, it happens; one day the flood begins in the Amazon and doesn't end. You have always wanted to be a writer, and the continuation is inevitable, just like the heroes of your first story, the one you published long ago and ignored.

And now it's your turn, to be absorbed in writing and marketing your products, the ones that will make you more money. Every three months publish a new book. You forgot about the readers you once used to woo. You replace the tremendous talent you once had, with another one — to write even faster. In the spare time you had left, you think about the dream you once had when you were a child, and now, you once again explain to yourself that "There is nothing to do with dreams today." Then, you wipe away a tear and add, "Without money, you cannot live."

Sunset
photo by Sarah Cortina

The Piano Song

ANDY PAPPAS

I can't put my whole life story into a 3-minute song
so I'll skip to the good parts, leave out the bad
and if you like it you can sing along
I can't put my finger on why I'm such a complicated, simple man
Live my life with no umbrella, and I'm soakin' it all in
This piano is my best friend

Used to spend all my minutes countin' up regrets
Wastin' time cuz I can't even count that high
Can't spend all life's moments worried 'bout what lies ahead
Save it for another time

I've been stuck in sticky situations
the truth is I'm a lucky man
And my heart is a sponge and I'm soakin' it all in
This piano is my truest friend

She don't judge me
don't criticize all the ill-advised things I've done
She's always here to lend an ear
I think maybe I'm in love

To summarize
I'm better with feelings than with words
And I've made a startling realization
I'm always gonna love 'til it hurts

Lord I couldn't dream this up
it's working out much better than I planned
And my heart's full of sunshine
and I'm soaking it all in
This piano is my best friend

Claim Your Nobility

RHONDA PARSONS

What's it like to be the Earth
Mother of life and light of the Divine?
What's it like to be crowned with the majesty of the mountains?
What's it like, what's it like, oh, what's it like to have the strength,
the stability to withstand the thunder and fire of life?

What's it like to live with heart,
to circle through the seasons,
to show off the beauty
diversity, color, regeneration, time, and
the seasons of life dancing with Father Time?
Sweet is the melody that moves the Earth to sway
this sacred dance with Father Time,
lifting the spirits of wildlife and humankind.

What's it like to be the sun,
the breaker of dawn and the promise of light?
What's it like to rise above the horizon,
to paint the sky with hope?
What's it like, what's it like, oh, what's it like
to shine so bright you melt the ice
and warm the heart of humankind?

What's it like to be the water,
flowing through channels and tributaries
with such fluidity and grace the desert blooms and rejoices?
What's it like to flow so fast, altering stone with velocity and speed?

What's it like, what's it like, oh, what's it like
to be the channel
the means others travel to the shore of eternity?

What's it like, what's it like, oh, what's it like
to rain down on the world and make flowers and trees grow?

What's it like to be the tree
with a towering trunk and yielding leaves
that blow in the breeze and change color with ease?
What's it like to be deep, deep rooted,
taking in nutrients,
making the soul flower with life?
What's it like to be evergreen,
branching towards the light,
limbs quivering for the touch of the Divine?

What's it like to be the rose
glorious in the garden,
petals unfolding to the sun?
What's it like to mingle with the others,
the tulips, the jasmines, and daffodils divine?
What's it like to grow side by side
the yellow, the white and hybrids of kind?
What's it like, what's it like, oh, what's it like
to be a rose on a bush, ok its neighbor isn't white?

What's it like to be the wind
wafting the fragrance of the love of the rose
wafting, wafting, wafting
that love through time, through space
no matter the distance?
What's it like, what's it like, oh, what's it like
to blow unrestrained sweet-scented musk
'til the Earth is a rose-garden and humankind its roses?

What's it like to be the eagle,
wings in full span, soaring on the winds of the Divine?
What's it like, what's it like, oh, what's it like
to circle in adoration,
scanning the field with sharp vision and clear perception,

to see what most eyes can't see?
What's it like, what's it like, oh, what's it like
to fly so high, to know such joy,
worldly treasures pale to a mouse?

What's it like, what's it like, oh, what's it like?
Stop wondering, and just be.
This is you though unaware you may be.
This is you, should you choose to be.
This is you, this is you, this is you,
the river flowing free,
the rose-scented breeze.
The towering tree limbs,
quivering for the light of the divine,
claim your nobility.

Denali: "The Great One"
photo by Matt Fillingsness

Witnessing America's Contents

CHARLENE PIERCE

The pilgrims set forth
God's providence
Some more welcome than others
Freeland
Farm workers
A warning
No Chinese
Not in New England

The slave trade
Runaways
Fur trapper
Tavern keeper
The Wild West

Lady's etiquette
Country school
Indian school
The school of manners
Private prayer
A hellfire sermon
Crusader
Simple remedies
Medicine man poison

Love on the trail
Pioneer wedding
A Puritan to his wife

A shiftless maid
Adultery punished
Another scarlet letter
A bigamist

Child labor
Indentured servants
Trouble makers
Slave law
A word of warning
Harsh punishment

Accident
Funeral in the gold mines
Hysteria
Asylums

Farmer's wife
In the kitchen
A famous dinner
Pocahontas throws a party
Virginia reels

The Gilded Age
Civil rights
All for the cause
True independence
Too true to be doubted

....

A Found Poem from *the Content pages of "Witnessing America" by Noel Rae 1996.* A "found" poem is one that is written using the text of another document. Here is a link to more info on the form: www.poets.org/poetsorg/poems?field_form_tid=412

When You Share the Diagnosis

CATHY PORTER

People offer platitudes and prayers,
quote celebrities who've beat it; throw
out statistics of why you should
stay upbeat and positive.

And you listen with one ear
store cuss words in the other that
find their way to your mouth
in private moments.

You know they're right — and they're wrong.
This is nothing like a movie; every day
is pre-stamped, and every moment is final.
The story of the 7-year-old, now 32.

The woman in Kansas who fought
and beat it three times, and now
sky dives for fun.
All relevant to the cause.

We all need to be strong
wild and free on summer
nights when time is endless
and winds never chill, or scatter

debris over the beach at sunset.

Potion

FABRICE POUSSIN

Treasure of treasures revealed in cold nakedness
it is given completely to the will of the other.

No cask full with holy nectars, nor golden fleece,
the diamonds are of glass and frozen rains.

Wrinkled bones perhaps under a sagging mass
of days gone without the care of a kinder soul.

A nickel too along with the last pennies made
all revealed wrapped up in a tired heart.

Soon to be departed in particles to a somber mystery
from dust to nothing, wealth of kings and goddesses.

On a plate large as the blue domain; invisible
it is offered whole to complete your coming days.

Take, caress, kiss, hold what still remains of the memories
they are made to fill crevasses others left behind.

With the blades slashing of unkind thoughts and cruel words
the present for healing, a potion to save at least your life.

Tikkun Olam

CHLOE RAY

Student at the University of Nebraska at Omaha

The phrase *"tikkun olam"* is Hebrew for "world repair" and is a key concept in Judaism. The term relates to the human responsibility to mend what is wrong with the world (*"Tikkun Olam*: Repairing the World"). It has become so well-known and meaningful that it was even used by Bill Clinton while pining for the Jewish American vote in the 2016 election ("Bill Clinton Targets Jews in Election Push"). Personally, it means to leave the world a better place than when an individual was born. I am a strong believer in *tikkun olam* and aspire to improve the world before my final day. *Tikkun olam* has a fascinating origin, major use in Judaism and everyday life, and holds a significance in my life.

Tikkun olam is believed to be originated in the second century and is a common belief in Judaism. The root *"tikkun"* is the idea that the world is extremely broken and can only be repaired by humankind. The first usage was in the Mishnah, the book containing oral traditions. *Tikkun olam* was used in the context of God preventing social chaos and fixing the world ("Origins of *Tikkun Olam*"). Although it is not mentioned in the Jewish sacred text, the Torah, the term is a pillar of Judaism. The phrase is used in a variety of age-old prayers and rabbinic interpretations (Jacobs). One of the most common Jewish prayers uses the term to remind followers that the goal of Jewish existence is to "perfect the world under the rule of God." *Tikkun olam* can also be interpreted differently by the Jewish mystic school of thought. It focuses more on the individual level of repair than on a grand scale and is used more abstractly and cosmologically. The mystic school of thought believes that the world contains both good and evil, and for

God to restore balance fully, humankind must work to fix it. No matter the interpretation, *tikkun olam* stands for reparation of Earth and has been a key aspect of Judaism for several centuries.

People of the Jewish faith have been following *tikkun olam* since nearly the beginning of time. The phrase can be interpreted into Jewish people's daily lives differently but is often incorporated with the word "*tzedakah*" meaning providing charity. This can be monetary, volunteering or providing aid for any cause or person with which a Jewish person would like to assist. The belief does not just mean Jews helping other Jews. *Tikkun olam* is inclusive of all people. Giving to the less fortunate is a key priority for Jewish people. The Jewish coming of age ceremony revolves around charity. In order to have a Bar or Bat Mitzvah ceremony, the child must partake in acts of giving to be considered an adequate Jewish adult. *Tikkun olam* first became associated with social action in the 1950s. Jewish people were fighting for social issues, such as desegregation because they rightfully believed that equal rights for everyone make society a better place. Helping others is a fundamental part of being Jewish, which the phrase "*tikkun olam*" encompasses.

Tikkun olam can be seen more than ever and is common today in liberal Jewish circles. Since, the 2016 election, the United States has exploded with social activism. Activists of all ages, religions, sexes, and skin colors responded to Donald Trump's presidential nomination through protests and marches all over the country by standing up for what they believe is right. Almost two years after the election, marches and protests for a plethora of issues continue. These social justice activists follow *tikkun olam*. This belief does not have to be a moral only pursued by Jews. *Tikkun olam* accepts everyone and is ubiquitous. Anyone who believes there should be an ounce of good in this world and works for that accomplishment adheres to *tikkun olam*. It is followed by Warren Buffett donating gobs of money to a variety of charities, a man holding a door open for someone else, and the lady who paid for the drink of the car behind her in the Starbuck's drive-thru. No act of kindness or generosity is too minuscule to make an impact and be considered *tikkun olam*.

Tikkun olam is essential in my lifestyle, not only because I was raised in a Jewish household, but also because I choose to stand behind the belief as an adult. Growing up, I had overheard the phrase by only half-listening in the synagogue pews on early Saturday mornings. Like most children, I recognized that being kind to others and giving to charity was important, but I failed to recognize how significant it was going to be in my life. As an adult, now able to make my own decisions on my beliefs, I grew a fascination and admiration for the concept. While trying to figure out where I was going to attend college, I became faced with a dreaded question. What did I want to do with my life? Slowly but surely it came to me by combining my love for traveling, researching, helping others, and social activism. I want to make a large-scale difference in the world by devoting my college degree to the care of others. I am majoring in international studies and double minoring in human rights and non-profit organization management. I hope to work for international non-profit organizations like Human Rights Watch or Amnesty International, so I can do my duty to better the world. I plan to dedicate my career to documenting human rights violations and calling for action on both the grass-roots organization level and government level. Public support and condemnation of human rights abuses are important to the success of these organizations and I hope to shed light on the unlivable conditions people around the world experience. The devotion to *tikkun olam* is ingrained in me.

The phrase "*tikkun olam*" is incredibly significant in modern times, my life, and throughout Judaism. It is a foundation for the Jewish people as seen through traditional ceremonies and the common value of providing charity. It is prevalent in today's society more than ever through the influx of social activism and has grown to become such a major focus in my life that I plan to dedicate my future to making the world a better place before I die. *Tikkun olam* may have originated as a Jewish value, but it can and should be followed by everyone.

Salt

DAVID REINARZ

If you can smell her hair without shampoo, without hairspray, maybe, with just a dash of salt from playing in the ocean that first time you were alone together, you want that. Always.

If you can smell her skin without deodorant, without perfume, maybe with just a pinch of salt from her perspiration as you chased her across the sand then tackled her and your nose ended up in the little hollow where her collarbone meets her shoulder, you want that. Always.

If you don't hold your breath when you kiss her and her lipstick was washed off in the sea and your nose is next to hers when she lets go and exhales and you breathe in her breath, the evidence of human life shared that is what you want. Always.

If you see her on the street and it's been so many years later that the polar ice caps have melted and the ocean has risen so there is no more beach and you call her name and she turns and there is a look of recognition in her eyes and you hold out your hand to her and she comes over to you and you embrace her and her hair smells like cigarettes and her skin smells like the cheap perfume that was probably a gift from the last of a string of faithless boyfriends and her breath smells like too many margaritas, but you taste just a little salt along the edge of her lips. That is what you want. Always.

Keeping a Journal

CASSIDY RENANDER

First of all, keeping a journal via a notebook and a writing stick is the only way to journal. Yes, there are other methods, like the typed format I am unfortunately using currently due to convenience. I think there's just something about writing words on a piece of paper, the pressure of the pen or pencil on the page and the quality of our handwriting. Like the back road I was driving on in a bus in Mexico was bumpy, and so my handwriting drifted and bumped along with my hand on every pothole and rock in the road. But I read those lines years later and remembered the exact moment, when the bump lifted my writing hand completely off the page. That exact time, when I was adventuring, bumping along, and transferring thoughts onto a page I will always remember. The stain in the corner from the cultural food I was eating, and it got a little messy. The flower I picked on the side of the path and tucked in my notebook. Those things cannot occur in the pages of a Word document.

Writing a journal organizes my thoughts. There's no pressure. These moments are not for anybody else's eyes, unless I decide they are. I don't have to use correct grammar, and if I misspell a word, it's okay. It's transferring thoughts onto a piece of paper, so I won't forget. I can reminisce. I can tell somebody, anybody, so I don't go insane by keeping it inside. I can confess things, pray, and share thoughts that come from a crevice deep, deep inside me, sometimes from places nobody else dares to go. Sometimes, the words come from places I didn't know I dared to go. Journal entries don't need to be complex and deep and philosophical. Sometimes, the simpler they are, the better. Writing a journal like this is something not everybody does. I think it's a healthy practice. Not necessarily daily, it doesn't have to be a set routine. Quite the opposite, in my opinion. Forced routine that becomes something I have to do kills the vibe, especially, in this technology-laden world. The simplistic-non-technology methods of doing things are extremely therapeutic and needed.

Erin Martin and Matt Fillingsness on Denali
photo by Erin Martin

Deep within a Cavern

MERCEDES RENKEN

Alice Buffet Magnet Middle Schoo

Deep into the depths of a cave rested thousands upon thousands of bats. The small creatures hung from the top of the cave by their feet, resting. They were waiting for the night to return. When the sun began to set outside, the cave of the bats awoke. One bat, in particular, was energetically excited to soar off into the night.

"Be careful," the small bat's mother chittered, knowing of the adventurous spirit the young bat had.

"Of course, mother," replied the bat.

As the other bats started to fly off into the night, so did Cavern. The night sky was dark. The stars glimmered brightly in the sky. Cavern's wings flapped energetically. Cavern flew through the trees catching small bugs with echolocation. Cavern used creative skills and tactics to catch the prey, like dive bombing moths and circling mosquitos.

Yet, in the far distance was a place Cavern wanted to explore. Cavern had been told hundreds of times not to go there. Cavern's mother never left the woods, but Cavern had heard stories of bats who had. "Someone has to want to go there too," Cavern thought. Cavern flew to the edge of the woods catching prey on the way. Cavern made sure no bat was around then left the safety of the forest. Cavern flapped on towards the town.

There were so many things in the town. Many things moving and changing. It was a bit overwhelming. Still though, Cavern wanted to explore. Cavern didn't want to wait until next year to take this marvelous opportunity. It was close to winter, in which there would be waiting for spring.

Cavern explored the town, investigating jack o lanterns and nearly crashing into traffic lights. Cavern caught swarms of moths high up, which were swarmed around light poles.

Cavern flew around buildings, wondering what they were for. As Cavern was flying around a house something moved. Cavern moved away then back in. Cavern heard a slight click. Then Cavern stopped, inches from a wall. Cavern flapped in place. Cavern studied the area. Indeed, Cavern was trapped. Cavern's mind raced, filled with worry, and non-relevant plans to escape. For some odd reason, this reminded Cavern of younger days, like when Cavern learned to master flying and echolocation. They were instincts, yet of need of mastery and understanding.

Cavern needed a way out. Cavern flew around the home. It was hard to maneuver around the small space. Cavern flew around a light in a main room searching for an opening to the outside. Then, a new problem arose. A man staggered into the room with a newspaper. He took a seat in a maroon colored recliner. He began reading his newspaper. Occasionally though, a dark shape would pass over his paper disrupting the ray of the light.

Cavern currently was still circling the light. The man glanced up this time finally wanting the answer to the shadow. He then noticed the tiny bat frantically flying around the chandelier. The man let out a howl and dashed out of the room. The man returned with a baseball bat. Three other people were there. The wife, the man, and his children were all dressed in pajamas. The man told them to leave the room.

Cavern noticed the moving figures. In the end, one remained. Cavern heard a light thump of something patting skin. In a last second event, Cavern dove, or he would have been hit by the baseball bat. He flew to a corner of the room, and his wings flapped, rapidly.

The man crept over to the corner and launched the end of the bat at Cavern. Cavern escaped the impact by mere inches. Cavern flew around the house, looking for an escape route more seriously than before. The figure chased after Cavern. Cavern nearly made impact with other objects and walls. A harsh truth drummed around inside Cavern. Cavern would die, if Cavern could not escape.

There were a couple close calls Cavern noted. The baseball bat had come close to smacking the bat out of the air. Cavern began to feel tired and desperate. The bat needed to find a way out quickly. Then, an idea sprung from the bat's mind. Cavern flapped in place by a window. Now, this was a life and death situation. This could kill Cavern, but Cavern would die anyway without it.

Cavern flapped in place in front of the glass. Cavern heard the footsteps of the man. The man approached and made a hefty swing at the bat. Cavern flew up in a streak of black. The window shattered. Cavern dove out the window. Cavern flew high as possible into the night sky, under the gleaming stars, flying back into the forest before dawn came.

"Anti-intellectualism has been a constant thread winding its way through our political and cultural life, nurtured by the false notion that democracy means that my ignorance is just as good as your knowledge."

ISAAC ASIMOV

Balancing Environments

ROBERT RICKER

Life is hard and
    finding your inner-voice or sense of self can
    be equally daunting

The journeys we are on have many avenues and encounters
    our beliefs, and social norms are formed from an early
    age by the external environment

The third-generation cop, or teacher, or baker
    the general store or farm that has been
    in the family for half a century or more

Those born of individuality and an adventurous nature
    struggle with these environments
    individuals must find their way

In the outside world one must choose
    what is the right decision
    while balancing the past

Truth, Beauty, and Grace

ELENA ROBINSON
Student, University of Nebraska at Omaha

Reading and writing are very important. Not enough people are able to read proficiently and understand what they are reading. In order to succeed in this world, you need to be able to read well enough to know what's going on, and a lot of people can't. Writing is good for the body and the soul, but not everyone is able to receive the education they need to be able to read enough, or want to read enough, to be able to write what they need to write. Humans crave the ability to communicate, and we all created our own letters and symbols and words to satisfy that need. Speaking is one thing, but before television, radio, and telephones, we used written words, elegant and impure, to express emotions to the people we loved who were far away. Books are translated into languages and sold in countries the author has never visited. Reading and writing connect us, but it can't connect us all. Some people never learn to read because they don't have the means to do so. Those people can only express themselves through speaking, and sometimes that isn't enough.

My dad never went to college and he taught me to read. I could spell encyclopedia by kindergarten, and I never felt better than when I was reading a *Trixie Belden* book. That's probably why I read them all. My father could have been a genius if he had pursued a higher education and skipped the drugs, but he didn't. And he isn't. Despite that, he reads everything he can, learns both sides of an issue, checks his own facts, and listens to opposing arguments with as little bias as he can manage before picking a side. He taught me to love reading by showing me how much it mattered to him. I learned in school how to write well enough to get by, but I learned from my uncle how to appreciate the power of poetry, how easy it is to pour emotion into writing, and how to understand what a person is writing about without them saying it. I learned how to comprehend what I saw by reading and thinking about it. English teachers insisting there was way too much meaning to *Lord of the Flies* forced me to see more than the words on the page.

Everyone should have access to the education needed to be able to read proficiently, and that should not be a subject of debate. We should not strive for greatness if we are refusing other people their chance because it is not convenient for us. I love to read, I love to write, but someone my age is insisting the opposite because they were never given a real opportunity to see either for what they really are. They did not have their eyes opened to the power. Sure, a bad teacher or two, dismissive parents or parents who are working too hard to have time, can all impact the ability of someone to discover the value of reading, but they should not stop it in its tracks. There is truth, beauty, and grace in everything we read and write. We just have to be able to see it.

"Dark words on white paper bare the soul."

MAUPASSANT

Mythology and Comic Aspects of Growing Up in the 1980s: A Sestina

JOHN ROBINSON

> *There is a somewhat comic, somewhat vulgar and mercantile, aspect to our serious and no doubt well-meaning endeavors to convince others and even possibly ourselves that the experience we are getting from poetry is certifiably profound, lofty, sublime, organic, harmonious... even pleasurable.*
>
> —Howard Nemerov, *Poetry & Meaning*

Part of growing up was the realization that fantasy stopped.
"Laughter is the best medicine," even if you are a goof.
"C" is a rounded shape that moves like a cradle toward sleep.
The story of Heaven, a castle and home is as old as earth.
The man in the moon was fictive. He had no scalp.
Unfulfilled American wishes line the bottom of this fountain.

Where is it written there is life eternal in this fountain,
along the coast of Florida, St. Augustine, a paradise of earth?
The brutal tales of natives, just as false — tree barks tacked with scalps.
Author Robert Price said by 1814 all American conflicts with Indians
    had stopped.
All these exaggerated aspects were a kind of sleep.
My grandpa used to talk about Red Skelton, Bob Hope, Milton
    Berle — all goofs.

Chaplin was perhaps America's greatest; a muted goof.
I never liked silent films or subtitles, so unfountainlike,
all that's obvious about its being, thrown forth, so unlike sleep.
Buddhists teach that we can learn from the silence of the earth.
If we are so advanced, when will our technical violence stop?
Tomcat steps on a rake; grows a bump in his smashed scalp.

Half a lifetime of humor is embedded in my scalp.
Situation comedies and stand-up improvs. Even Sam Kinison
     was goofy.
For some, to annihilate American ignorance with insults stopped
the pain that all of us have known. That inner fountain
overflowing with repressed anxiety. For some, the fallen heights
     of earth
have shaken us to make us see and wake us from our sleep.

I used to stay up all night when I was young; forget sleep.
I didn't have the same kinds of American dreams in my scalp.
I wasn't caught up in those real excesses of the Earth.
Still, I didn't plan, didn't map my future. I was never a goof.
I am thankful for laughter like Chevy Chase; a fountain
of memory against those tragedies we could not stop.

On weekends we made pizza and watched Chiller movies, stopped
believing the dark concealed monsters of our sleep.
Who knew they collected all the money from the fountains?
Changes in my thinking were more gradual, no scalpel.
Carson, Letterman and Saturday Night Live were the greatest
     American goofs
in fact *because* they seemed to us so human, so earthly.

Clowns of this earth made us whole because they never stopped.
They believed through their goofy beings in satire and parody of sleep.
Renew us to ourselves, these injured scalps anointed with living
     fountains.

A Scottish Farm

ROBERT S. RUNYON

> *Knowing that you love the earth changes you, activates*
> *you to defend and protect and celebrate. But when*
> *you feel that the earth loves you in return, that feeling*
> *transforms the relationship from a one-way street into a*
> *sacred bond.*

— Robin Wall Kimmerer

Meeting us at the ferry boat dock in Stranrear, Scotland were Sheila's younger brother James and his wife Liz. We had not seen them in five years. Quite unexpectedly in this summer of 2018, there was a prolonged drought coupled with the highest temperatures on record. We loaded our baggage into the trunk of his BMW and set off briskly for Stepend, the McCrae family farm. With confidence, James maneuvered through the complex interurban traffic network among foreign lorries, as well as, tractors, trailers, and cars of all sizes. Highly efficient roundabouts allowed speedy directional changes at road intersections without the delays of traffic lights. Massive lorries were moving goods between Europe and Ireland. Some of these contained enormous loads of timber that towered high above the driver's cab. The journey was about one-hundred miles, finally tapering down into narrow, one-lane roads with occasional laybys for passing among the cultivated fields. Contrary to Ireland, where green landscapes prevailed (from which we just came), Scottish fields and pastures were brown with sparse new growth. There were media reports of possible water rationing being considered by public authorities.

"How was Ireland?" Liz asked from the back seat.

"Quite hot," replied Sheila. "I didn't bring any shorts or other warm weather clothing. We never used to have weather like this in Scotland even in the warmest summer months.

"It's just like Omaha," I added. "For me, July is the worst month to be in Omaha, so I thought this would be different. Nevertheless, we had some great excursions to scenic and historic sites in the Irish countryside,"

James was totally focused on the changing highway conditions.

I told him that I would like to join him on his morning inspection journeys around the farm and surrounding pasture land. I wanted to absorb as much as possible of the farm life and rhythms. From many previous trips I was familiar with the basics. But now that James was seventy-six and I was eighty-four, I was sure there would be interesting new insights to share.

At 8 AM on our first day on the farm, I climbed into the passenger seat of his Mitsubishi station wagon. We wended our way cautiously up a winding, single-lane road. At a slight turn in the road, we were suddenly confronted by a red Royal Mail van coming from the opposite direction. It was on a delivery trip to the farm. Both drivers quickly braked and swerved in opposite directions into the roadside scrub. We passed slowly with inches to spare and continued on to Wood Park. It was one of several farms that James rented to provide supplementary pasture land for bullocks and young calves.

The hilly fields were partitioned by ancient drystane dykes (stone walls) with wide swinging steel gates. Each one had to be separately opened to allow our entry and closed on return. We bounced along rough terrain to a high point on the hill. It was from there that James could observe and count the beasts to confirm all were well and none had migrated to other fields. The animals in each field formed a different age and breeding cohort. They were closely monitored throughout their productive life spans. James provided descriptions and explanations regarding the parsing of animals in each of several fields. He related the financial history of the several rented farm lands we passed through. I had my hearing aids adjusted to maximum acuity, but James's Scottish brogue and guttural tones eluded some of my best efforts to absorb and understand his full story. I remember one morning coffee break many years earlier in his farm kitchen, a bulk milk tank driver had joined the McCrae family around the table for morning coffee. After several minutes of animated conversation, he looked at me and remarked: "My, but you sure have a funny way of talking."

"The feeling is mutual," I said. "So do you." This was a pithy reminder that I would always be a foreign interloper in Sheila's native world deep in the Scottish countryside.

I continued to probe and to learn as I followed James about his duties as a helpmate to his son Jim, to whom he had turned over ownership of the family farm. James gave me tours of the barn and milking parlor. He pointed out the sturdy metal yoke neck restraints that held each cow in position for milking and winter feeding. Twice a day, the cows were herded into stalls where electronic sensors read an ear mounted and number-coded tag identifying them to a modern computer management system. A customized diet was then metered out according to each cow's recorded condition and specific needs. Current data stored in a database helped to monitor the health, productivity and gestation cycle of each of two-hundred milking cows. As James explained earlier, this farm's milking herd was relatively small according to current standards. Small farms were increasingly being bought up by larger ones and consolidated into corporate enterprises. There were nearby Scottish farms managing milking herds of over one thousand cows.

Such farms would all have large staffs of permanent workers who could fill in at jobs for one another during off periods and vacations. James and his son currently had only one permanent employee. He was a Polish immigrant who lived in a neighboring milker's cottage with his family. If James or his son wished to take a trip or vacation, the twice a day milking routine must still be done. There could be no alternative. For every such absence they were obliged to call upon other family members or friends to help out with the daily milking. The cows could not be left untended in the fields with full udders. The life of a dairy farmer is akin to exercise upon a treadmill or elliptical exercise machine from which the owner can never get off. It can lead to fatigue and exhaustion. Fortunately, with good health, humor, and cooperation many robust farm families are able to make a go of it. Some don't. And some like James's son start planning for retirement and sale of the farm and its fixed assets in their fifties. In James's case, this will cause a regretted rupture in continuous family ownership of several hundred well-tended acres over a period of two-hundred years. Change can be difficult.

Diverse tasks in the life of a farm family are demanding and complex. Some of these relate to the management of the required food and waste products of the cows that produce the milk.

Very large and expensive equipment is required to conduct the practical and seasonal operations that assure a dairy farm's steady income. Three cuttings of the feed grass are required every summer to produce the silage or feed that sustains the herd during winter months. Heavy machinery must be purchased or hired to perform serial operations of cutting, collecting and assemblage of grass into string tied hay bales or compacted grass rolls that are hermetically sealed in black plastic wrapping. These were the operations of the first cutting that Sheila and I witnessed during our early July 2018 visit to Stepend Farm.

A recurring ritual of farm operations relates to the disposal of animal waste products. The cows' excretory products (urine and fecal matter) are mechanically collected and pumped into massive slurry tanks. This odorous process yields a liquid fertilizer for recycling. The stored solution is later transferred to mobile tanks that pump a brown spray onto the pastures to enhance grass growth

The overview provided here is but a small glimmer of the daunting complexity of life on a modern dairy farm, big or small. Changing technology, staffing, market fluctuations, and consolidation of small farms into large corporate entities provide challenging economic realities for farm managers.

For me, on my first visit to Scotland, fifty-two years ago, it all had the aura of a simple agrarian life in nature. This recent trip opened my eyes to what now seemed like complex, overwhelming farm family tasks and temporal demands. This city boy's naïve view of a bucolic existence on family farms was rudely shaken. It was an illusion that any pragmatic Scottish farmer would find laughable at best. It has led me to revisit once again the life and work of the bard of Scotland, Robert Burns.

As mentioned in an earlier chapter, I was married to Sheila McCrae in a wee Scottish kirk on June 29, 1966. At that time, I discovered the poetry and life story of Burns. On repeated trips, I visited his home in Alloway, the meeting hall in Ayer where he first read his poems within a unique Bachelors Club of young male cohorts, his rented Ellisland Farm on which he strived vainly to prosper for several years before it took a disastrous toll upon his health and livelihood, and later his Dumfries home where he lived while working as a much-maligned tax collector, and later died (age 37) as a universally beloved poet of the people. In a nearby cemetery in the same city is the grave where Burns lies in a white marble mausoleum. Like many readers before me, I was entranced by Robert Burns' story. During my first visit to Scotland, I had resolved to memorize and read his poetic *Address to Jesse* (my future wife's middle name) at our wedding reception. I was politely informed that protocol did not allow the groom to make such a declaration.

My interest in Burns stems from the role and importance of nature and relationships in his life and poetry. As mentioned in earlier chapters, I had a fragmented personal family experience. Anger, depression, and rancorous separations were the order of the day. I had little sense of belonging, anywhere. My debut experience of life on Sheila's family farm (called Straith) highlighted a very different world.

I discovered that farm families grow up and work together throughout individual life spans. They acquire basic survival skills of cooperation, mutual support, and sharing. They study and hold dear the natural processes of plants and animals. They acknowledge and reciprocate nature's gifts of beauty and belonging. Elders and youth live and share meaningful lives together. Tough conditions inspire fierce loyalty to territory and the extended family. Relatives and neighbors commonly share intimate bonds of affection, back-handed teasing, and dependable support. Farms are given historic names that are retained for generations through thick and thin. Interior grounding and stern discipline occur within farm families. For entire lifetimes, a family may be strongly attached to specific pieces of land marked off by ancient stone walls. These drystane dykes, with periodic restoration, may persist for over hundreds of years and multiple generations.

There is a five hundred foot high, multi-tiered, manmade earthwork on the McCrae family farm, which itself was long known as Milton of Buittle. The oblong mound sits at the intersection of two flowing rivers. It was originally created in the eleventh century as a Norman mote-and-baily fortification. Its purpose was to provide defense and a lookout point for foreign invaders. This high ground was once proposed as an historic monument. It was long known as the *Motte of Urr* and remains in use today as pastureland for cows. It is also a tourist destination for history buffs and archeologists.

Selected farm related verses from Robert Burns's writings:

> *My father was a farmer upon the Carrick border O*
> *And carefully he bred me in decency and order O*
> *He bade me act a manly part, though I had ne'er a farthing O*
> *For without an honest manly heart, no man was worth regarding O*
>
> *Then out into the world my course I did determine. O*
> *Tho' to be rich was not my wish, yet to be great was charming. O*
> *My talents they were not the worst; nor yet my education: O*
> *Resolv'd was I at least to try to mend my situation. O*

My dear, my native soil!
For whom my warmest wish to Heav'n is sent,
Long may thy hardy sons of rustic toil
Be blest with health, and peace,
and sweet content!

Gie me ae spark o' Nature's fire,

That's a' the learning I desire.

The simple Bard, rough at the rustic plough,
Learning his tuneful trade from ev'ry bough;
The chanting linnet, or the mellow thrush,
Hailing the setting sun, sweet, in the green thorn bush;

The soaring lark, the perching red-breast shrill,
Or deep-ton'd plovers grey, wild-whistling o'er the hill;
Shall he — nurst in the peasant's lowly shed,
To hardy independence bravely bred,

By early poverty to hardship steel'd.
And train'd to arms in stern Misfortune's field
Shall he be guilty of their hireling crimes,
The servile, mercenary Swiss of rhymes?

Or labour hard the panegyric close,
With all the venal soul of dedicating prose?

James Barke, a noted Burns scholar, wrote this about Robert Burns:

> *He could read and write and remember. He was*
> *surcharged with emotion, awareness and sensibility. And*
> *despite his background and foreground of poverty and*
> *hunger and never-ceasing toil, he could laugh.*

Pride and Prejudice and Online Dating

JOSIE RUTAR
Elkhorn, NE, High School

Based on *Pride and Prejudice* by Jane Austen

The Bennets were a respectable family, they really were. They occupied Hertfordshire at Longbourn, near Meryton, and basked in the glow of an upper-class English lifestyle. So why were the Bennets, a truly respectable family, crowded around a glitchy computer from the future, each Bennet sister yelling at the other? Simple — the Bennets had discovered the wonderful world of online dating.

In the early nineteenth century, it had become fashionable for donors from the distant future to send gifts back to families, so they could enjoy what the future had to offer. Many of these gifts were strange technologies, such as the computer gifted to the Bennets from their future donor. The two youngest girls, Lydia and Kitty, were engrossed with the contraption. In fact, Elizabeth recalls, the entire online dating incident had been all Lydia's fault. She had always been the flirt of the family, batting her eyelashes at any boy who had the misfortune to be near her. It was really no surprise then, when Lydia burst into Elizabeth's room one morning with "terribly exciting news."

"Lizzie! Lizzie! It's incredible! It's the perfect tool to create everlasting love," Lydia cried, bursting through Elizabeth's bedroom door. Elizabeth groaned, quite used to her sister's antics, and not looking forward to this one.

"What is it, Lydia?" The eldest sister, Jane, stepped out of the washroom, her hair neatly pinned and her complexion as lovely as ever. Lydia grinned at her sister.

"It's called Perfect Match!" she exclaimed. Jane shot Elizabeth a confused look, to which Elizabeth responded by shrugging and picking up the nearest book. "It's a website-on the computer thing-that matches you up with your one true love!"

"I'm not sure I understand what you mean," Jane stated, nervously laughing. Lydia huffed.

"All right, just let me show you!" Lydia seized Jane by the arm and started to drag her down the stairs.

"Lizzie!" Jane shrieked with feigned terror, as she whirled away from her young sister. It was Elizabeth's turn to huff. She threw down her book and chased her sisters to the drawing room. Lydia and Jane were crowded around the clunky machine, and Lydia was already clicking away.

"Here," Lydia breathed, as both older Bennets peered over her shoulder. What they saw was a brightly lit screen welcoming them to "Perfect Match." "Now," Lydia said clasping her hands together, "we need to create your profiles." Jane clapped her hands as Elizabeth rolled her eyes. Lydia turned to Jane first. "What should your screen name be?"

"My screen name?" Jane asked.

"The name that people will see when they view your profile," Lydia explained. "Honestly, Jane, keep up."

"Oh, well, how about 'Not a Plain Jane?'" the eldest sister suggested.

"I like that one!" Lydia grinned. She began to type rapidly, asking Jane all types of questions about herself, but Elizabeth zoned out. Love had not been a much thought about topic for the second eldest Bennet. She believed she didn't need to validate her worth based on what a man thought about her, and the men did think about her. Mrs. Bennet had been desperately trying to get Elizabeth married, but her efforts were in vain. Elizabeth would marry when she felt inclined, or she would not marry at all. "Done! All right, Lizzie, hope you're ready for your turn!" Lydia squealed. "Screen name?" Elizabeth drew in a breath.

"Miss Elizabeth Bennet," she replied.

"Boring as ever," Lydia scoffed, as she began to type, again. Thus followed the same sequence of questions that Lydia asked Jane. After what seemed like centuries, Lydia stopped the onslaught of queries, and Elizabeth was free. "And we wait," Lydia hummed, as Elizabeth plopped down on the family sofa. After only five minutes, Lydia squealed and shouted something incoherent. Startled by the commotion, Elizabeth hopped up from the sofa and rushed to her sisters.

"Lizzie! I got a match!" Jane cried, pulling her sister into a tight embrace. "It's from a Mister Bingley," she beamed, letting Elizabeth go.

"Wonderful, Jane, really!" Elizabeth forced a smile and started to slink back to the sofa when Lydia grabbed her arm.

"Not so fast. You've got a match too, sweetheart," Lydia cooed, pulling the frowning Elizabeth back to the computer. Jane stood holding a hand over her mouth, stifling giggles with each passing second.

"Oh, Lizzie, good luck," she laughed. Lydia took one look at the screen and burst out laughing.

"What? What is it?" Elizabeth cried, a blush finding its way onto her pale face. She pushed Lydia out of the way and stared at the screen. "My match is…" Elizabeth's jaw dropped as she stared at the computer in disbelief. "My match is," she repeated, "Mister Darcy."

We – 2018

CHRISTINE SALHANY

- Considered New Year's goals.
- Were in awe of the beauty of God's creation and the devastation and havoc nature can impose.
- Gave and received.
- Planted gardens inside and outside.
- Recognized and were refreshed by youth and their level of artistic capability.

- Read books.
- Completed long-term goals and set new ones.
- Learned new recipes, celebrated various ethnicities through culinary contributions, and shared meals together.
- Celebrated family and friend's birthdays.
- Rejoiced in our accomplishments and those of others.

- Challenged ourselves to puzzles.
- Mourned the passing of family members and friends.
- Learned and took on family financial responsibilities.
- Challenged ourselves to new professional collaborations.
- Found the joy in finding new scrabble buddies.

- Welcomed first time guests to the United States.
- Traveled for business and pleasure.
- Organized a lifetime of photos.
- Traveled to the Amen Clinic to get an illness diagnosed.
- Challenged ourselves to new ways of living.

- Learned about the functions of the brain and how aspects of our daily habits can influence its function in ways that can be crippling and need to be modified through a holistic approach to lifestyle.

- Challenged ourselves to new ways of living. Food is medicine.
  Found joy in physical exercise. Nature is illuminating physically,
  mentally, and spiritually.
- When life seems perfect, faith lies dormant.
- Challenges can breed enlightenment through the resurrection of
  faith.
- *Met and fell in love with a horse!*

Cranes at Sunset
photo by Ron Boerner

The Room

JAMES M. SALHANY

Separation revealed
a cathartic deprivation
Manifest in a room
suddenly barren.
A room once filled with life,
But now a temple
To a failed relationship.

At first, passion was life.
Time could not count
The intervals of emotion.
There was no time
While embracing
In the palm
Of "Rodin's Hand."

Then came
"The Wake of Heraclitus,"
Where change was so stark
It jolted the soul.
A lasting relationship,
Became a vulgarity,
Stripped of its essence,
Lying there alone,
In a room.

After the Climate Changes

SALLY SANDLER

A hundred thousand years… what will they find?
After lapping hungry at our feet
the creeping seas rise, and then retreat.
Will humankind be fossil over time?

What traces from the life of our tribe —
like ancient middens buried in sandstone
with hidden bits of pottery and bone —
what part of modern man survives the tides?

Perhaps the plastic shovel washed away
from a child's castle on the shore,
the unicorn tiara that she wore,
the pink jelly shoe she lost that day.

Or from a boy's kite, the nylon string —
the dragon kite that tangled, you remember?
Will they leave a trace, my family members?
Please, the great-grandchildren. Anything?

Those relics by themselves won't tell the story
of how we feared the changes… powerless
when politics devoured our progress,
or why we failed to save the planet's glory,

left ruins for our grandchildren, and theirs,
and finally betrayed our planet's heirs.

The Path of Experience and Responsibility

STUART SEDLAK

Belgian born essayist Marguerite Yourcenar wrote, "Wisdom, like life itself, appeared to be comprised of continuing progress, of starting over again, of patience." Wisdom comes to people in many different ways. In my life, my path to wisdom appeared to me just over twenty-one years ago. It was the day my father died. My father, Dave, was a healthy forty-seven year old who was full of energy and filled with vigor. February 16 was an unseasonably warm Ash Wednesday afternoon. My dad, a small business owner, went out for his daily run that afternoon, but he never returned. He dropped dead of a heart attack

My father's business was a bowling center. Bowling had been the family business since 1943, when my great-grandparents, Vince and Hazel Kelley, opened Kelley's Bowlatorium on the corner of Sixteenth and Harney. The members of the Kelley family were pioneers in the Omaha bowling scene. In 1956, the family expanded, and built Kelley's Hilltop Lanes in Dundee. My grandfather took control a few years later, and subsequently in 1979, my father took over day-to-day operations of the bowling alley.

The evening of February 16, 1994, my father did not show up to work. I was just beginning my second semester of college in Lawrence, Kansas, when I rushed to Omaha. It was time for the fourth generation to take over the daily operations of the business. The fourth generation was me. Unlike my predecessors, I was not groomed for the job. The only thing I knew about bowling was how to keep score, and the optimal path a ball must take in order to get a strike. This was the day that a completely new path began in my life. The day my path to wisdom began.

My mother and sister were as strong as they could possibly be. My sister was only a freshman in high school, so she was not mature enough to help out. In the beginning days after my father's death, my mom was a great help. She tended to the business, while I tried to finish my semester of college. I failed every single class. My depression, combined with commuting back and forth from Lawrence, to Omaha, was too much to handle. Meanwhile, my mother was having an increasingly more difficult time at the bowling alley. It was time for me to step up, move to Omaha, and take charge.

I wish I could find another word for "responsibility," which is not strong enough to describe what was set in my lap. I not only became a small business owner, but I became a janitor, handy man, bookkeeper, and human resource director. I was only nineteen years old and had no responsibility in my life. Hiring and firing workers became an art form. I became an amateur psychologist, when employees had issues outside of work. I bailed employees out of jail. I worked seven days a week, and it was overwhelming.

A big part of wisdom is patience. Dealing with customers who are often intoxicated can be a challenge. I have been thrown to the ground, punched, and kicked. I have had patrons scream and throw trash cans at me. Over the years, I learned the best way to deal with these customers is to be overly patient and kind, no matter how awful they act. Putting a smile on my face in these situations is a true test of inner strength.

One evening about five years ago, there was a disturbance at our facility. It was a busy evening, and I was getting happier with each dollar that was going into the register. The noise level had risen, and there was a feeling of panic in the air. A young man was shot and killed. What was I supposed to do? The media arrived right away. I had to preserve the reputation of the business, because I knew this would scare off customers. I had to craft a statement that showed empathy for the victim, but at the same time showed that this activity would not be tolerated in my bowling center. I told the media that this was a safe neighborhood, steps were in place to add more security, and this was an isolated incident.

At that time, I had fifteen years of wisdom to help me deal with the situation. Although I only have one semester of post-secondary education, I feel that I now have wisdom. I am no longer in the bowling business. Nearly two years ago, a religious institution made an offer to buy the bowling alley and convert it into a church. Selling the business was by far the hardest decision I ever made. My stress level was as high as ever, and the facility needed $750,000 in capital improvements. I chose not to take the alley of debt and stress. Instead, I chose the lane of freedom and uncertainty.

I am a college student once again after a twenty-one year absence. Now that I am back in college, I feel no task assigned is as difficult as the situations that I had to encounter when I managed the business. Writing a paper is relaxing compared to filing sales tax reports and dealing with employee theft. After being in private business for half of my life, I am not sure what my strengths and weaknesses are. Like a professional boxer gets ready for a prizefight, I want to get my brain into top academic condition. I want to master the heavy bag and speed bag, and do daily mind calisthenics. Once my mind is back into shape, I am going to apply my wisdom and experience to my studies, and whatever path my life takes.

Words on Yellowing Paper

SUE SHELBURNE

They called to me for months, the handwritten words on yellowing paper, lying dormant for years, in cardboard boxes in the basement. They called to me on unproductive days and sleepless nights, begging for me to remove them from their dusty stacks.

I had files of more current renderings, alphabetized and neatly typed, which I had written and shared but, every time I read them, I'd think of those other words I'd written years before and wonder if I had remained true to the essence of who I believed myself to be in those earlier years.

I feared more than anything, that I would find the person who had written all those words, did not exist anymore. I feared that if I read them again, I would find they were written by a stranger, and it would break a truth I believed about myself, as well as, the common thread that held my life together.

Finally, one rainy day, like an archeologist, driven by the need to know the past, I begin to uncover the words on yellowing paper, from their dark prisons. As I carried stacks of loose leaf papers into the sunlight, I caught a glimpse of some of the words I had written, in now faded ink years before. "One day, I will know why I write these words on paper."

It did not take long after that, as I sorted and deciphered and reconnected phrases to phrases, to reclaim whole years of my life. The fear I had felt was replaced by a feeling of victory. I was older now, definitely more cynical because of hard lessons learned and battle weary dreams, but there was no doubt, I had written them. I was there among the words, a younger more naive and idealistic version of me, but not the stranger I feared I might find.

The natural progression of life is change, and I had changed, but the core of who I have been since the fourth grade, an individual driven to express, evaluate, understand, celebrate, and grieve my life's experiences in written words, runs strong and victoriously through the tapestry of my life.

Funny how it is often the small victories which gives us the greatest gifts. Who knew, here and now, shortly before my 72nd birthday, these hand written words on yellowing paper would be mine. Maybe, I somehow knew that truth deep down in my younger self. Maybe that is the reason I am compelled, even now, to write words on paper. They are little victories for future rainy days.

Lake Bed
photo by Michael Campbell

The Smoke from All the Fires

D. N. SIMMERS

I would like to fly up
country and count
the fires but there
are too many
careless ones.

So let's start
with the smoke
that is here.

Clouds of it
hanging off the trees
as I look out the window
in the morning.

Rude patches,
haze that is like
left over Halloween cobwebs.

The smell is of old shoes that
were left there
after a good fire
was put out.

Pus and barf
combined and
mixed shadows
in daylight.

Cotton candy that
would be hard to
swallow.

And easy to wheeze
and sneeze
from throughout the day.

//

*I sing the praise of the unknown teacher. Famous
educators plan new systems of pedagogy, but it is the
unknown teacher who delivers and guides the young. He
lives in obscurity and contends with hardship. He keeps
the watch along the borders of darkness and makes the
attack on the trenches of ignorance and folly. Patient in
his daily duty he strives to conquer the evil powers which
are the enemies of youth. He awakens sleeping spirits. He
quickens the indolent, encourages the eager, and steadies
the unstable. He communicates his own joy in learning
and shares with boys and girls the best treasures of his
mind. He lights many candles which, in later years, will
shine back to cheer him. This is his reward. Knowledge
may be gained from books, but the love of knowledge
is transmitted only by personal contact. No one has
deserved better of the republic than the unknown teacher.*

HENRY VAN DYKE

//

What If…

OLIVIA SIMMS
5th Grade, Alice Buffett Middle School

What if magical pencils could fly,
    dogs could say bye, bye?
    humans lived under water,
    Arizona got even hotter?

What if animals could talk,
    vegetables could walk,
    books had eyes and ears,
    papers had huge fears?

What if a sock became art,
    a race ended at the start,
    a key went with no lock,
    a marker was shaped like a rock?

What if rulers ruled the world,
    my brother's hair was curled,
    dictionaries were filled with pictures,
    the whole world spoke in whispers?

What if a gymnast couldn't bend,
    this poem wouldn't end?

For Mark

BOBBI SINHA-MOREY

The autistic child counts
the beads, so rapidly on
the lampshade, but his mind,
hidden away inside its own
envelope, so seldom unfolds
to open itself, and find its way
out. I try to reach him, my
ten-year-old son with crayons,
cards, brain teasers he loves
to decipher. I give him a book
of famous quotations, listen to
him, patiently, while he reads
his favorite ones out loud.
Other days he'd box himself
up inside his room, hold onto
his strange silences for half
the day 'til *Animal Planet*
was on TV, and he'd draw their
likenesses on paper napkins,
eating sticky plums. I taught him
kindnesses, not to disrupt
parental conversations, not
to paint the walls of his room
with messy palms. Often, he'd
wander the house on his knees
'til his sister, father, or I would
pick him up. One night I dreamed
of him: an average kid on a bike,
and I saw the dot of him, meadows

away, growing in sight, as he
peddled home in the late daylight,
my heart rejoicing like a fountain's
rainbow.

Winter Fields
photo by Sue Shelburne

Seaspore

PHILIP SMITH

Droplet
spawned by bursting spray
child of many seas.

Ascend
above the unthought shores
brief prism for glorious sunlight.

Ebb
knowing not the tides
pleading with the waves.

Plunge
Into briny torrents
amid the roaring flux

Dissolve
into vast anonymous plasma
into liquid silence deep.

We encourage submissions to *Fine Lines*. We have printed writing by an eight-year-old third grader, a ninety-four-year-old great, great grandmother, students, teachers, professors, janitors, doctors, lawyers, ministers, truck drivers, nurses, and scientists. If you want to read interesting ideas, *Fine Lines* is for you. Send us a submission, and you could become a published writer, too.

What to submit: We welcome articles on topics of interest to our readers about interesting life experiences. Our editors encourage a variety of styles. We accept articles and practical submissions that describe innovative views of life's challenges. We are glad to receive work encouraging stimulating dialog that crosses traditional rhetorical and disciplinary boundaries, forms, and roles. We provide a forum for writers of all ability levels. We reserve the right to reject submissions that use profanity, abusive violence in all forms, alcohol, and drugs.

What we disclaim: The views expressed in *Fine Lines* are solely those of the authors. Therefore, *Fine Lines* is not intended to represent any author's political or religious point of view. Our purpose is to be a capable writing vehicle for all serious, intelligent, and compassionate thinkers.

What we require: Submissions must be sent via email file-attachments or laser-quality hard copies. If replies are requested, include a self-addressed, stamped envelope, or mention this in the submission. Use the MLA format with all submissions. To complete your submission, include a one paragraph autobiographical statement and a digital, head-shoulder photo. When sending submissions via email, submit all work in Microsoft Word (.doc) or in Adobe Portable

Document Format (.pdf). Send correspondence to Fine Lines, PO Box 241713, Omaha, NE 68124. Send your questions, comments, concerns, and letters to the editor at fine-lines@cox.net.

Fine Lines Summer Writing Camps: Our week-long "campers" range in age from third grade to senior adults, and every session is filled with comedy, art, dance, music, history, and writing. These week-long workshops are filled with inspiration. They motivate authors to tackle their writing projects. Check our website for more details.

Remember, if it is not written down, it did not happen. Improved literacy adds clarity and passion to our lives. Composition is hard work, and it brings order to chaos, beauty to existence, and celebration to the mysterious.

Write on,
David Martin

*"From one person to another,
one candle to another,
one page at a time,
may we share our light of understanding."*

DAVID MARTIN

Practice What I Preach

ANDREW SPRAGUE

We all can increase our creativity. In order to be creative, we must have a problem that needs to be solved or a goal that needs to be met. Albert Einstein's Theory of Relativity came to him as a result of personal challenges.

Teachers and parents structure children's lives to revolve around rules and conform to social norms. Many schools and institutions have set us up for a life of conformity because they do not allow students to be creative.

I can relate this to my own life because with music, if there is no creativity, then you do not have music. I now know what I can do to improve my musicianship in one way or another. For instance, putting myself in a new and different place while I practice really helps cultivate good ideas. The idea of being able to not only have the ability to be creative but hone and perfect that ability is something that I, as a musician, will always work towards. Another way being creative is important in music is when I'm improvising. If I were to play the same boring lick over and over with no direction, it would not only be boring to myself but for whoever is listening. Taking suggestions and ideas from other players and making them my own is a really good way to boost my creativity. I hope to inspire people with my creative music. If I could help someone get out of a creative block with my ideas, then that could lead them to do the same.

I am working to get my degree in music education. This is a profession in which I have to not only stay creative but also teach my students how to do so. The list of creativity killers has given me something to avoid when teaching, and also to avoid when trying to get more creative myself. Also the list of things that could spark creativity has helped me map out a plan of attack for when a student is just not feeling creative. The only way I can help show them how to be creative is if I practice what I preach, which is leading by example. Not only would I implement these tips for creativity into my teaching, I'd implement them into my daily life, so I can better understand them and be able to share them with my students.

"When you're tired of writing, you're tired of life."

WILLIAM SAFIRE

Image Over Everything

GARY TAYLOR

how am I
to overcome
a life lived high
and on the run
I'm trying to change
all bridges burned
it seems to me
my past shouldn't
bring my future to its knees
I'm forced to bow
upon old practices
and ways of living
I'm tired of taking from a world filled with giving
I want to stand on my own two feet
to be in the position to help others like me
it's hard to flourish
because when people look my way
what do they truly see?
my accomplishments and improvement
or just the criminal attire
watch as others ignore
as I'm in agony
all due to what I used to be
the life I had
has a never-ending fee
but please God,
just look at me

Poetic Interlude

JAMES TILLOTSON

I write when I talk
When I rant and rave alone
Like a mythic madman casting
Ill-boding auguries and forsaken foretokens
At household appliances and electronic images.

I write when I am depressed
Deep diving into melancholy oceans
The weight of the ink
Black oceans so great the bones of my soul
Creak and groan in protest.

I write when the voices fill my head,
A chorus of alien personalities and worlds
Pulling my attention from this world
Into vistas that drip from my fingers described
In painfully inked sentence after sentence.

The Cinnisnail Tale

CARTER TIPLER
Grade 5, Alice Buffett Middle School

It all started off one day
where the clouds were gray
like a rainy day.

The Cinnisnail was on the ground,
that's when I noticed a strange smell.

It was cinnamon it's the best
So, I put my nose to the test.
I must find this pest
who smells better than the rest.

I followed my nose.
Suddenly I found it on a rose.

There it was, a snail with a cinnamon roll for a shell.
It looked peculiar but smelled divine.
It was really, very fine.

Then as my mom called my name
he was gone in the grass roaming free,
nothing to worry about, but me.

To Forgive Is Good

DILLON JAMES VANORNAM

Grace is something many people lack. Our society ignores it, because we think it feels better to hold onto grudges. It may bring immediate gratification, but long term, it is the least beneficial thing to do. I associate grace with forgiveness. To me, grace is what we give to people when we forgive. Another word I associate with grace is mercy. I heard once, that grace is giving something good that is not deserved, and mercy is not giving something negative that is deserved. For example if someone killed people, one might think that person deserved to die, but giving them mercy would be not giving them death. That might be true, but for the sake of simplicity, I am going to call them synonyms.

Why do we find it so hard to give people grace? It comes from a combination of entitlement and self-preservation. The entitlement in people tells them they deserve to be treated with respect, and no one has the right to do them wrong. If people do, they have to pay. Entitlement is ugly. The other thing is self-preservation. Somehow, humans have come to think that forgiving people shows weakness. The misconception of forgiveness is that you are saying, "I accept what has been done to me."

People think if they forgive, it is like letting people walk all over them, and leaving the power in the hands of others. This is not the case. Forgiving does not mean what has been done is acceptable; it means the forgiver will not hold it against the forgiven. Though forgiving means we are giving up the power we have over others, it does not mean the forgiver is left powerless. As long as we think that forgiving people shows a lack of strength, there will be an eternal struggle. Another misconception is that not forgiving will hurt the offender, and we have to avoid forgiving to make them hurt like they made us hurt, but not forgiving hurts the not-forgiver much more than it hurts anyone else. It stays with them. It holds on to a part of them and won't let go.

AMERICAN NATIONAL BANK *PRESENTS*

OMAHA GIVES!
powered by the Omaha Community Foundation

DONATE TO *FINE LINES!*
MAY 22, 2019

Fine Lines offers:

- Readers a quarterly literary journal
- Writers a place to submit their work, hone their craft, and have a community.
- Students of all ages a summer camp that is inspiring and educational

Learn more at:
www.omahagives.org

Battle Scars

CORA VOBEJDA

5th Grade, Alice Buffett Middle School

When I was seven, I did a lot of idiotic things. One day, I was playing with my friends in my front yard. We were having fun on the hot summer day, by getting a bucket of ice cubes and playing with them. We put ice cubes down each other's shirts, left them in each other's socks, and stuck ice in their shoes to find later. The usual things.

Then, the neighbors came out. Keep in mind, my friends and I were seven. The boys we lived next to were at least three times older. For some reason, that is still unknown, my friend thought it was a good idea to throw an ice cube at the older boys. One of the boys at the neighbor's house threw it back, not hard but hard enough to reach us. Both my friends looked at me, expectantly. I was the leader of the group, so I responded by chucking an ice cube back at the boys.

That's how the Great Ice Cube war of 2014 started. Shimmering blocks of ice sailed past me. I flew in and out of the garage, my only cover. My two warriors and I worked hard, but we never hit the boys. Two buckets of ice later, the sun thought it would be funny to blind me, temporarily. My friend yelled my name and told me to duck, but it was too late. I felt the impact and fell back. My eyebrow felt like it was on fire. Water trickled down my face from ice and tears. A sticky, red liquid oozed down the right side of my face and into my eye. The boy who hit me sprinted over, apologized, and asked if I was okay. Yes, I'm great, just fantastic! Since my right eyebrow was torn open, I was probably feeling awesome! The ice cube that punctured me rested in my lap, laughing at me. My blood soon dyed that ice cube red.

My mom must have heard me crying, because she rushed out, scooped me up, told my friends they should go home, slapped a bandage on my cut, and drove me to the doctor. I got my eyebrow glued together and went home. I looked at the scar and sighed, because it was right next to my other cut on that eyebrow.

"They are your battle scars," Mom said. After that, all I did was watch TV and eat ice cream. Just before I went to bed, she handed me a glass of water. I looked into the cup and saw small clear cubes staring up at me.

Temporality's Death

JULIE WUTHRICH

When Temporality fell, it was like a dream. There was no way such a thing could be real. There was no way Temporality (the great Temporality, greatest superhero of the world, the one who had taken down Lithium and Keystone, the one who stopped Skyshift several times, the one who carried world peace upon her shoulders) could have died.

Temporality was there. Protected the world. In people's minds, Temporality would always be.

But Temporality was human, and all humans died, eventually.

"I can't believe it," Len said. "She's dead. Temporality is dead."

Seira was still watching the TV screen displaying the bad news in shocked silence.

"It's not possible," Len said again, shaking his head. "Not possible. She was always there. She can't just… die."

"She was only human," Shesheri spoke up from behind Seira. "Humans die. We're gonna die, too, you know." But Shesheri was as shocked as Seira. Their words weren't as biting as usual. "She was 73 already."

"She died saving an entire city," Seira whispered. "It was a good way to die, for her."

Temporality was always calm and composed, even in the worst situations. She was strong, and she held her ground no matter what. She smiled fondly, would go to extreme lengths to help people, and she didn't fear for her life.

She arrested over three hundred villains during her life. Defeated many more. Only the current most powerful villains escaped her, but she always stopped them whenever they attacked, and it was no doubt she could have defeated them at some point. She held her ground against Skyshift. Because she was there, the world felt safe.

Seira had heard about Temporality since she was born, because Temporality was the world's hero, the person everyone admired. Temporality was nearly revered as a god, in some places. She controlled time, could distort space, held a power greater than anyone else's, but was always using it for good.

Like everyone else, at that time, Seira wished to be such a person.

But she would soon learn that there could only ever be one Temporality.

"People are scared," Shesheri informed them, slipping back into the apartment. "I talked with some executives of the Nations Assembled, and they fear a massive villain attack, because villains have been quiet since Temporality's death."

It still felt like a dream. It was still hard to swallow. Seira had hoped that this morning, when she would turn on the TV, she would learn that it was all a joke and Temporality was still alive, still in activity, still ready to arrest villains.

"It's only been a day since the announcement, though," Len raised a brow.

"Temporality was the world's greatest protector," Shesheri shrugged. "Without her, the Nations Assembled fear that the world is going to turn to chaos."

"Everyone relied on her way too much. Now that she's not there... well, it's like there's a hole, you know. Something amiss."

Seira got up from the couch. It felt too much.

"When are Temporality's funerals?" she asked softly.

"Two days from now," Shesheri replied. "What are you going to do?"

She shook her head. "I need some fresh air."

Len and Shesheri didn't stop her. Shesheri put a hand on her shoulder when she passed by them, nodding in understanding.

"She was really your hero, wasn't she?" Len remarked, quietly.

"Of course, she was." Seira opened the door with a sad smile. "She was everyone's hero."

Temporality was really recognized as a hero and raised to the level of a legend, when she defeated Lithium. She was only eighteen. She just graduated from a hero-specialized high school and was preparing herself to go to a hero college; but fate decided to put her under the spotlights earlier.

Her youth struck people hard. She wasn't a professional hero. But that didn't prevent her from saving the world. That didn't prevent her from being powerful.

Seira studied this event when she was six. With her class, she watched the recording of the fight, filmed by a security camera that was still working despite the chaos.

Lithium, the most dangerous and prolific villain of that time, attacked a commercial center with an army of villains. Temporality happened to be there at the same time, and upon seeing how much damage was done, she decided to interfere.

People called her reckless and foolish. Suicidal. Some said she was arrogant. None of them understood.

Temporality knew heroes would be stuck fighting the army of villains. Only someone inside the commercial center could fight Lithium, and it happened she was the only one willing to try.

Temporality wanted to save people. She just couldn't let them die. So, she became a hero.

Seira kicked her legs back and forth in the air like a child, sitting on a rooftop. She should have gone back home an hour ago, but she wasn't hungry, no matter how good Shesheri's cooking was. They wouldn't resent her for that. Or they would save her some food, or Len had already devoured everything.

Temporality's death left her empty. Temporality's death surely left everyone empty, but she had a special place in Seira's heart.

Temporality was everything Seira would have wanted to become. Temporality was a hero. A real, true one.

She wasn't looking for glory, fame, or anything like that. She genuinely wanted to help people. She genuinely wanted to keep the world safe, because she loved the world. She was wise, and she knew to admit her mistakes and reflect upon them.

She was someone you could admire.

"Why did you die, old lady?" Seira asked the night. Part of her wished Temporality could answer her, even after her death. "Not you. You just couldn't. You didn't have the right."

But Temporality was gone.

Seira sighed and brought her legs against her chest, resting her chin on her knees. The city was strangely peaceful. It was as Shesheri said, the villains were quiet. It seemed the entire world had come to a stop with Temporality's death.

"I bet you're still watching over us," Seira whispered. That sounded like Temporality.

Seira took a deep breath and jumped down the building.

Temporality defeated Keystone when she was fifty, four years before Seira's birth. Seira also studied that event, but she really learned more about it when she met Shesheri, who was five at the time, right in the heart of the action. (Len was three and only recalled hearing about it on TV.)

Keystone intended to take over the world. He was considered Lithium's successor: just as powerful, if not even more, but way greedier. Where Lithium solely intended to bring chaos, Keystone wanted to be the ruler of the world.

Lots of heroes tried to stop him. Many died. So when the threat became too great, Temporality stepped in.

The world trembled, the day they fought. They were of equal strength. They battled in a camp of refugees Keystone attacked, and after a fight that lasted hours and seemed lost in advance, Temporality defeated him.

Temporality had a tendency to beat the odds, and she was determined. Keystone had barely anything to lose, and Temporality had everything to lose. There lay the difference. When Keystone began to tire, it showed.

Temporality hid her pain and her exhaustion, until she was sure Keystone would never get up again.

"She was amazing," Shesheri told Seira. "I watched her with stars in my eyes. We all thought we were going to die, but she brought us hope. She brought us safety."

Seira suspected that it's after her fight with Keystone when people began to think Temporality would never leave them.

Seira pushed the door of the apartment open. All quiet. Shesheri was probably sleeping. Len was reading; she was sure of it. Seira had lived with them long enough to know their night patterns by heart. They were family.

She went to her room and sat on her bed. The funerals would be in two days, and yet Temporality's death still felt surreal to her.

She sighed. In a way, she should have known. Temporality was part of the old generation. Seira was part of the current, young generation. They hadn't lived in the same world for more than eighteen years. It was bound to happen.

"How could you love this world so much, Temporality?" Seira sighed again. "It doesn't deserve you."

The world was a mess. Temporality had protected this mess, never giving up on it, no matter how dark it truly was. The Nations Assembled were a viper's nest. Had Temporality been less powerful, less wise, they would have tried to manipulate her.

Temporality knew.

And yet, she kept on being this broken, dark, messy world's hero.

Seira met Temporality several times. Many things Temporality said remained in Seira's brain and would probably always remain.

"What have you seen to have such eyes, young one?"

Temporality's voice was always soft but determined, incredibly compassionate as she talked to thirteen year-old Seira. It was the first time they met.

"Too much," was Seira's answer.

Seira realized that day no matter how bright Temporality was, there was no way Seira could feel bitter, jealous, or have any negative emotion towards her. Temporality was her hero and would always be.

Temporality was powerful, but not omnipotent either. She had her defeats, her failures. She would entirely take the blame for each of them, even if it would have been impossible for anyone else, and she always swore she would be better.

Her first real defeat was against Marion.

Marion manipulated and played with people like puppets. He infiltrated the Nations Assembled and declared himself the rightful heir of Keystone. Just as there was one greatest superhero, there was one greatest villain. If the greatest superhero's place remained stable, the greatest villain's position was more unstable.

Lithium, Keystone, now Marion. But even Marion knew his time would come. Temporality defeated his predecessors. Other strong heroes were rising. He could not remain the greatest villain forever.

But should he fall, his goal was at least to take Temporality down.

Seira was twelve. It was around that time when she met Len and Shesheri, briefly, but hadn't thought much of them yet — that would come later.

Marion defeated Temporality, because he used people against her, people she had sworn to protect, and even with all her power, she couldn't hurt him without hurting someone else in the process. And she refused to. She decided not to fight. To let herself be defeated. Because she refused to sacrifice people to defeat Marion.

She nearly died.

She was only saved because another villain killed Marion just before Marion could kill her — but no one knew who it was.

Some claimed it was The Ghost, a villain who infiltrated into the Nations Assembled, who knew everything because he could phase through walls and step everywhere, manipulate people's minds and then disappear, not remembered by anyone, erased from their memories. A real ghost. A real, current danger for the Nations Assembled.

Some thought it could be Regulate, with his temperature-control power. He was said to be more powerful than Marion, at that time, and some villains apparently complained that it was Marion, who placed himself in Keystone's lineage, not Regulate. Regulate was doing incredible damages, freezing cities, or putting them under unbearable heat, and taking great pleasure in destroying things.

Some speculated it could be Skyshift, but that seemed unlikely. Skyshift had appeared way too recently. The rumors about Skyshift being the next greatest villain were, at that time, yet only jokes and wild guesses.

At any rate, those three names were raised, as people thought they were the most likely to become the next most powerful villains.

People were right.

They could have never imagined it was those three villains' combined actions, working together a bit by accident, which defeated Marion.

"Seira. Wake up."

Seira grumbled, pulling her covers over her head.

Len sighed.

"Wake up, brat. Shesheri made breakfast."

"Did you eat my food last night?"

"You know I did. Come on. Shesheri left early, but I kept breakfast warm."

Seira, reluctantly, got out of bed. She still felt a little dull and empty because of Temporality's death, but she suspected neither Len nor

Shesheri were doing any better. They were less affected than she was. She was the one who met Temporality the most, after all.

Three months ago, last time I saw her, she was perfectly fine, Seira thought. How could someone so strong die?

But as Shesheri said, Temporality was only human. Seira needed to accept it.

"I still can't believe it," Len said.

Seira smiled weakly. She definitely wasn't the only one affected. "Same."

"Temporality's funerals are tomorrow, at night," Len brutally reminded her. "At Time Hero's Place. What do you want to do?"

Seira looked at him. He already knew, because he knew her too well. Like Shesheri: they started living together when she was thirteen. She couldn't hide anything from them.

She sighed.

"I'm going to be busy today. But first, breakfast."

Temporality might have failed to defeat Marion herself, but she definitely marked the future generations, heroes and villains alike. Especially villains. The new villains respected her. Were tamer. Less driven by the call of power and greed, because they knew if they went too far, Temporality would be there to stop them.

Temporality helped a lot of young villains find their way back to the light. That was something many villains admired in her, though they disagreed with her positive view of the world.

The world was a rotten apple. It wasn't ambition which devoured new generations into villainy, it was utter despair. But Temporality wasn't rotten, and she was hope. It turned out some villains just needed a bit of hope.

She was old, though. Immensely powerful, but old. And yet, the only villains who managed to escape her were still stopped by her and were the most powerful of them.

She could never catch The Ghost. They were always there, in the Nations Assembled, roaming around, an invisible threat. She stopped

their worst attempts at creating chaos, though she never even saw
them. They seemed to respect her greatly, preventing one or two
machinations aiming to manipulate her. They were toying with the
Nations Assembled, happily, but never went too far and left Temporality untouched.

Regulate was another story. He liked causing havoc, liked
destroying entire cities and didn't care about people's lives, but whenever he heard she would go for him, he would run away and remain
hidden as long as he needed to. He played hide and seek with her,
always knowing when she would arrive, and when it was all rumor.
Only her presence stopped him. Only her presence was enough for
him to disappear, or to leave people alone. That showed how powerful
she still was.

And then there was Skyshift.

Seira went home feeling like she had run a thousand miles. She had, in
a way. Her throat was sore from talking over the phone so much, too.
She felt exhausted, though her legs were still functioning and taking
her back to her place.

"I shouldn't have procrastinated that so much," she grumbled,
pushing the door open. But the announcement of Temporality's death
had been a real shock. Her hero. Dead. That wasn't something you
could recover from in one second.

"Welcome home," Shesheri greeted her.

"I'm home," she smiled, tiredly. "Thanks for your help. You too, Len."

Len perked up from his book and winked. "Anything for you."

Family, she thought once more. They were everything she had.
Especially now that Temporality was dead, and she had no one to
admire so much anymore — only her family.

"I'm beat," she declared. "I'm going to sleep."

"Cuddle night?" Shesheri suggested. Len cheered.

She laughed.

"I could do with one."

Villains turned into villains for many reasons.

Ambition, greed, personal revenge, bloodlust, and fantasies of power were reasons which belonged to Temporality's generation. She couldn't do much against those.

Utter despair, poverty, grudge against the world, abuse, violence, and hopelessness were reasons which belonged to the new generations, and as strange as it seemed, Temporality understood those reasons. She tried many times to fight against them, as hard as she would fight against villains themselves.

"Those young people are in a world which isn't good to them," she one day declared. "They're like wounded animals. And believe me, wounded animals would do anything to survive."

Fortunately or unfortunately, Temporality was never aware of the Scums.

The Scums were a small district hidden from the world by the government. The Scums were right under everyone's nose, yet only its inhabitants really knew about them. Most people didn't. Most people could never imagine they existed. The Scums used to be called Eden and were the project of districts created specifically to raise heroes from birth.

The Scums were the government's failure.

It didn't work. Many tragedies happened. The government tried to hide everything by completely giving up on the Scums, when people needed help the most, leaving the place to ruthless inspectors desperately trying to finish their jobs. The Scums weren't slums, so to speak, yet, it was a place where people didn't really matter, where the world ignored their existence, where everyone manipulated everyone, where killing was as random as breathing, where children were raised to be machines, and where behind the normal façade hid a dark, dark reality.

The Scums were made to create heroes, but they created villains instead.

People of the Scums were praying, every day, that someone would change this situation that someone would show the Scums to

Temporality, and she would save them. The hope she represented kept many people alive.

But it would have been the end of the Nations Assembled if Temporality ever heard of the Scums, so they did everything, including the worst, to make sure she remained ignorant.

The villains who hated the government the most came from the Scums. They were the ones who had seen the darkest part of the world, who had seen hatred and despair and injustice. Who had seen people executed just for being suspected of wanting to escape, who saw children raised to become the dogs of people treating them like garbage, who had seen too much.

The Ghost didn't come from the Scums. Neither did Regulate. The Ghost was a refugee from a country attacked by Keystone, who was then oppressed because the Nations Assembled did nothing to help their people, and Regulate ran away from a wealthy but abusive family and lived in the streets.

Skyshift, however, was the perfect example of how badly the government had failed the Scums.

Skyshift was the current world's greatest villain. Greater than Marion, Keystone, or Lithium. Greater than Temporality herself, some said — but now that Temporality was dead, this theory could not be verified.

Skyshift was strange. Never seen. No information about them. Skyshift ravaged cities like the wrath of a god falling upon humanity. Unstoppable and merciless.

As any child raised into the Scums, Skyshift held no hope for this world and took special care to destroy anything related to the Nations Assembled, like the Scums themselves.

"Skyshift is the representation of the despair rampant in this world." Temporality's words were pronounced in a severe voice, after Skyshift destroyed a hero college. "I am not condoning their acts and will do anything to stop them, but you must understand there are thousands of other future Skyshifts in this world right now. We must do better."

They clashed many times. Temporality was the only hero able to stand against and stop Skyshift, though never able to win, and they seemed to have a strange respect for each other.

But here again, every villain respected Temporality. No villain really hated her. She was the embodiment of hope, and everything they had failed. Even Skyshift, who could never share her love for the world, held her in great esteem.

The last time Seira saw Temporality, she said, "Thank you for being my hero."

"I wish I could have done better," Temporality answered sadly. "I wish I could be stronger and do more for this world. Not only protect it. But also help it. Save it. Unfortunately, I am only human."

Temporality was the kind of person Seira would have wanted to have as part of her family. Kind and earnest, aware of the darkness, yet believing in the world and always trying.

Always.

Even if that's what took her life in the end.

When the government learned that Skyshift had been talking to Temporality during their fights, they grew scared, terrified, that the world's greatest hero would one day discover how rotten they truly were.

But Skyshift never spoke about the Scums. Skyshift and the villains from the Scums, though they would have wished for Temporality to save them, were paradoxically glad she didn't discover the truth.

Temporality was too good for this world. She didn't deserve to discover that the government she had worked under hadn't respected any of the principles of life Temporality tried so hard to maintain.

She deserved to die knowing she had done what she could. Not thinking there were people she could have saved, had she known about them.

It was the night of Temporality's funerals. They were held at night on the Time Hero's Place, the former commercial center where Temporality defeated Lithium. The place was crowded. All executives of the Nations Assembled were there, making speeches about her.

People were crying, honoring her, talking about her. But people were also scared.

It had been two days without any villain attack. The entire world was holding its breath, the threat for a massive attack during the funerals imminent, bracing itself against a crime spree.

And it happened.

Wind slipped between people, a stronger gust twirling above their heads, and slowly, descending from the sky, hundreds and hundreds of villains arrived. They remained floating in the air, supported by the wind, standing above the civilians, until a figure in a black cloak landed and made its way up to the stage where the executives of the Nations Assembled were giving their speeches, and where a memorial for Temporality had been set up.

"Who–" an executive started, fists clenched.

"We came here to pay our respects to a fallen foe," the cloaked figure said. Wind was keeping people away from it, gently but firmly. "And the greatest hero."

"This is Skyshift!" people whispered to themselves. Only the world's greatest villain with the power to command the weather and the sky could make an entire legion of villains come here, carried by the wind.

"Farewell, Temporality," Skyshift said. "May you be well. Thank you for having been our hope during all this time. Hope doesn't do much for this world, you know. But it kept us alive. You will be missed."

Skyshift and the entire crowd of villains bowed in front of the memorial.

Seira was eleven when she tried to die. She wasn't Skyshift yet. She had just flown away with the Scums, after killing the guards trying to execute her because someone tried to escape. They would kill someone else. It didn't matter. There were no friends in the Scums. Seira did not care about them.

Or about anything at all.

She was flying, and she realized there wasn't anything for her. She had been raised to be a hero. That had failed cruelly. She wasn't anything. There was nowhere for her to go, nothing for her to do.

Just die.

Seira cancelled her power and let herself fall into the sky, into the storm she created, to die.

In her fall, she passed in front of a giant screen. Though there was no one in the streets at that hour and with that weather, the screen displayed the extract of an interview with Temporality.

Seira stopped falling. The wind carried her softly to the ground, where she lay, breathless, listening to Temporality.

To her hero.

Temporality was hope. She was what kids in the Scums were taught to become but couldn't, because there was only one Temporality. She was Seira's most admired and respected person, what Seira tried, but failed to be.

Seira cried, watching her hero talk softly about everything good in the world. Those were things Seira did not know. Seira did not know anything good in the world. Temporality said she loved the world, and Seira did not understand how you could love the world.

Seira realized she didn't know how to help people, how to want to protect them. That was where the Scums failed in their hero education: they taught kids to be destructive but never gave them the desire to protect anyone.

Seira had no hope for humanity. Had Temporality not existed, Seira would not have had any at all.

"How can you love this world?" she cried, that night.

As Temporality spoke about what there was to love in this world, Seira saw. She did not understand, but she saw. She saw how

Temporality could want to protect the world, could cherish it, and could think it had beauty. For the first time, she saw there was more than her dark and broken life, though she did not understand how to see it.

Temporality loved the world. She protected it.

"I cannot love this world," Seira murmured. "So, I'll destroy it. Stop me, Temporality. Prove to me I'm wrong."

That night, Seira became a villain.

"I'm going to miss her," Seira admitted, flying into the sky. Beside Shesheri and Len, she had dropped everyone at their meeting point, and they would all go back to their place by themselves. "I don't think there will be another hero like her. They don't understand."

"Give them time, brat," Len shook his head. "The new generations will arrive."

She smiled. "Hopefully. But there'll only ever be one Temporality."

"You loved her," Shesheri remarked. "Temporality. I know how much you liked to confront her, because she understood you. She didn't judge you. She wasn't seeing you as an enemy."

"She was trying to save me," Seira nodded. "And I'm sorry she couldn't save me. I'm sorry it was too late. But she kept on trying, and talking with her was one of the most healing things in the world."

Another of those things being her family.

"And I wanted her to save me, too. "

Seira told Temporality she found a family. It must have been during the second time they battled. She felt proud. She cared about them. She did not know why. After having spent so long barely feeling anything, it was good to have emotions over despair, anger, or the will to destroy.

"I found a family, Temporality. I found one."

"You did well," Temporality answered, smiling, though they were fighting, though Seira was Skyshift and was an enemy.

"It's okay that you couldn't save me," was the last thing Seira told Temporality.

It was during their last fight, as Seira was retreating, once more unable to defeat Temporality, but not defeated either.

"I should have," Temporality replied. "You deserved to be saved. I hope your family can save you, my child. If not from villainy, then at least from your own darkness. There are beautiful things around you, dear. I hope you can see them."

"I was wrong," Seira smiled through her tears.

She was cuddled between Len and Shesheri. She looked at them, thought they were what was good in her life, her family, her happiness, what she loved and cared about, what she thought was beautiful in this dark, messy, broken world.

She would have never noticed this beauty if Temporality hadn't existed.

"She had already saved me."

WRITING UNITES US!

"Anything that you do not give freely and abundantly becomes lost to you. You open your safe and find ashes."
— *Anne Dillard, The Writing Life*

"Believe your writing is worth it." — *Margaret Lukas*

"The first discipline is the realization that there is a discipline. All art begins and ends with discipline. Any art is first and foremost a craft." — *Archibald MacLeish*

"Live with Intention." — *Mary Anne Radmacher*

"It is not lack of time that is holding you back. It is fear."
— *Sherri Shakelford*

"If I waited until I felt like writing, I'd never write at all." — *Anne Tyler*

"Write with nouns and verbs." — *E.B. White*

"So long as you write what you wish to write, that is all that matters; and whether it matters for ages or only for hours, nobody can say." — *Virginia Woolf*

CONTRIBUTORS

TRACY AHRENS lives in Illinois, has been a journalist/writer for over 25 years and has published seven books, including two books of poetry. As of January 2018, she had earned 60 writing awards locally, statewide, and nationally. She is a member of the Illinois Woman's Press Association, National Federation of Press Women, Dog Writers Association of America, and the Cat Writers' Association. Her author statement reads: "Poetry is an escape for me from journalistic writing. It's a time to play with words as life moves me. It's the ultimate brevity a pen stroke — a signature that etches lasting impressions."

DUANE ANDERSON is currently living in La Vista, NE. He graduated from Augustana College in Rock Island, IL, and worked at the Union Pacific Railroad for 37 years. After his retirement in 2013, he started writing poetry. He had his poems published in *Saga, Poetry Now, Telephone, Lunch, Touchstone, Pastiche: Poems of Place,* and the *Omaha World-Herald* in the late 1970s and '80s.

SARAH ASAD is an immigration lawyer who grew up in Japan and now is practicing her degree in Orlando, FL. She loves to write and feels very happy to write for *Fine Lines*

CATHY BECK is a first time writer for *Fine Lines*.

JOSEPH S. BENSON is a veteran, retired educator, and writes from Hiawatha, Kansas.

RON BOERNER is a native Nebraskan, born in Nebraska City and now living in North Platte, where he moved in 1969 to take a teaching job at North Platte High School. That is also where he met his wife-to-be, Sheila, an English teacher there at the time.

KRISTI BOLLING "My story is, well, stories. I have been writing them for as long I can remember. I'm always going on adventures with my writing. I'll never forget the first work of mine that was published. I was so excited that I couldn't stop talking about it. Later in high school, I was told to make a portfolio for English class. I wrote the first two chapters of a book that other kids would finish for me. I'm still writing stories. There's just something about writing that opens up a secret part that I never knew I had in me."

J. ELEANOR BONET writes fiction as J Eleanor Bonet to honor her Aunt Eleanor, who encouraged her to "just be as crazy as you want to be and don't give a hoot about what others think." She writes non-fiction as Janet E. Bonet, for academic and community activism purposes. Her educational background reaches to the "all but thesis" level in anthropology/sociology, and she has a BA minor in Spanish. She is a freelance professional translator and interpreter, because she loves words and is dedicated to social and environmental justice. She resides in the house she was raised in on the edge of South Omaha's Spring Lake Park. She is happily letting her yard revert back to the wildwood it was meant to be. In her mind, nature should be natural.

DEREK BURDENY is an award winning, internationally recognized photographer from Omaha, Nebraska. Derek's main photographic passions are chasing severe weather through tornado alley in the central USA, to chasing solar storms and the aurora borealis in far northern Norway. See more of his photos at www.derekburdenyphotography.com.

STU BURNS has studied history and folklore at three of the fourteen Big Ten universities. His work has appeared in *eTropic, Laurus, Montage,* and *The Dictionary of Literary Biography.* He is a Municipal Liaison for National Novel Writing Month, has been an editor for *Fine Lines* since 2010, and works for an insurance company in Omaha.

JAYME BUSSING graduated from Yutan, NE, High School and Metropolitan Community College with a major in Creative Writing. This fall she will begin a Bachelor's Degree in English Literature (major) and Creative Writing (minor) at Purdue University. She enjoys writing short stories the most, and she was our *Fine Lines* summer intern.

AMANDA CAILLAU is past President of the National Art Educators Association, University of Nebraska at Omaha student chapter, a graduate of UNO, and teaches art in the Omaha area.

MARY CAMPBELL a native of Omaha, NE, is a writer, musician, writing coach, and certified meditation instructor, whose award-winning poetry has appeared in scores of periodicals, including publications of the Kansas Poetry Society and the Arizona Poetry Society. A longtime writer and editor at the University of Arizona, Mary is the author, coauthor, and ghostwriter of more than twenty books. She has written or co-written hundreds of songs, poems, stories, essays, news and magazine features, blog posts, and podcasts. Mary has composed for and directed children's and adults' choirs; has led church-school, preschool, and meditation classes; has taught in a nationwide children's ballroom-dance program; and produced three children and, indirectly, nine grandchildren.

MICHAEL CAMPBELL is a humor writer and musician. *Of Mice and Me,* Campbell's 2017 collection of humor essays, is now available in print and eBook editions, as is his previous book, *Are You Going To Eat That?* His "Dumpster" column closes every issue of *Food & Spirits* magazine. Campbell also has four albums of original songs. The 2015 album *My Turn Now* includes a title track with a hilarious cameo by former game show host Richard Dawson. Learn more at michaelcampbellsongwriter.com.

BUD CASSIDAY is an artist and English teacher. He works at Metropolitan Community College in Elkhorn, NE. Some of his artwork and writing may be found at http://artbycassiday.blogspot.com/.

DAVID CATALAN is the founder of Catalan Consulting. He was the executive director of the Nonprofit Association of the Midlands from August 2002 to February 2008. David is the President of the South Omaha Business Association and the author of *Rule of Thumb: A Guide to Small Business Marketing.* He is working on an autobiographical collection of poems drawing from relatives, friends, and locations.

STUART CODD is a first time *Fine Lines* writer and lives in Washington state.

SARAH CORTINAS began to develop her photography skills while growing up in Omaha, NE. She now resides in the mountains of Western North Carolina where the vastly different landscape has offered a new perspective. She is currently working towards her graduate degree at Appalachian State University, where she also received her undergraduate degree, which included a minor in Commercial Photography. Photography and the arts have always been influential in her life, and she hopes to continue to use her work to promote the ecological preservation and appreciation of the Appalachian Mountains.

JACK DONAHUE has had poems published in journals such as *North Dakota Quarterly; Laldy (Scotland); Prole (U.K.); Poetry Salzburg Review (Austria); Armarolla (Cypress); Bindweed (Ireland); Opossum* and others throughout North America, India and Europe. Mr. Donahue received his M.Div. degree from New Brunswick, Theological Seminary, NJ, in 2008. He is married and resides on the North Fork of Long Island, NY.

WILLIAM DORESKI went to Goddard College and Boston University, has a PhD in American and New England Studies, has written two books on Robert Lowell and one on modern poetry in general, and reviews poetry regularly for *Harvard Review Online.* He taught at Emerson, Harvard, Goddard, BU, and Keene State College.

ROBERT KLEIN ENGLER lived in Omaha, NE, and sometimes New Orleans, LA. He was a writer and artist. His many publications are available in print and on the Internet. He held degrees from the University of Illinois at Urbana and the University of Chicago Divinity School, where he studied religious art. He was an Ed Tech Assistant at the Joslyn Art Museum in Omaha, NE.

MATT FILLINGSNESS is an underwriter at Aetna Insurance.

GEOFF FITZGERALD is an artist, photographer, and Wolverine Watch Biologist in Montana.

KRISTI FITZGERALD had her first poem, "The Great Big Lion from Nastle," and accompanying illustration published in the local newspaper when she was nine years old. She has bachelor's degrees in English and theater with graduate work in costume design. She is a member of Willamette Writers, is a finisher of NaNoWriMo for two years running, and belongs to two writer's groups. She has had two articles and two poems published in *Renaissance Magazine* and a story in *Chicken Soup for the Soul*: "Here Comes the Bride." She's currently editing her first novel, a young adult fantasy, with dreams of publication. She lives in Hamilton, Montana.

MARCIA CALHOUN FORECKI lives in Council Bluffs, IA. Her academic background is in the Spanish language. She earned a Master of Arts degree from the University of Wisconsin-Milwaukee. Her first book, *Speak to Me*, about her son's deafness, was published by Gallaudet University Press and earned a national book award. Her story "The Gift of the Spanish Lady" was published in the *Bellevue Literary Journal* and nominated for a Pushcart Prize.

DOREEN FRICK: "Hello from Nebraska. I am 64, originally from the Philadelphia area, but now, I live in Ord, NE. We've moved a lot, and that's the beauty of my life, meeting and working with others. 'Oh, Nebraska,' is a true story."

NANCY GENEVIEVE is a Special Editor for *Fine Lines* and an Emerita Associate Professor of English at the University of Illinois at Springfield (UIS). She taught creative writing for ten years at Eureka College (IL) before teaching creative writing for ten years at UIS; she retired in 2010, and she and her husband live in Massachusetts.

AMANDA B. HANSEN-WEIGNER is proud to call herself a recent graduate of UNO. She holds her Bachelor's in General Studies and is certified in English Lit., Music & (of course) Creative Writing. She is a recent addition to the *Fine Lines* Journal Editorial staff (and posts for their Social Media sites) where she feels she is part of a team. She is currently a stay-at-home mom who owns an Etsy shop called Stitchery Poetry, where she cross-stitches her own poetry. She currently resides in Omaha with her husband, newborn son, and their family dog, Max. Her poetry can be found in countless issues of *Fine Lines,* as well as *13th Floor Magazine.* You can find more about Amanda at her website, www. amandabeatricehansen.com.

JEAN HART: "For most of my long and rewarding career, I worked in high-technology, primarily in developing countries. I have a BA and an MB, and have taken numerous creative writing classes, gone to many workshops, and still attend a weekly writer's group. Although I grew up in the rural South, I'm most at home on either coast. In addition to publishing my short fiction in literary journals, I've been invited to read at various literary events in Portland, Oregon, a serious writer's town if there ever was one. I'm a book junkie, a dog lover, and enjoy old, amber liquids."

KATHY HASTINGS is a multi-media artist and writer who lives in Snohomish, WA.

NIA KARMANN: "Having the opportunity to share my outlook on life and the amazing beauty and wonder that God has given us is my passion. I receive great pleasure in capturing a fraction of God's awe-inspiring canvas while taking photos, and, in doing so, it allows me to express my freedom while escaping the box that Spina Bifida creates. Shooting from a wheelchair gives my work a unique perspective of unusual angles, shapes, and scenes, and I am very willing to do whatever it takes to capture the right angle. I am an award winning photographer and have been published in magazines and hope my work inspires every reader of *Fine Lines.*"

DESHAE E. LOTT taught English courses at one of these universities: Louisiana State University in Shreveport, Texas A&M University, and the University of Illinois at Springfield. Spirituality and living with a disability both infuse Deshae's professional scholarship, essays, and poetry. In 2011, Lott received for one of her essays an EXCEL Gold Medal from Association Media and Publishing. She has served as a co-editor of the American Religion and Literature Society Newsletter and has published on a variety of nineteenth-and twentieth-century Americans including Margaret Fuller, George Moses Horton, Mary Mann, Julia Smith, Walt Whitman, Jack Kerouac, George Oppen, Maya Angelou, and Annie Dillard. A mixture of syncretism and individualism appears in mysticism, and Lott's teaching and publishing primarily highlight mystics who concurrently endeavor to and model how to contribute constructively to their communities.

NORMAND LUND is a retired Omaha businessman.

WENDY LUNDEEN retired from teaching in the Omaha Public School District, where she taught Spanish at Central High School and at Alice Buffett Middle School. Señora Lundeen is a "Yaya" to six grandchildren and is writing a book about her two grandsons' struggles with Duchenne Muscular Dystrophy, a terminal illness. Her passions include writing poetry, singing in the church choir, traveling, acting, and dancing every year as "Oma" in *Nutcracker Delights*. For more than a decade, she has led a group of young writers every year at the *Fine Lines* Summer Creative Writing Camp.

DAVID MARTIN is the founder and managing editor of *Fine Lines*, a non-profit quarterly journal that has published creative writing by "young authors of all ages" since 1992. All writers are welcome to submit their poetry, prose, photography, and artwork. This publication has printed work by authors from all fifty states and forty other countries. The website (www.finelines.org) has more information about submission guidelines and a sample journal to view. He has published two books of essays and poetry (*Facing the Blank Page* and *Little Birds with Broken Wings*), which may be found at Boutique of Quality Books (www.bqbpublishing.com).

ERIN MARTIN is an orthopedic physician's assistant at OrthNebraska Hospital in Omaha, NE.

YOLIE MARTIN is a counselor at Anderson Middle School in the Millard, NE, Public School District. Every day, she comes home from school exhausted and claims to be the "Grandmother" for 300 children, and she loves it.

JEROME MCALLISTER was a scientist after graduating from Texas Christian University in 1967 until his retirement in 2004. Then, he took a large number of creative writing courses (fiction) from The Loft in Minneapolis, Minnesota. Jerome grew up south of Houston, Texas, near the Gulf of Mexico. Discovering Jim Crow arose from his childhood experiences. His current residence is New Richmond, Wisconsin.

VINCE MCANDREW is retired from the Omaha Public Schools, where he was a teacher, counselor, and administrator. He is now giving full attention to his grandchildren and his poetry.

JERILYN MCINTYRE is a retired university professor and administrator whose personal essays about her family have appeared in several literary journals, including *Fine Lines*. In addition to those reminiscences, McIntyre has also published two novellas for middle grade readers: *Paws in the Piazza* and *The Shadow of the Unscratchable,* featuring the adventures of a charismatic black cat named Harley.

BRETT MCLAUGHLIN is a first time writer for *Fine Lines*.

BARB MOTES: "As a retired educator, I plan to spend time exploring the life and environment around me. Being a Colorado native I have always had an appreciation for nature and its beauty. The use of photography enables me to express that passion for nature."

KRISTEN NORMAN is a poet who writes in Edgartown, MA.

ANDY PAPPAS is a manager at Valentino's Pizza. His passion is writing lyrics and playing music that make people want to get up out of their chairs and dance.

RHONDA PARSONS is a first time writer for *Fine Lines*.

CHARLENE PIERCE is a local sales manager of the *Omaha World Herald* newspaper.

CATHY PORTER her poetry has appeared in *Plainsongs, Chaffin Journal, Kentucky Review, Hubbub, Homestead Review,* and various other journals in the US and UK. She has two chapbooks available from Finishing Line Press: "A Life in the Day" and "Dust and Angels." Her most recent collection, "Exit Songs", was released in 2016 from Dancing Girl Press in Chicago. She is a two-time Pushcart Prize nominee. She works at Iowa Western Community College and lives in Omaha, NE with her husband Lenny, their golden retriever Lucky, and the king and queen cats Cody and Mini. Feel free to contact her at clcon@q.com.

FABRICE POUSSI: "I'm the advisor for *The Chimes,* the Shorter University award winning poetry and arts publication in Rome, GA. My writing and photography have been published in print, including *Kestrel, Symposium, La Pensee Universelle, Paris,* and other art and literature magazines in the United States and abroad."

DAVID REINARZ has been writing fiction short stories and poetry since October 2015, when he participated in the "7 Doctors Writers Workshop" sponsored by the University of Nebraska Medical Center and The Nebraska Writers Collective. He continues to participate in a "7 Doctors" Alumni Group. He lives in Omaha with the love of his life, Lynne. He graduated from Benson High School, attended the University of Nebraska at Omaha, and graduated with a BA in Philosophy and Religious Studies. He is retired from a thirty year career of managing professional retail bicycle shops.

ROBERT RICKER has a Bachelor's Degree in History from UNO. He served four years in the U.S. Air Force, is a voracious reader, and likes politics, economics, and Tolstoy.

JOHN TIMOTHY ROBINSON is a graduate of the Marshall University Creative Writing Program in Huntington, West Virginia. He has an interest in critical theory of poetry and American formalism. He is an educator for Mason County Schools, WV, and is working on a creative dissertation in contemporary poetry.

ROBERT RUNYON grew up in Summit, New Jersey. At Wesleyan University, he studied philosophy, psychology and the French language. He later received a Master's Degree in Library Science from Rutgers University. For over thirty years, he served as an academic library administrator. Sometime after retirement from UNO's Criss Library in 2001, he returned to UNO to take courses in Creative Nonfiction. Now an octogenarian, he is working on a memoir of travel, family, nature, and aging.

CHRISTINE SALHANY is an artist, singer, and historian. Recently, she finished a book of family research that is a detailed outline of her mother's survival during World War II.

JAMES M. SALHANY is a retired professor of internal medicine and biochemistry at the University of Nebraska Medical Center, where he taught and performed research in molecular biophysics. He did his graduate studies at the University of Chicago, where he obtained his Master's and PhD degrees. His poems attempt to present scientific concepts in humanistic terms. Now, he spends most of his time writing and producing song recordings. He has 110 original songs on Reverb Nation, where his songs are ranked #1 in the nation. He is on the *Fine Lines* Board of Directors.

SALLY SANDLER gives voice to her generation of Baby Boomers and their elders. She illuminates their shared concerns over the passage of time and fading idealism, the death of parents, and loss of the environment, while maintaining hope for wisdom yet to come. Sandler writes in classic forms to honor poetry's roots while also addressing contemporary issues. She is a graduate of the University of Michigan and lives in San Diego, California.

STUART SEDLAK is a student at Metropolitan Community College in Omaha, NE. There's no place he would rather be than at a ballpark. A huge baseball fan, he enjoys attending Kansas City Royals and Omaha Storm Chasers games. He looks forward to taking his new son, Carson, to future contests.

SUE SHELBURNE is originally from Kentucky but now lives in Omaha, NE. She enjoys decorating, photography, acrylics, and writing, which has been a constant companion in her life for as long as she can remember. Writing is her therapist, her friend through lonely times, and her mirror that reflects best. Putting words together has never been a laborious thing for her because she writes the words that want to be written and in the way they want to be expressed. It is her responsibility not to censor them. When she honors that responsibility, they read back to her with a light of their own truth.

D. N. SIMMERS lives in British Columbia, Canada, and writes poetry. He is an on-line *Fine Lines* editor. Widely published in the USA, he has also been published in England, Wales, and New Zealand.

BOBBI SINHA-MOREY'S poetry has appeared in a variety of places such as *Plainsongs, Pirene's Fountain, The Wayfarer, Helix Magazine, Miller's Pond,* and *Old Red Kimono.* Her books of poetry are available at www.Amazon.com and her work has been nominated for Best of the Net. She loves aerobics, knitting, reading, and rock hounding with her husband.

PHIL SMITH: I am a recently retired physician, who practiced Infectious Diseases for many years, and directed the Ebola Unit at the University of Nebraska Medical College. Poetry has always captivated my imagination. Although my time for writing has been limited, I was a participant in the "Seven Doctors" project at UNMC and in the writers' group at First Central Congregational Church in Omaha, NE.

KIM MCNEALY SOSIN was a professor and department chair of economics at the University of Nebraska at Omaha, until her retirement a few years ago. She published numerous articles in economics journals and created and continues to maintain several websites. She enjoys photography and writing and has been focused on reading and writing poetry. She also collects vintage fountain pens.

GARY TAYLOR is a new writer for *Fine Lines.*

JAMES TILLOTSON is a student in Omaha, Nebraska, currently working on a degree in English literature and creative writing. He is working on writing and publishing his short stories. His preferred genres to write in are horror and romance.

JULIE WUTHRICH is an 18-year-old, second-year university student at Université d'Orléans in France, majoring in English and Japanese.

PLEASE SUPPORT OUR SPONSORS

Silver Departures

Kathy Hastings

Traditional paintings and photography
www.kathyhastings.com • email: dkstudios@aol.com
(360) 920-6634

Now Available:

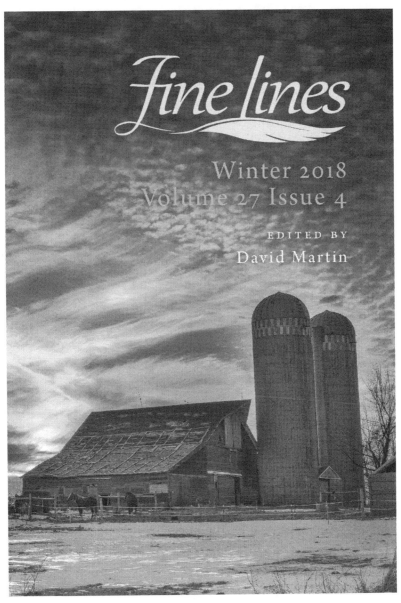

Print Edition at Amazon.com
Full-Color PDF Edition at FineLines.org

NELAC
Nebraska Language Arts Council

Nebraska Language Arts Council (NELAC) is a statewide professional volunteer association of language arts educators who join together to network through conferences, meetings, journals, and conversation. NELAC is Nebraska's official state affiliate with Nebraska's Council of Teachers of English, and membership is open to all educators of language arts, kindergarten through college level.

NELAC Promotes:
- Excellence in Student Magazines
- Young Writers' Programs
- Achievement in Writing Awards
- Promising Young Teacher Award
- The Nebraska English Journal
- The Nebraska Student Journal
- Nebraska Literary map
- Guide to Nebraska Authors
- Annual Nebraska Poetry Month
- Annual High School Quiz Bowl
- Plum Creek Children's Festival
- SLATE (Support for the Learning and Teaching of English)
- AFCON (Academic Freedom Colation of Nebraska)
- Nebraska Center for the Book

JOIN NELAC this year!

Send $10 to:
NELAC
PO Box 83944
Lincoln, NE 68501-3944

Contact:
Clark Kolterman
Ckolte00@connectseward.org

AFCON
Academic Freedom Coalition of Nebraska

Academic Freedom Coalition of Nebraska promotes academic freedom in education and research contexts. This includes freedoms of belief and expression and access to information and ideas.

As a Member, you can help us:

- Support applications of the First Amendment in academic contexts, including elementary and secondary schools, colleges, universities, and libraries.

- Educate Nebraskans about the meaning and value of intellectual freedom, intellectual diversity, mutual respect, open communication, and uninhibited pursuit of knowledge, including the role of these ideas in academic contexts and in democratic self-government.

- Assist students, teachers, librarians, and researchers confronted with censorship, indoctrination, or suppression of ideas.

- Act as a liason among groups in Nebraska that support academic freedom issues.

To become a member:

Send dues, organization or individual name, address and phone number to:
Cathi McCurtry
15 N. Thomas Avenue
Oakland, Nebraska 68045

AFCONebr.org

www.finelines.org

Made in the USA
Columbia, SC
19 March 2019